P9-EJZ-519

WITHDRAWN

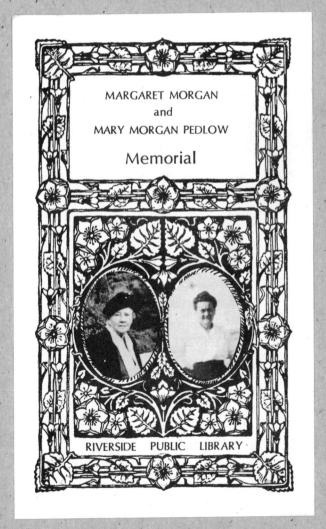

MARGARET MORGAN
and
MARY MORGAN PEDLOW

Memorial

RIVERSIDE PUBLIC LIBRARY

THE SEARCH FOR

Isadora

The Legend & Legacy
of Isadora Duncan

Lillian Loewenthal

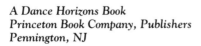

A Dance Horizons Book
Princeton Book Company, Publishers
Pennington, NJ

The Search For Isadora: The Legend & Legacy of Isadora Duncan. Copyright © 1993 by Princeton Book Company, Publishers. No portion of this book may be reproduced in any form or by any means without written permission of the publisher.

A Dance Horizons Book
Princeton Book Company, Publishers
P.O. Box 57
Pennington, NJ 08534

Interior design by Anne O'Donnell

Library of Congress Cataloging-in-Publication Data
Loewenthal, Lillian.
    The search for Isadora : the legend & legacy of Isadora Duncan / Lillian Loewenthal.
        p. cm.
    "A Dance Horizons book."
    Includes bibliographical references (p.) and index.
    ISBN 0-87127-179-6
    1. Duncan, Isadora, 1877–1927. 2. Dancers—United States— Biography. I. Title.
    GV785.D8L64 1993
    792.8'092—dc20
    [B]   92-50754

For Leo

husband, lover, collaborator, critic
and dearest friend,
who urged this book into existence
and saw me through
to the finish line

CONTENTS

PART III:
The Legend and Legacy

PREFACE

WHEN I FIRST BEGAN my journey to discover the sources that could feed my lifelong fascination with Isadora Duncan, there existed but a limited literature available to me.

The documentation of Isadora's extraordinary life began to accumulate only in more recent decades when her contemporaries began to publish their own recollections of her unique personality and presence as an advocate of dance reform during their era. I well recall my frustrating, almost inhibiting, search for information on dance, which in prior years had been peripheral to our culture and an uncommon subject for specialized investigation. Library personnel, less than familiar with this topic, more often than not lacked the proficiency to deal with the rare requests. Determination and patience were necessary when wading through the miscellaneous boxes and folders of unsorted papers and mismarked photographs, in hopes of stumbling across an item of value.

Almost more significant than the pursuit of written and pictorial materials were the impressions and insights provided me by Isadora's remarkable disciples, Irma, Theresa, and Anna Duncan, and the pleasure, beyond measure, of observing their perfection and eloquence in the performance of Isadora's work. Further revelations of this work came to me through Irma and

Anna's gifted pupil, Julia Levien, who was my teacher and who embodied the heart of the Duncan esthetic.

Finally, in the early sixties, my longtime desire to go abroad was realized. It would be the first of a series of trips to Europe in the next two decades, taken to satisfy my inquisitiveness about that other distant world through which had flowed the principal streams of Isadora's life. I had hoped that this journey would consummate my personal commitment to search for a fuller comprehension of the individual and her art. Inquiry into less studied aspects of the multi-faceted Isadora also presented a powerfully attractive challenge. That fresh discoveries awaited me I had no doubt and I welcomed the added mystery and intrigue to my self-styled odyssey.

With a largely improvised itinerary, my wanderings and explorations were guided as much by hunches as by the unexpected. A few schedules were pre-planned; one was my decision to retrace certain locations that had cradled the young Isadora and her not yet fully realized ideas for the dance. Something about standing before the Grecian antiquities in the British Museum as she did in 1900, or circling the Louvre's *Victory of Samothrace*, taking in the admirable spirit and forceful thrust of the sculpture that had so stirred her at the turn of the century, or facing Botticelli's *Primavera* in the Uffizi Gallery in Florence, which had inspired one of her earliest dance arrangements, bonded more firmly this pilgrim to her subject. Past and present lost relevance. "Then" fused with "now."

And if in the United States the mention of the name Isadora could at times elicit the response, "Isadora who?," France was altogether a different story. Without question, a visit to that country merited major concentration. I returned there as frequently as time and money would allow. This was particularly true of Paris, the cultural mecca of the world Isadora considered her home. In the sixties there still lingered in memory some of the more flagrant fragments of the vibrant life long since vanished from its midst. The Sorbonne student, a marketing housewife, a café bartender, an antique dealer, with flickers of recognition in their eyes responded: "The woman with the shawl?," "Didn't she dance in veils?," "Oh! the Bugatti car!" [in which she was killed], "Weren't her children drowned in the Seine?" [in 1913]. Paris and Isadora Duncan in the twentieth century were part of each other's history. An invisible monument, one could say of her, the imagination playing with a vision of the dancer, sculpted in one of her life-affirming postures, atop a high granite pedestal overlooking the Seine. Among Parisians she had lived as a neighbor and as a celebrity. Conserved in the vast library system of Paris were reservoirs of printed material that had tracked the details of her private and professional existence.

Because there already existed biographical and numerous other accounts that have dealt with Isadora's life, both personal and professional, with the highlights of her career, and with the social and cultural implications of her revolution in dance, my priorities directed my research along less ventured routes. I placed much emphasis, for instance, on the need to look more closely at artists and sculptors for whom Isadora's dance had revealed an exciting range of gestures of which the human form was capable, and through whose perceptive eyes and facile hands was provided the visual key by which subsequent generations have come to know her. Most fascinating to me was the magnet that drew artist to muse. There were the galleries, the private collections, and the museums with their considerable collections of artistic impressions of the woman and the dancer. Not to be overlooked as well were innumerable—and knowledgeable—dealers in books, art, and theater memorabilia.

Fortuitous indeed were my successful efforts to find surviving associates and friends who had had long-term affiliations with Isadora—themselves prominent figures in the literary and art avant-garde of her period. They were now few in number but as I was to discover, still visible on the French intellectual scene, none more so than Jacques Hébertot whom Anna Duncan suggested I try to locate. Hébertot, who assumed directorship of the Théâtre des Champs-Elysées in late 1920, featured the dancer there during the week of January 25, 1921. At the time of my meeting with him in the sixties, he was in the process of staging a new dramatic production in his own Théâtre Hébertot (so in keeping with this man who had had a lifelong determination to create a center of international art such as Paris had not known). My meetings with these distinguished Frenchmen and their evocative tales of another time are among my own treasured memories. Through them, as they shed the shadows clinging to their past and refreshed their unveiled reminiscences, I moved closer to that other world I had come to find.

Topping my inventory of sources to explore concerning Isadora Duncan's dance legacy were her own choreographies. Incongruous as it might appear, motion picture filming was alive and well during the latter part of her life, but the technology had not yet sufficiently matured to adequately document dance. For all the rumors that had made the rounds among Duncanites to the effect that here, there, somewhere, lay reels of film of the dancer in the execution of her own dances, with the exception of a brief, inconsequential strip of film recently uncovered, nothing has surfaced to date which can insure for posterity the luxurious vision of the dancing Isadora. The annals of our century's progress in dance has suffered in this regard.

Almost as an act of compensation for the absence of filmed record, what the French public actually saw of Isadora's dances and how the critical community appraised those performances assumed heightened importance in my search for clues to her choreographies. Her many seasons of dance and her large number of performances in Paris were regularly well attended by a siz-able network of reviewers from newspapers, art journals, and literary, musical, and political periodicals. It is reasonably safe to conclude that the entire gamut of her concert repertory had been viewed and reviewed as in no other city.

In discussing dance criticism during the first quarter of this century, one must note that the advent of Isadora Duncan brought reviewers to a sophisti-cated dance medium whose style and character were contradictory to conven-tional orthodoxies and were far removed from dance's customary function as an adjunct to opera, theater, and music hall entertainment—the territorial experi-ence of most reviewers. There were the few, rare critics, whose distinctive back-grounds in the realm of esthetics gave them a critical expertise to produce a few masterpieces of keenly discerning observations. Fortunately, they have been published and made accessible in English translation. Instead I carefully perused the voluminous reporting of the large corps of active French theater journalists and critics who were well regarded at home, if unknown abroad. Surprising and welcome facts concerning the particulars of certain choreographies came to light. Without getting a step-by-step, phrase-by-phrase analysis, I was able to weave together a sense of Duncan's intent and the content of some of her more effective dance compositions and their impress upon her spectators.

Like all voyages, the quest abroad came to an end. On a deeply personal level the years of involvement at home and abroad yielded incalculable gratifi-cations. In my search to better define the life and meaning of another, I had also given definition and purpose to my own existence. The objective to enlarge my comprehension of Duncan and her dance as an esthetic phenomenon had been accomplished. It was while assembling and filing the visual and printed materi-als I had collected over the years that I questioned myself. I had given little thought to the ultimate utility of my experiences, findings, and understanding. Yet my confidence in the value of this material prompted the decision to share it. This book is the result.

It has come together through the efforts and generosity of many people in varying but significant ways. To my editor, Debi Elfenbein, of Princeton Book Company, Publishers, for her responsive and professional editorial labors on behalf of this book. For granting interviews, conversations, correspondence, and consultations, my special gratitude to dance historian Selma Jeanne

Cohen; George Dorris of *Dance Chronicle* for his prudent guidance; editor Barbara Palfy for her valuable advice and skill; Jacques Hébertot, director of the Théâtre Hébertot, Paris; journalist Michel Georges-Michel, Paris; Aia Bertrand of the Raymond Duncan Akademia, Paris; Mme. Langevin, daughter of artist Jules Grandjouan; artist A. Dunoyer de Segonzac, Paris; sculptress Antoinette Shulte, Paris; Jean-Jacques Poussier of the National Center for Scientific Research, Bellevue, France; Gilberte Cournand, Paris; Mary Meerson of the Cinémathèque Française, Paris; Janet Flanner (Gênet); Eva le Gallienne; Edward Steichen; Max Eastman; Abraham Walkowitz; Dr. Rogesin; Angus Duncan; Louis Untermeyer; Maxwell Stewart Simpson; Helen Farr Sloan; Palmer White; Leonard Baskin; Kathleen Hinni and her School of Creative Arts; Mr. and Mrs. Stefan Salter; Louise Craig Gerber; Sylvia Garson Doner; the Coty salon, Paris; Mme. Dan (Princess Rounling), Peiping; Marguerite Tjader Harris; Mother Superior Christina of the Sisters of Birgitta Convent, Darien, Connecticut.

For the invaluable knowledge and recollections of their roles in the history of Duncan dance they shared with me, my indebtedness to the original disciples of Isadora Duncan—Anna Duncan, Irma Duncan (Rogers), Maria-Theresa (Bourgeois); to Anita Zahn, director of the Elizabeth Duncan School in the United States; and to the contemporary dancers and teachers in the Duncan tradition—Hortense Kooluris, Ruth Fletcher, Nadja Chilkovsky Nahumck, Mignon Garland; and Lady Madeline Lytton and Odile Pyros, Paris, disciples of Lisa Duncan.

Special thanks for their kind permission to quote extracts from their published material to Wesleyan University Press, Middletown, Connecticut, for *Duncan Dancer*; Marcel Dekker, Inc., New York, for *Dance Perspectives* issue #64; Louis Untermeyer for his "Iphigenia in Aulis" and "Isadora Duncan Dancing (Chopin)" poems in Alfred A. Knopf's *Poems of the Dance*.

My deep appreciation for the foreign-language translators who smoothed a rough task: Maria Milne and J. H. Van Ammers (Dutch); Gisella Barcelone, Ruth Cohen, and Frieda Szwebel (French); Ruth Wertheimer (German); and Norma Shikman (Russian).

Grateful thanks to the individuals, departments, and institutions for their assistance in locating sources and permitting access to and use of specialized materials: Dr. Julia Sabine of the Art and Music departments, Newark [New Jersey] Public Library; The Print Collection of the Newark Museum; the Print Archive of the Philadelphia Museum of Art; the art libraries of the Frick Museum and Metropolitan Museum of Art, New York; Samuel Pearce of the Department of Theatre for use of the Arnold Genthe Collection of

Photographs and the Mary Fanton Roberts Collection on Isadora Duncan in the Museum of the City of New York; the Department of Photography, Museum of Modern Art, New York; Genevieve Oswald and the staff of the New York Public Library Dance Collection, Performing Arts Research Center at Lincoln Center, New York; the Robinson Locke Collection in the New York Public Library Billy Rose Theatre Collection, Performing Arts Research Center at Lincoln Center, New York; the Isadora Duncan and Arnold Genthe collections in the Prints and Photographs Division, Library of Congress, Washington, D.C.; Mary Doering of the Media Archive Department, American Red Cross, Washington, D.C.; Karen Haas, Curatorial Assistant, Isabella Stewart Gardner Museum, Boston, Massachusetts; Mr. Kastner of the Achenbach Collection (James Rambo, curator), Palace of the Legion of Honor Art Museum, San Francisco, California; Brooke Whiting of the Department of Special Collections, University of California at Los Angeles; Ellen S. Dunlap, research librarian, for use of the Craig Archives in the Humanities Research Center, University of Texas at Austin; the Francis Robinson Collection of Theatre, Music and Dance in the Vanderbilt University Archives, Nashville, Tennessee; Mme. S. Coron for use of the Gordon Craig Collection in the Département des Arts du Spectacle, Bibliothèque Nationale, Paris; the Auguste Rondel Theatre collection in the Bibliothèque de l'Arsenal, Paris; the dance collection in the Bibliothèque de l'Opéra, Paris; Cléopâtre Bourdelle and Rhodia and Michel Dufet of the Bourdelle Museum, Paris; Cécile Goldscheider, curator, Rodin Museum, Paris; Musée des Beaux Arts, Nantes, France; the public library of Nice, France; the Greek and Roman departments and the library, British Museum, London; E. Alexander av Toneel of the Theatre Museum, Amsterdam; the State Central Theatrical Library, Ministry of Culture, Moscow; Allegría Manegat of the Museo Clarà, Barcelona, Spain.

Indispensable were those who became extensions of my eyes and ears, seeking items and ways to facilitate this undertaking: Alfred Loewenthal, William Dworkin, Saul Schwarz, Henrietta Katzin (Moscow), Claire Destrée (Belgium), Leslie Getz, and Raymond Zimetbaum.

Immeasurable is my indebtedness to my parents, Essie and Berel, whose striving for lives of knowledge and fulfillment led me to Isadora Duncan; to my own family—Dan, Jeff, Eben, and Faye—for their patient encouragement toward this undertaking; and to Julia Levien, who brought the poetry and music of Isadora's dance into my life.

PROLOGUE

THERE IS A SINGULAR moment of magic when the drift of a new melody
enmeshes us and becomes a refrain that echoes for a lifetime. Such was the
moment when an eleven-year-old, in her first theater experience, tumbled
out of her seat in the Manhattan Opera House in 1928 at the sight of young,
lithe bodies in rhythmic and exhilarating motion. They were Isadora
Duncan's Russian girls from her school of dance in Moscow, on tour in the
United States with their gifted teacher, Irma Duncan, one of Isadora's famous
adopted disciples and I was that eleven-year-old.

I found myself in the midst of a riveting enchantment of bare legs and
arms moving so deliriously free as they danced the dances of Isadora. The
rhythmic life of their running and skipping across a seemingly limitless space
in playful freedom and blissful joy produced an intoxication in itself. The
graceful contours of their more contained and deliberate movements, like the
freezing of motion by a photographer, firmly set images in my mind. Around
this memory circled the thoughts that would attach me to the subject of
Isadora Duncan—her dance and her music. I was moved to seek what there
was about this art that had touched me so.

From early in this century, when the young Isadora, fresh from her
native America and in search of artistic freedom in a supportive climate
abroad, was stirring up large theater audiences in Germany and France, her
elusive art, indefinable, yet touching, sparked frequent rhetorical discourse.

The curiously different manner in which she moved her body and the physical and psychic impact it engendered, turned out to be, in effect, her pronouncement that the dance of modern times had arrived. It was the prelude to the dance of the future.

Surviving and prevailing for succeeding generations since her death in 1927 is an image of a compelling woman of enormous charm and flamboyant personality, whose life was driven by an undeviating passion for the dance and its power to delight the senses, to quicken the pulse, and to provoke the creative imagination. On stage Isadora projected beauty, charisma, and drama. From her stages around the globe she assumed the role of arch propagandist for her natural and expressive dance, believing it to be vital to the fulfilled life. To enthusiastic, if somewhat bewildered, audiences, she carried her message through speeches that were usually impromptu, brief, and to the point, or drawn out and off the track, superbly wise or embarrassingly sophomoric, utterly disarming or vehement and volatile. But it was the human aspirations of her dance and her pleas for all nations to make an education of dance for all children, for all people, that made her a symbol of liberty and egalitarianism for political and social reformers of the first decades of this century. In the final reckoning, she permanently recast the world's perception of dance from an entertaining diversion to an intelligently illuminating art expression.

The post-Duncan years, from the thirties through World War II and beyond, saw a radical transformation in all the arts. Dramatic alterations of form, style, and content emerged as artists experimented with new ways of communicating, interpreting, and reflecting our society's transition into the age of industrial technologies and behavioral psychologies. The modernism manifested by the new dance may not have brought much comfort to partisans of Isadora's more romantic and idealistic efforts, but unmistakable to them as they viewed the new expressions were the results of the stylistic and artistic freedoms that she pioneered during her esthetic renaissance. Almost osmotically, her influences were integrated within the multi-channels of contemporary innovations. Only through years of hard struggle did modern dance finally define and establish itself and gain its own loyal audience. What there was about the art of Isadora Duncan that had so touched countless lives in the preceding era all but disappeared from the mainstream of dance activity. Amid the enveloping strong currents of change, Isadora slipped into virtual obscurity.

Today, more than six decades after her death, Isadora appears to have risen, rebounding into the contemporary consciousness as a ponderable entity for biographers, dance estheticians, scholars, historians, and young dance students. The latter, in all probability, will continue to do what their predecessors have done—fall in love with the idea of Isadora Duncan, with her passion and her fearlessness to dance freely and boldly.

PART I

The Dance of
Isadora Duncan

CHAPTER ONE

Dance and Dancer

THE DANCER

A grave and ancient rapture
She has brought our troubled times —
Bearer of mystic treasures
With magic in her measure
She comes, her light steps lyric
And her white feet shod with rhymes.

SHAEMAS O'SHEEL
Jealous of Dead Leaves

EARLY ON ISADORA DUNCAN declared her dance to be an encounter with life through the movements of the human body: waves, spirals, circles— undulating, radiating, spinning—the patterns and directions of motions inherent in the natural world. It was from nature's rhythmic impulses and decorative forms that she shaped her life's invocations and revelations.

Movement has been described by Edward Gordon Craig, actor, theater director, and renovator of modern stage design, as "that infinite and beautiful thing drawn from space."[1] For Isadora Duncan, that beautiful thing was lost in the formalization of the reigning dance of her day: ballet. Her numerous discourses on this subject make clear her distaste and resistance to ballet with its conventional style unaltered from a long historical tenure in theatrical spectacle.

When Isadora posited that ballet perpetuated a thoroughly implausible format for a twentieth-century art, new ideas and forms were already emerging in the other arts. Ballet alone remained a complacent, insular institution of archaic forms and constraining movements floundering "in a maze of intricate artifice."[2] This dance institution, Isadora argued, continued its insensitivity to the need to delve into "the development of dance and what makes up the essence of dance." There was preoccupation with inventing when there should have been the drive for searching. Ballet ignored art's highest mission: "the human need to transmit and express emotions." What was unacceptable to Isadora's concept of a true dance art was the exploitation of physical action without addressing intelligent substance; gesture was not to be isolated from inner motivation.

Academicians of the period railed with anger and sarcasm against the controversial cubists, for instance. Sculptor Auguste Rodin, known for his advocacy of those in revolt against stylistic decadence in the arts, reacted. He supported the new artistic vision and accepted the cubists' deviation from accustomed perspectives and tastes. They were something different. "So much the better," he asserted. "They are something else."[3]

With her own "something else," Isadora presented herself as a redeemer come to deliver the dance from its shackled state. Leaping over the boundaries of entrenched dance orthodoxies, she landed in the new century armed with a manifesto illuminating her dance of the future. Into a theatrical atmosphere thick with tales of princely fantasies, of winged sylphs and dragonflies, she introduced a human art premise: a philosophy of life as art, beauty, intelligence, and moral purpose integrated through the dance experience.

For Isadora Duncan the root of all artistic creativity was born of man's idealization of the human form and his consciousness of its divinity. Curious about how her own movements came into being, she subjected herself to long periods of scrutiny, analyzing her manner of moving and gesturing. This analysis helped clarify the relationship of her body to the gestural product it issued. She further sensed that all her movements seemed to be generated from a central source, the base of her motile power, which she located in the solar plexus region of the body. This center of feeling, when initially activated by an idea or emotion, impelled her toward movement. Like a streaming current her gestures flowed out in visible responses: "Working much like a motor does—in a progressive development—a single movement from an initial impetus gradually follows a rising curve of inspiration, up to those gestures that exteriorize the fullness of feeling, spreading ever under the impulse that has swayed [the dancer]."[4]

The body's motion was then capable of heightened expressive function, shaped and channeled into a kinetic language. In both psychological and artistic terms, the body behaved as an agent or carrier of the individual's identity with the self and its conscious and unconscious universes. In terms of dance it had to do so for Isadora "by means of the motions which are natural to it." Movements not corresponding to the basic function and design of the human form were unnatural; unnatural was ugly and equated with wrong, and conversely, natural was beautiful and therefore right. True dance, or correct dance, sprang from those undulations of the body's rhythms that, though separate, were sympathetic to the organic rhythms of the natural world and to the universal energies of the earth. Conceptually, she translated nature's rhythms into human rhythms.

The most potent catalyst for triggering Isadora's artistic imagination was music, its alternating rhythms of action and repose corresponding to her rhythms of tension and relaxation, her ebb and flow. Music that "combined with absolute perfection both terrestrial and human rhythms"[5] was her first choice, and from it she composed dances that were a unity of elements, much as music was an organization of sounds and pulses. This unity of music and dance, sensitized by interpretive insights, became Isadora's credo of art as revealed truth.

The particular form, style, and exaltation of spirit that gave Duncan dance its distinctive character have largely been credited to the art of ancient Greece and the Italian Renaissance. These beguiling representations engulfed Isadora and gave credence to her still-gestating ideas and impelled her search for stylistic identity. Although the splendor of Hellenic culture had captivated historian, scholar, and artist for centuries and was at the root of Isadora's intellectual nurturing, its visual perfection and spiritual essence left a permanent impression on her when, in 1903, she personally beheld the magnitude of Greek legend in pictorial artifacts, as well as in the surviving monuments of stone. "I studied them . . . to discover the secret of their ecstasy."[6] She savored each preserved relic as a portrait of unexcelled grace of bearing and physical beauty. Natural, uncomplicated movements in positions of action or repose demonstrated that the ancient Greeks danced with all the body—head, torso, arms, legs, feet, hands, and fingers.

As worshipped by the Greeks and evidenced in their sculpture and architecture, praise of physical beauty is echoed from generation to generation. Returning from a trip to Greece, French sculptor Aristide Maillol described how "under the pellucid skies . . . contours [of statues] seem to move, to live, to melt away like sugar only to reappear immediately and more sharply . . . it is very moving."[7]

In 1982 art critic John Russell wrote of his "personal awe . . . the Parthenon is majesty, lucidity, serenity never surpassed."[8] It was in the portico of the Parthenon that Edward Steichen photographed Isadora Duncan in 1920 as "she made a gesture completely related to the columns";[9] she appears to be intoning her hymn to the eternal rhythms of the universe. Philosophically and physically, Isadora embodied Terpsichore's joy in the dance. Undeniably, she evoked in her forms the graceful line of Hellenic bas-reliefs and vase paintings, but it was their physical character and quality of gesture that rooted her dance in nature rather than in archeology.

Out of her fascination with the naturalism of the human form that adorned ancient relics, Isadora advanced for her artistic purposes an engaging hypothesis: If these figures, long frozen in time, were to suddenly thaw and animate, they would proceed in their motions with natural grace, in harmony of body and spirit, and with supreme dignity. The almost palpable sensation of these ancient beings, poised to step into the present, underscores the remarkable durability and timelessness of their classical splendor and certifies their adaptability for contemporary expression. "The dance of the future is the dance of the past and the dance of eternity, and has been and will always be the same."[10]

Through sylvan glades Echo, Pan, Bacchus, and Ariadne romped invisibly in the creative fancies of Isadora's early career. The classical scholars in her audience readily noted the dionysiac thrust of her head in executing a rhapsodic sequence, the brandishing of the thyrsus during a bacchanalian frenzy of motion, the classical stateliness of body line in the modulation of movements, and the sublime poise of the figure in repose. To many she became a reincarnation of classic antiquity, an animated Grecian frieze.

While Greek art exerted a developmental influence on the visible form and spirit of her movements, Renaissance art imparted the interior life of her gesture. Isadora observed in the masterful strokes of painters Botticelli and Mantegna how the moving line of gesture was enhanced by feeling. In the works of the former—in particular his Three Graces from the *Primavera*—she found the simulated motion of the contoured figures evocative in their pronounced decorative and physical appeal. Though depicted with simplicity, their expressiveness was fully revealed. One needs but a quick glance at the scene of dancing nymphs in Mantegna's *Allegory of Parnassus* to understand the dancer's interest in the arrangement of his moving figures. Moreover, the lightly draped garments that softly grace their spirited bodies could well have served as models for Isadora's lyrical forms three hundred years later.

The working premise for Isadora and many other artists in the pre-World War I years was to recreate one's adoration of beauty and nature through a medium of art and render it esthetically comprehensible to its own era. The artist's mission and responsibility was to make a universal work that espoused the moral and social considerations governing art. Only then would the resulting product be faithful to enduring human values and ideals. The creative mission was the faithful commitment to truth, goodness, and beauty.

Although later in her life Isadora smiled at her own youthful naïvetés and "apostolic sentiments" for her art, her striving for an art that would enrich all people was uncompromised. During the twenties she voiced her concern about the trendy avant-garde movement in the arts around her. Basically unsympathetic to the unsettling currents of the period, she did acknowledge, with some admiration, the skillfulness of the new young artists, but believed her own work beyond their transitory and superficial nature, their lack of "heart and head," and the absence of a human ideal.

The interpretive revelations of Isadora cast a spell over a large spectrum of European intellectual society early in this century. Her movement images suggested subtleties of meaning that were startling in their originality. Through the body lay a capability to translate infinite realms of experience into a potent, metaphoric language, superseding that of verbal communication. With the individualism of her approach to art, the demarcating line between the traditional dance and the modern esthetic she proposed was irrevocably drawn.

NOTES

1. Edward Gordon Craig, "Artist of the Theatre of the Future," *The Mask*, Vol. 1, #3–4, 1908, p. 68.
2. Isadora Duncan, "Les Idées d'Isadora Duncan sur la danse," *La Société Internationale de la Musique*, January 1912, pp. 9, 10.
3. J. Cladel, ed., *Rodin—The Man and His Art*, p. 249.
4. Isadora Duncan, "Depths," *The Art of the Dance*, p. 99.
5. Isadora Duncan, *My Life*, p. 89.
6. Isadora Duncan, "Depths," *The Art of the Dance*, p. 139.
7. Aristide Maillol in Michel Georges-Michel, *From Renoir to Picasso*, p. 280.
8. John Russell, "Puzzle of the Parthenon," *New York Times*, January 3, 1982.
9. Edward Steichen, *My Life in Photography*, chapter 6.
10. Isadora Duncan, *Tanz der Zukunft* (The Dance of the Future), p. 12.

CHAPTER TWO

On Stage

THE DANCER
I saw dear countrymaid
How soon shall spring
From this our native land
Great loveliness.

WILLIAM CARLOS WILLIAMS

DURING HER APOGEE, ISADORA'S dances were seen by French architect Louis Sue as "the most stunning, the most original . . . they passed over
Paris like a breath of Spring."[1] Sue credited them as having affected all the art
developments in the first decade of this century: ballet, haute couture, painting, sculpture, and dramatic arts as related to movement.

Motion shaped the basis of Isadora's dance forms and their powerful and
emotional appeal lay in their fluid interactions. Blending the visual (dance)
with the tonal (music), she presented architectural designs of breadth and
touching beauty. The course and continuity of her movements were orches-
trated like a symphony of contrasting tempi, rhythms, and tonal colors. In

9

their gentle and fluent transitions in and out of one another, in their smooth-ness of execution, her sculpted freestyle gestures flowed like oil.

In his *Sketch Book* Gordon Craig wrote: "All she did was done with great ease—or so it seemed. This it was which gave her an appearance of power."[2] In moments of stillness Isadora could generate countless undetectable ener-gies that steadily deepened the resonance of her postures. Her more fleeting motions brought pulsations to the stage extremities in a matter of moments. Spectators accustomed to a more conventional theater of the period had to focus and orient themselves differently to interpret her symbols. Eyes had to shift frequently in order to follow quick turns of direction and to keep abreast of an accelerating momentum. Backs straightened and necks craned to catch each of her unobtrusive stirrings, lest her utterance be lost. The action and color on stage suggested to Futurist Emilio Marinetti, "many points of contact between Isadora's art and pictorial impressionism."[3] Onlookers were enveloped in the mysteries and abstractions of her images, yet found in their forms engaging and recognizable human qualities, chaste and forthright in their appeal and completely devoid of the erotic.

She walked, ran, strode, skipped, jumped, leapt, knelt, reclined, fell, spun, crouched, lunged, galloped ("Go, then," an astounded critic exclaimed, "go ask of a ballet dancer to gallop!"[4]). With these movements, wonderfully wild or gracefully tender, she created memorable portrayals of grandeur, solemnity, desolation, or joyousness.

The program notes for Isadora's 1909 New York appearance with Walter Damrosch carried the following descriptive excerpt by French play-wright Henri Lavedan: " . . . with the motion out of the very Parthenon itself, with splendid freedom of action, the young woman draws herself up to her full height and steps out into dance, limbs nude, strong, firm as Greek marble in the light, the folds of the tunic falling away as a background to the flexible, finely modeled knees; in the firm, clear flesh, the head alert, the eyes insa-tiable, every pore exquisite."[5] American painter John Sloan, returning from the dancer's Carnegie Hall matinee on February 15, 1911 entered the follow-ing in his diary: "Isadora as she appears on that big simple stage seems like all womanhood—she looms as big as the mother of the race. A heavy solid fig-ure, large columnar legs, a solid high belly, breasts not too full and her head seems no more important than it should be to give the body the chief place."[6]

Of particular fascination were Isadora's arms and hands: the arms "grace-ful, passionately impulsive, subtle, irresistible," or "significant as a line of poetry." Her arms, beautiful in moments lyrical and serene or powerful when exhorting to battle, remained beautiful to the end, when her body itself had changed. Wrists and hands were manipulated with exceptional grace and flexibility, fingers "trembled to catch ecstasy." "Gestures are an art in themselves, her hands weave contoured colored patterns in the air, her countenance . . . can set a mood eloquently, as of joy, or fear or hate, or vengeance. . . ."[7] All of her gestures resembled some natural organic process of emerging, evolving, and growing. "Everything harmonious . . . gestures always spread from the center like a flower unfolding its petals, the arms part from the body first gradually opening the hands and letting the fingers unroll."[8]

Largely disregarded by ballet masters of old, the torso and the chest played a dominant role in the projection and quality of the Duncan élan. Her use of the flexible trunk gave the impression, through the inflated thorax, of a body buoyant, light enough to soar. (Arthur B. Davies made a study of the Greek theory of inhalation which he applied to his painted figures; the lifted thorax produced a more vital appearance.)

From the moment of her discovery that a creative dancer must speak in movement that springs from the self, Isadora began to create for that self. Essentially, and at her most magnetic, she was a solo performer. There is striking testimony to the phenomenal command of her artistic forces when alone on stage. More focused and intense in the projection of her material, Isadora, as a solo artist, could hold the attention of her viewers without one's eye momentarily wandering to take in the customary paraphernalia of other stage spectacles: the corps de ballet, the costumes, the stage sets. Yet, from the outset, she claimed never to be dancing alone. In this context it is of interest to refer to the collection of miscellaneous dances—long since gone—which the ambitious novice brought with her to England from the United States in 1899. There were her mimed interpretations of Greek poems, as in Pan and Echo, and her gestural responses to pictorial subjects such as *Bacchus* and *Ariadne* and the *Allegory of Spring*, where by innuendo of gesture, facial expression, reversal of directions, or a quick adjustment of costume, the presence of another, or others, was made felt. Her unusually strong mimetic gifts could beckon a companion, inveigle a lover, escape a pursuer and later, in her more substantial works, summon a throng or lead an army into battle. And there were those moments as she danced that an unsuspecting audience would be included in her communication. Steadily moving down to the stage edge, her arms opening wide, she would envelop the enchanted viewers in a metaphoric embrace.

An eyewitness to Isadora's earliest public dance recital in London's New Gallery in 1900 described the *Primavera*: "Isadora impersonated, one after the other, all the figures in that full canvas. Now, the head inclined, hand uplifted, she was the pensive spring herself, then with draperies billowing 'round her bounding limbs she was the Zephyr; again she glided through the exquisite postures of the Three Graces in their rondo."[9]

Uncommon levels of strength and elasticity marked her interpretations to musical scores that were frequently of trying length, complex rhythmic structures, and fluctuating emotional intensities. Confidently she drew from enviable reserves of energy for the endurance needed to sustain the momentum and shape of movement without fuzzing the details. Her vitality and her labors to attain a disciplined and superbly supple body are recalled by Marie Kist who worked for Isadora in Holland in 1906. Unable at certain periods in her accelerating career to maintain a regimen of exercise, she would compensate "by going at it with thirty times more power when she did."[10] (Kist also recounted a lesser-known fact of the very human side of Isadora: She suffered stage fright for the first few minutes on stage and was steadied by Kist's hands from behind the curtains.)

Despite Isadora's declared aversion to the muscular and acrobatic emphasis placed on a traditional dancer's preparation for her craft, she made use of her own extensive gymnastic groundwork for making the bodily apparatus pliant and responsive, "making it docile to the rhythm of the soul," as poetically phrased by actress Ellen Terry. One of her admired assets was her nimbleness and lightness of tread. The disciples who later shared the concert stage with her would eventually outdo her in the physically demanding executions, but they would not rival her lighter-than-air feats. "She comes as if not touching the ground, as on a beam, as on a high note of a flute . . . her steps make no more sound than do flowers nodding earthward by a gentle breeze."[11]

The absence of precedent for what she represented and the implications of the modernism in her work stirred up a steaming brew of enthusiasm, skepticism, and confusion. There was no dearth of journalistic satire to puncture the merit of the new and different. The German magazine *Jugend* printed an item about Isadora's first appearance in Munich in 1902: A group of cloakroom attendants gathered to voice their curiosity about the much bruited dancer. One of them boldly volunteered to steal a peek into the auditorium to see for herself. Returning moments later, she shrugged her shoulders and reported to them: "I don't know—when I looked in she seemed to be catching flies."[12]

No less baffled were those professionally assigned to judge her. They had no precedent by or context in which to evaluate her advances in dance style. To what could one compare an artist whose creations were so anarchic and antithetical to conventional disciplines as to negate established criteria for assessment? They relied on the prevailing norms *for* virtuosity, and failed to comprehend her fundamental repudiation and movement *against* it. Thus, she was found to be "inadequately trained" for her profession, her technique "deficient," her dance vocabulary "limited," her choreography virtually nonexistent. Some critics considered her "steps" and "poses" redundant, producing monotony of movement, although they acknowledged the power of expression as formidable. Still others responded to her dance forms and range of movements as effective and sufficiently varied to articulate her expressive intent; they marvelled at her economy of means and at the artful use of them. There were the few who from the outset cautioned against dissecting this unusual art lest the heart of its mystery be "plucked out."

It would be a mistake, André Marty wrote in 1909, to compare Isadora to anything else: "It is an art in itself . . . she attains the beautiful by means all her own. There was most surely a discipline, a Duncan discipline, that admirably served her artistic ends."[13] A firm, resilient technique structured the design of her motions and facilitated the body's fluent transitions. Her technique seemed so effortless and flawless that its presence went unnoticed, as though absorbed into the esthetic creation. "Such dancing is, of course, not lawless, but deeply lawful, the artifices of dancing are thrown aside, the great rhythms of life are enabled to play through the physical instrument."[14]

To watch Isadora move with her inimitable ease and freedom of gesture, likened to some liberated bird, was to feel drawn into a spontaneous unfolding of the moment. As a result, she had to repeatedly explain that her dance was not suddenly inspired. Nonetheless, she earned a reputation as an improvisor whose random creativity lacked both an underlying discipline and a preconceived choreographic organization. Tenacious as the proverbial barnacles clinging to the ship, this notion persists even to this day.

Quite plausibly, the force of Isadora's performance, coupled with the effervescent spirit and physical loveliness of her body in motion, tended to obscure other esthetic considerations and in themselves stood for the sum of her artistry. The misperception and popular myth of her improvised dancing style become understandable upon further examination. A specific insight from critic André Levinson observed that "at the base of [Duncan's] art lies an unconscious sense of formal creation."[15] There is little doubt that she was endowed with the unique aptitude for producing almost instinctively what for most artists is a lengthy and laborious endeavor: she could swiftly synthesize from disparate elements a semblance of intelligent order. Isadora's artistic precociousness almost rivalled that of Johann Strauss who was reputed to be able to compose a waltz in the morning, rehearse it mid-day; and première it at night. Reliable anecdotes tell of instances when she baffled her assigned conductor or piano accompanist slated for a pre-concert rehearsal with her. She listened to the music but once or twice, until she mentally structured and set the dance role to her satisfaction. And that was the rehearsal!

Nevertheless, it was more than "an unconscious sense" that governed the final outcome of Isadora's creative efforts. The freshness and sense of aliveness that her dancing imparted may have appeared spontaneous, but John Dewey was closer to the mark when he attributed spontaneity "only to those who have long been absorbed in observations of related material and whose imaginations have long been occupied with reconstructing what they see and hear . . . "[16] Spontaneity for Isadora was the result of long periods of familiarizing herself with music and of plotting dances to musical works well in advance of the dates these dance compositions were completed, as was the case with Gluck's *Iphigénie,* and Wagner's *Tannhäuser* and *Parsifal.* "My art has been growing in me for years," she frequently commented. With her dancer's passion to dance and her artistic need to create, her fluent ideas were always at work. Movement fragments sprang to her fertile mind in much the same way that great composers mentally preserve melodic phrases until they can be committed to paper.

For indefinite periods Isadora internalized the music with her envisioned gestures until they grew into a promising conception. These previously conceived thematic fragments or movement motifs became the starter fabric of a dance. Then with imagination, heart, and artistic conscience, she wove her sketches into a tapestry of movements and forms. Only then, in a state of artistic and conceptual coherence, was it acclaimed a fresh creation.

As important as music was to Isadora, it was not her accompaniment, but rather an independent artistic entity from which she drew her dancer's will and sustenance. Even when she became a celebrity and the headlining attraction of her dance events, she shared her prestige with the noted conductors and orchestras who performed the great scores to which she danced. The conductor alone assumed responsibility for interpretation of the music, and once Isadora conferred with him on his overall approach, she attuned herself to it. No particular tempo or phrasing markings would be deliberately disturbed to accommodate or facilitate her actions on stage.

Historically, choreography has been part of the very fabric of theater, a spectacular mélange of music, mime, dance, acting, costume, and stagecraft. Isadora rightfully considered her dance not of the theater in that sense. She was uncomfortable with the designation "choreography" because that conveyed a contrived framework for technical display, a pre-planned scheme that threatened to exercise a constraining effect on the independent physical action and interpretive scope of the dancer. Choreography as a blueprint for Isadora was purposely flexible, never intended to disguise, dominate, or compromise the primacy of expression in dance. In contrast with our era, in which choreography, performance, and production are often in the hands of different people, Isadora alone created, interpreted, and produced her esthetic product; her artistic and professional judgment prevailed.

A more sophisticated and elaborately devised choreography would have been needless from a dancer who could subtly be in control of all she was achieving. She balanced the gestural and musical dynamics, finely shading her rhythmic emphases. In repetitions of a music and dance phrase she produced such subtleties of variation that a critic compared them to the palette of eighteenth-century French painter Jean-Baptiste-Siméon Chardin, with his "three gradations of white pigment."[17]

Fans who returned to the theater to see a favorite work knew well that she would not appear as before in the same dance—a transient mood, her physical energies, or a variation of response to the music could modify an anticipated moment, but the structural outlines and the inherent character of the dance's content would remain essentially unaltered. She left little to chance with regard to the technical aspects of her composition design.

A contemporary, authoritative source, Julia Levien—teacher and professional performer of Duncan repertory and dance technique—has offered her specialized observations on Isadora's dances that have survived, in most instances, more than seven decades. Originally taught the Duncan repertory by Irma and Anna Duncan, Levien has long analyzed, evaluated, and demonstrated this body of work as "transmittable entities of art." The dances bear an unmistakably clear choreographic framework, an individual architecture that exists for each, a well-defined floor pattern, and a vocabulary of movements of varied shape, volume, textures, and dynamic contrasts. These underlying structural elements, Levien points out, have given Isadora Duncan's known compositions the capacity for survival and for transmission.[18]

Costume

Dramatically different as Isadora's style of dance was from other dance genres of that era, the Duncan costume was no less an unusual departure. The pendulum of stage dress swung from the ballet's form-fitting outfits, designed to portray a story-line character, with traditional tutus and slippers in tow, to the voluminous yards of fabric that virtually eclipsed Loie Fuller's body as she ingeniously concealed the mechanical appendages that produced her illusionary effects, to the cobweb airiness of garment that barely covered the barefoot and bare-armed Isadora.

Society's stringent dress code was not the true deterrent to Isadora's dancing in the nude, frequently but erroneously cited as her first choice of costume. Eccentric as she may have been for the social moralists of her period, she was quite pragmatic where her professional judgment was concerned. While she divested her dance of the traditional theatrical trappings surrounding her, she retained a keen awareness of dance as a visual medium, conscientiously seeking and selecting the apparel that most enhanced her esthetic creations.

Honoring the plasticity and beauty of the human figure demanded that all the motions of her free body be revealed. Lawsuits brought against her on grounds of indecent exposure were not uncommon in the early years. Isadora could never understand what all the fuss was about. The same people who protested her revealing coverings admired the painters and sculptors who drew dancing figures clad in similar light draperies. Once the audience's initial shock had subsided, however, Isadora's unshod foot was welcome after centuries of what one apparently grateful reviewer described as coverings of "ugly pink satin shoes which make a foot resemble a shapeless parcel tied with ribbons."[19]

A loose and filmy garment that did not obstruct the body's freedom of movement, that was designed simply and visually beautiful when in motion, became Isadora's choice of covering. The classic tunic she adopted and wore throughout her career in modifications to suit her artistic purposes or ingenious fancies, was based on the Greek Ionic *chiton*. Favored by sculptors of the classical age, it was worn by *maenads* (seen on antique red-figure vases) and was a one-piece garment which, when authentically worn, was gathered at the shoulders and held by a clasp, brooch, or cameo. The chiton could be softly bloused by belt or cord around the waist. Isadora and other Duncan dancers used elastic band crisscrossed between the breasts, and wound around the waist and often around the hip to keep the light material from billowing up too high. Several slits extending from below the hip allowed for free pelvic and leg movements.

From European importers of Indian and Chinese silks, Isadora selected fabrics of luxurious fibers and colors for her diaphanous veils. "Greek art abounds in representations of modest and beautiful young girls dancing hand in hand or independently, sometimes carrying light veils or scarves, often cloaked in flowing garments whose folds add to the charm of [the] choreographic pattern."[20] Their fluctuating lines and delicacy of colors swirled about her in the spirited dances of youth and joy. Henri Lavedan described her "clothed in chiffon flowing about her . . . sometimes fluttering back from the beautiful body as a shadow clinging to her."[21]

The world of *haute couture* took notice of the unadorned simplicity and elegance of Isadora's loose and graceful costuming. Isadora inspired many designs, including Parisian designer Paul Poiret's tunic dress and Count Mariano Fortuny's chef d'oeuvre, the Delphos gown—a luxurious, finely pleated silk dress, suggestive of the classical age as represented on stage by the dancer.

*Figurine of Dancing Girl, Greek,
Third century B.C. (Collection
of the Walters Art Gallery,
Baltimore, Maryland)*

*Figurine of Dancing Woman,
Greek, Second century B.C.
(Collection of the Walters Art
Gallery, Baltimore, Maryland)*

Program, F.R. Benson's Shakespearean Theatre Company, February 15-April 11, 1900. Miss Isadora Duncan is listed as dancing in Henry V and A Midsummer Night's Dream. (Collection of the author)

A series on Isadora in Pan and Echo at the Sarah Bernhardt Theatre, Paris, 1903. Drawing by Valentine Lecomte from Album of Line Drawings of Isadora Duncan.

Isadora, sketch attributed to Aristide Maillol. (Collection of the Bibliotheque de l'Opera, Paris)

Isadora, drawing by José Clará

Isadora Duncan, oil painting on canvas by John Sloan, 1911. (Collection of Milwaukee Art Museum. Gift of Mr. and Mrs. Donald B. Abert.)

Isadora, etching by John Sloan, 1911. (Coourtesy of Helen Farr Sloan and Delaware Art Museum)

Isadora Dancing Chopin, *lithograph,*
by Edward Gordon Craig, 1906.
(Collection of the author)

Isadora, London, 1908. (Collection of the author)

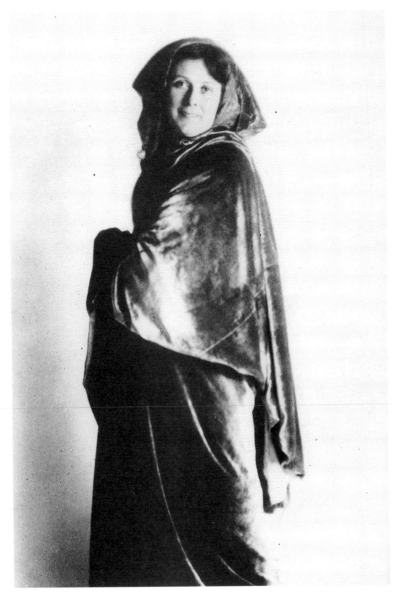

Isadora in cloak designed by Mme. Babani. Cloak in the collection of the author. (Roger Viollet Collection)

These lighter, less confining costumes influenced subsequent choreographers, as evidenced by the performances of the Russian Ballets in France. Strongest of the impressions created by Isadora on the principal young choreographers of Russia at the turn of the century were the *plastique* of her more expressive arms, their softer, more flexible line, and the fascinating use of her light and simple costuming that seemed to flow in harmony with her moving body. Among the Russian ballet productions in which historians of that era have traced influences of this plastique and stage apparel were Michel Fokine's *Eunice* (1907), Anna Pavlova's costume in Nicholas Legat's *La Nuit* (1909), Vaslav Nijinsky's *L'Après-midi d'un faune* (1912) with its Grecian-styled costumes, nymphs, and bare feet and Alexander Gorsky's version of *Swan Lake* (1920) with its loose tunic style reminiscent of Isadora, whose impact on that choreographer was a lasting one.

Isadora's basic costume consisted of a tunic, over which might be draped a *chlamys*, or cloak, of varying length, fullness, texture, and weight. In Isadora's knowing and talented hands, the draped overscarf was said to be an art in itself, contributing its own movement in harmony with her physical motions: "She seems to transfer her magic even to the fabrics she works with; no one who has ever seen it can forget the beauty of the slow sinking of her cloak to earth in one of her dances; the ripples in it move the spirit like a series of soft mysterious modulations in music."[22] When standing still, enveloped in her robes, Isadora left a lasting impression of majesty and classical splendor.

For Gluck's *Orpheus* Isadora appeared in a robe of flowing gray; in the *Dance of the Furies*, a deep red, short tunic. In *Parsifal* she was garbed in white silk, beautifully draped, her hair adorned with pink flowers. For Scriabin's *Poem of Ecstasy* roses edged her white silk tunic. Her *Marche Slav* and *Redemption*, choreographed later in her career, presented her in a plain sheath of coarse dark-brown material, or draped in fabrics of somber colors when interpreting the graver, more liturgical character of the music. "Where now," a critic wondered, "have I seen those strong folds of dark material? Perhaps in the figures which decorate the tombs of the Dukes of Burgundy."[23]

Stage Design

Isadora would step onto the concert stage which, of her own volition, she left bare, empty except for a backdrop and, on occasion, a piano. In her early days, there were times when neither stage nor platform set her off, only a square area separated from the spectators and carpeted for her bare feet. "This was the whole of her paraphernalia, all the rest is Isadora Duncan," a Munich correspondent wrote to *St. Louis Gazette* in 1902.

Isadora projected into the challenging emptiness of space—much as an artist puts his first markings on a blank canvas—the unfolding visions and concepts of her imagination. Publisher Mary Fanton Roberts described: "A great space, silent and high, separated from the world by curtains of blue—as she walked, ran, opening, extending arms, spreading fingers, she penetrated space as it penetrated her."[24] Spanish sculptor José Clara related that there was no stage set "except long, neutral curtains which disappeared up into darkness and left the imagination full play."[25]

The color blue has been characterized as the color of water and of sky: It is said to evoke a sense of space and an ethereal quality; as used in medieval religious painting, it represented faith. Perhaps Isadora considered these traits in choosing a background color for her dancing. The known fact is that throughout her performing years, on stage as well as in her studio, she performed before a light blue backdrop which gave the illusion of spaciousness, of limitless scope . . . simple draperies that seemed to rise to a vast height, "as high as the eye could reach and lost in cathedral-like distance,"[26] creating the effect not only of space, distance, and time, but of "ancient trees that guard the vaporous cleft of the Pythoness in the forests of Delphi."[27]

One takes lightly Isadora's own claim in her *Art of the Dance* to have invented her blue curtains when she was five years old and "danced before them ever since."[28] Her disciple Irma stated, more realistically no doubt, that during Isadora's active early years as a performer in Europe, she danced to whatever was available in the theater—but the simpler, the better. References to "plain curtains" and "blue backgrounds" are common in the accounts of this period.

Isadora's lover, Gordon Craig, recorded seeing (and sketching) in 1904 a stage backed by a few gray curtains hung between short pillars. In 1905 and 1906, when he acted as her manager of sorts, his notebook entries pertaining to her engagements specify for the decor, "plain blue sky at back and at sides, if possible." For her landmark appearance in Russia late in 1904, there is mention in the St. Petersburg press of a thick rug on stage, a sky-blue backdrop with "cigarlike poplars and fragments of classical columns" at the sides. Isadora's own memory of this event has her dancing before a simple blue curtain.

Seeking to clarify the ambiguity of the curtains, I consulted Isadora's disciple Maria-Theresa, who described the famous drapes this way: "Horizon blue—the sky at dusk—the blue of the sea—the blue vert of the forests and mountains from afar—the blue of night—endless space—infinity. All this was Isadora's (our) curtains. They suggested everything—shadow and light—

all depth and all heights and they changed color according to the light."[29] If her reply left me no further enlightened on the subject of the color blue, it did help solve the quandary about why the critics, reporting on the very same performance, could refer to the curtains at the same time as blue, green, gray, light, dark.

American scenic designer Robert Edmond Jones nostalgically recalled the backdrops as "dreamy blue filled with illusion, warm and soft"; a "robin-egg blue," contributed Mabel Dodge Luhan. Readers of Carl van Vechten's reviews learned that there were green curtains falling in folds from the heights at the back and along the sides of the stage, leaving a semi-circular space in the floor's center illuminated by a dim, rose-colored light. Minimizing the use of footlights because they threw ugly shadows on stage, strong light projectors instead were placed in the front corners of the platform, making more uniform the light distribution and deepening the folds of the curtain backdrop. Tinted lights effected a mysterious alchemy that transformed the atmosphere into the delicate blue of dreams or the pale pink of joy.

Critiques on Isadora's art and reviews of her appearances rarely excluded mention of the distinguished draperies, considered innovative for the times. As she traveled the great distances to the countless destinations her celebrity demanded of her, the curtains were sometimes delayed, misplaced and retrieved, damaged and repaired, lost, even replaced—but always remained that same shade of near-blue.

NOTES

1. Louis Sue, "Isadora Duncan—Météore de Génie," in *Sous le Signe d'Isadora*.
2. Gordon Craig, *Sketch Book*.
3. R. W. Flint, ed., *Marinetti: Selected Writings*, p. 137.
4. Pierre Mille, "Miss Isadora Duncan," *Le Théâtre*, February 1909.
5. Carnegie Hall program, December 2, 1909. Translated from the French *L'Illustration*, February 6, 1909.
6. Bruce St. John, ed., *John Sloan's New York Scene*, p. 507.
7. W. Anthony, *San Francisco Chronicle*, November 26, 1917.
8. G. Etscher, *Forum*, September 1911, p. 326.
9. M. J. Meeus, "A Star Danced," *Cornhill Magazine*, May 1932, p. 545.
10. Interview with Marie Kist by Dutch journalist, 1936.
11. Maurice de Faramond, unidentified source, April 10, 1920.
12. *Jugend*, Number 13, 1904, p. 257.
13. André Marty, "Miss Isadora et son école d'enfants," *Comoedia Illustré*, February 1909, p. 122
14. John Collier, "The Stage, a New World," *Survey*, June 3, 1916, p. 251.
15. André Levinson, "The Art and Meaning of Isadora Duncan," *Ballet Review*, Vol. 6, Number 4, 1977–78, p. 9.
16. John Dewey, *Art as Experience*, p. 72.

17. Ovion, "Les danses d'Isadora Duncan," *Mercure de France*, March 1, 1910. p. 80.
18. Julia Levien in conversation with author, 1983.
19. Etscher, p. 326.
20. Lillian Lawlor, *The Dance in Ancient Greece*, p. 102.
21. "Mme. Isadora Duncan," *L'Illustration*, February 6, 1909.
22. Ernest Newman, "Dances of Isadora Duncan," *Living Age*, June 4, 1921, p. 607.
23. Michel Georges-Michel, review of *Funeral March* (Chopin), unidentified source, April 5, 1920.
24. Mary Fanton Roberts, "Isadora Duncan—My Friend," in *Art of the Dance*, p. 28.
25. Jose Clara, "Isadora Duncan," *L'Art Décoratif*, August/September 1913, p. 107.
26. R. E. Jones, "Gloves of Isadora," *Theatre Arts*, October 1947.
27. *Ibid.*
28. Shaemas O'Sheel, "Isadora Duncan—Artist," in *Art of the Dance*, p. 33.
29. Letter from Maria-Theresa to author, September 7, 1967.

CHAPTER THREE

The Lyric Muse

"Music not merely reproduces the individuality and mood of a particular composer: It becomes also the echo and resonance of the time, of events, and of social and ethical standards."

ANTON RUBINSTEIN

IN 1906, SIX YEARS after her arrival in Europe to launch her career, Isadora told a young Dutch writer what she thought the perfect dance should be. For her this was an unaccompanied dance, a self-sufficient expression, independent from all musical support. Such a dance would have the dancer moving in accord with her own bodily rhythms, in dialogue only with an inner voice—no music, no text. It would be pure dancing for oneself to the "rhythms of some invisible music," not interpreting but creating expression and taking place in privacy or "before a group of knowledgeable insiders."[1]

Isadora's concepts were original for the period in which they were expressed. She articulated dance as intimacy, mystery, and wonder at the rhythmic body. She drew a distinction between meanings that result from interpreting existing subjects and those that come with the moment of spontaneous creation.

Ideally, she suggested, dance should contain its purity in the privacy of the creative act and in its autonomy from other imposing factors. Pragmatically, she did not always apply these notions of a consummate art, but they were not entirely visionary. Discernible in her subsequent writings and in the dances she presented to the public were echoes of her early precepts, albeit in moderated form. Isadora's particular intellectual focus and emotional nature had discovered in music the decisive and mandatory inspirational element that brought high excitement and full realization to her artistic powers. Her dance would partake of music's emotional and physical energies.

The era of romanticism had begun to alter the character of ideas and esthetics of the period, gradually disencumbering the arts from their rococo formalities and artifices. The spirit of change grew to favor simpler, more natural, and more subjective expressions. If not necessarily predictable, it would not have been unexpected for Isadora, as a product of nineteenth-century Western culture, to gravitate toward and absorb the new spirit of her time. For Isadora the development and richness of symphonic music and the expanded literature for the piano during her century provided the reservoir from which she drew a repertory of dances that sustained the momentum for her evolving career.

One might reasonably suppose that Isadora was musical in our customary understanding of that term—the presence of some demonstrable technical and theoretical knowledge or competence in the performing of a musical instrument. Her autobiography contains an isolated reference to "instruction in piano and theory of orchestral composition," which to date remains unexplained and uncorroborated. There is testimony, however, from several valid sources—musical collaborators, musician friends, and those associated most intimately with her work—of her extraordinary musicality (although not all critics shared this opinion), intuitive feeling for music, good musical ear, and phenomenally retentive memory for musical details relevant to her choreography. "In each of her interpretations of music there is a self evident rightness which silences censure."[2]

The story of Isadora's life in dance is firmly interlaced with music. "She penetrated into the realm of music . . . permeating her psyche with its pulsating ebb and low."[3] Perhaps the most direct source of the dancer's deep-rooted affinity for music is the literate and intellectually oriented environment of her youth, her enterprising, creative, literary father and her musician mother, a pianist of respectable competence. Isadora recalled her mother playing with great feeling and insight. For her young listeners, Dora Duncan made accessible and lovingly familiar the music of Bach, Chopin, Schumann, and

Mendelssohn. Her suggestion that they concentrate on illustrations of paintings—Botticelli's *Primavera* during Mendelssohn's *Spring*, for example—while she played, initiated for Isadora, the youngest and most gifted of the Duncan children the concept of sounds relating to images. Isadora herself traced her ideas for "visional movement created from music" to those childhood sessions with her mother.

For years Isadora continued to ponder the organic relationship between dance and music. The elusive interconnection between these two arts and their complex kinship both intrigued and perplexed her. To Gordon Craig, she wrote early in her career: "I would like someone to help me learn more about music and study more exactly its different relations to dancing." Still later, she asked of Craig, "Does the dance spring from the music, as I think it does, or should the music accompany the dance . . . or should they both be born together . . . or How?"[4] (Craig believed all things sprang from movement, even music.)

Out of music's inherent rhythmic vitality, Isadora perceived varied shapes, colors, and motions, all symbols for her. When listening to the great composers, she inwardly visualized a dancing "orchestra of shadows." A crescendo swell in the score could effect a comparable dynamic sensation within her: "The life in me mounted and overflowed in gesture."[5] Maria-Theresa believed that she "metamorphosed in her dance the tonal image," that the whole dramatic action "rose before her inner eye," and that she was able to see "the fantastic figures of the composer's imagination."[6]

At no time did Isadora regard music as a commodious solution for the business of making dances. Profoundly respectful, if not worshipful, of the intrinsic genius of the musical giants, their music remained a sacred preserve, as did her dance. She was dependent on it as nourishment for her soul and, during her life's upheavals, as consolation. She turned to it as much for healing, meditation, and therapeutic refuge as for pleasure, inspiration, and art. She strongly advocated Wagner's vision of dance as a free art born from the body of music and she conceived of this unity as a romantic rapture formed from an embrace of the two arts. Her immersion in music's deeper currents with the sensitivity and passion attributed to her may partly explain the secret of her powerhold on her audiences.

For the dance to attain the supreme height of an expressive art, it had to avail itself of the finest music of the master composers, Isadora reiterated. Dancer Elsa Wiesenthal wrote that until Isadora's advent, music for dancers at the turn of the century was barely more than a "shallow accompaniment for synchronizing balletic movements; deplorably trite, it had no genuine merit and was notorious for its banality of content."[7]

Music diehards considered it pure folly to ask a serious art like music to accommodate a supplemental means of expression like the dance. It was altogether alien to music's original intent. A dancer was expected to dance that music written for the dance. How could one produce movements and arrange poses on a musical phrase unless it was so indicated by the composer himself? To illustrate: Appending dance steps to a musical work designed to be sung might be considered a novel stunt, but in a meaningful way it could have no artistic value. If to some sensibilities Isadora's insistence on her selection of music was an error in judgment, she asserted nothing more than her right to such choice, having placed high value, thought, and study of the music she assigned to her dance.

Music was not only the mainspring for Isadora's inventions in movement but also offered, from its own underlying construction, a buttressing framework for the structural properties of her dance. Harmony of interpretation with the music was of prime importance to her. A secondary objective was to render the dance's structure discernible from that of the music—neither one dominant, neither subordinate. Dance critic Edwin Denby, in his analysis of Isadora's disciple Maria-Theresa, touched on this concept. He observed how her body "seemingly yielding to the music, was yet not passively 'carried' by it, but actually carried itself while yielding"[8]—two disciplines coexistent and related but autonomous.

The spacious range of Isadora's music bridged the eras from before Bach to the late nineteenth and early twentieth centuries. Like Nietzsche who formulated a philosophy of art derived from the two deities, Apollo and Dionysus, Isadora characterized the rapturous, exalted emotion and vital life essence of her dance as Dionysian. Nietzsche's statement, "Man now expresses himself through song and dance as a member of a higher community; he has forgotten how to walk and speak and is on the brink of taking wing as he dances. His gestures speak enchantment. He feels himself a God,"[9] reverberated in Isadora's "Man must speak, then sing, then dance. But the speaking is the brain, the thinking man. The singing is the emotion. The dancing is the Dionysiac ecstasy which carries all away."[10] The search for beauty from more lucid and orderly experiences led her to the music of Liszt, the Apollonian. In contrast was the exhilaration of the music of Scriabin, whose creative strength—the Dionysiac source—came from within.

The new vogue of impressionist music by composers like Ravel and Debussy left her dissatisfied; they did not speak to her spirit. One can only surmise her irritation with the more radical forces within the modern music camp—Schoenberg, Webern, Berg, Stravinsky—who were dissolving the tonalities and harmonies of traditional music theories.

Deep and lasting was Isadora's attachment to the music of Gluck. She identified in this composer the harmonious blending of music and dance as it was known to have existed in the performing arts of antiquity. There were solid philosophical convictions that bound the twentieth-century dancer to the artistic ideals of the eighteenth-century composer. The immutable tenets of her esthetic credo were equally operative factors in Gluck's creative thinking, embodying "simplicity, truth and naturalness as fundamentals of beauty in the production of all art."[11]

Referring to her own contribution to the development of a new dance as a renaissance of the art of line and movement, Isadora appreciated Gluck as a renovator of the opera of his epoch. She applauded his remarkable unity of voice, instrument, and sound, and his singular aim of expressiveness. Each element, the music and the lyric, was shared equally—the poem as much a part of the music as the music was a part of the poem. Introducing the dimension of dance into this harmonious union produced for Isadora the ultimate synchronization of all esthetic elements. In this way the ancient "orchestic" concept that merged these arts in the pre-Christian eras could be reconnected in hers. More than anyone else, wrote Isadora, Gluck "understood the Greek chorus, its rhythms, the grave beauty of its movements, the great impersonality of its emotion . . . [and] spoke in passionate terms of sincere movements, of true gestures."[12]

In his *Orfeo* with its themes of love and song triumphing over the barriers of death, Gluck created music of a haunting simplicity and purity, his dance airs suggesting classic bas-reliefs. His tale of chaste Iphigénie contains many ballets or dance melodies, attesting to the important role given dancing in Greek dramas. Highlights of her repertory were the choreographic adaptations of Glucks' operas *Iphigenia* and *Orpheus and Eurydice*.

As important as Gluck's music was to the Duncan repertory was the music of Frédéric Chopin. Stretching from the earliest beginnings of her career (London, 1900) to almost the very end (Nice, 1926), she interpreted in dance a wide variety of his compositional forms from the fragile, melancholic, joyous, and militant moods of this most elegiac of composers.

From the pale-tinted mood miniatures of his preludes to the dances of the soul, the mazurkas, to the melancholy mysteries of the night, the nocturnes, the stately and heroic polonaises, and the charming waltzes, Isadora's poetic movement images to the music of the "Poet of the keyboard" became one of her most popular program offerings. Over the years she explored this music's subtleties and melodic richness ever more fully, re-interpreting and refining it with deeper insight. As it had been said of Chopin that all possible expressions were to be found in his compositions, so too were many who held the opinion that there was not a human emotion in his music that Isadora did not express in her dance.[13]

The grace, sunniness, and charm of Schubert, his "bewitching wistfulness," also captivated the lithe, ebullient young Isadora. To the joy of her audiences there were choreographic delights from his waltzes, marches, and German dances.

The titanic force of Beethoven and the sweep of his sonatas and symphonic music became the vehicle through which the dancer projected her own bold rebel's voice of emerging selfhood. Often Isadora tried to reassure the disgruntled music connoisseurs in her audience that the composer would not have been disturbed by her renditions. To the contrary, she would have expected him to applaud her. Not so, resounded the rash of satiric comments and caricature sketches published in the German magazine *Jugend* in 1904; in one issue there appeared a drawing of a scowling Beethoven looking helpless but resigned to the sturdy little Isadora prancing on his head. Objections to Isadora's use of the revered classics also came from more serious quarters and in more subtle fashion. One particular grievance concerned her choreography to movements from Beethoven's Seventh Symphony. Conducting its Russian première in February 1905 was the eminent music teacher, Leopold Auer, who, while leading the orchestra, averted his eyes from Isadora's "profanation!"

The womanly Isadora also became magnetized and exhilarated by the sensuality of Wagner's dramatic works and their lure of sublime faith and transporting love. She introduced new movements designed to conform to the character of the composer's rhythms, as indicated and notated in his scores, which Wagner's son, Siegfried, and widow, Cosima, gave her permission to examine and study. Indicated for his opera *Tannhäuser* were "large delirious gestures of Bacchantes." These gestures captured her imagination, haunting her for years until they were set within her danced version of his "Venusburg" music. Her excerpts from Wagner's *Tannhäuser, Parsifal, Die Meistersinger, Tristan,* and *Die Walküre,* as well as from his songs contributed handsomely and substantially to her active repertory. Venturesome, to say the least, were her festivals of dances to Wagner's music in Paris, for example, where for years he had been banned from the French Opéra and where he was yet to acquire respectable acceptance and support among musicians and critics.

As Isadora attained greater artistic control and mastery of her medium, she replenished and fortified her interpretive scope by turning to Tchaikovsky, Liszt, Berlioz, Franck, and Scriabin, challenging herself to glean more profound insights from their technically complex structures, opulent orchestrations, and emotionally charged melodic themes. Maturity created a need for music fortified with moral strength and intelligent content: Franck's symphonic interlude, *Redemption;* Liszt's *Les Funérailles* and his *Bénédictions de*

Dieu dans la Solitude; and large-boned music from the symphonic literature, such as Schubert's great Seventh Symphony in E major and Tchaikovsky's Sixth Symphony, the *Pathétique*.

The deepening stresses of Isadora's own life and the social and political turbulence enveloping her world drew her to music that channeled her awareness and concern for the human condition. "She meant her dance to be an act of healing the spirit's bruises," poet Shaemas O'Sheel said of her.[14]

Along with her expanded range of music, Isadora's art in transition could also be observed. For her enlarged version of Gluck's *Orfeo*, completed in late 1910, the "Dance of the Furies" in Act II bore a theatrical, dramatic element and an intensity that could be seen in more specific movements, more explicit expressions, and more distinct characterizations. The entire body became a force of "concentrated venom and malice . . . savage . . . " in its portrayal of the underworld's demonic creatures. "Muscles harden in the face and limbs, the movements are abrupt, fierce, now bowed and now angular. The carriage of the body is stiff and inflexible; and then quivers and vibrates like a bowstring loosed from the hands. This dance is something of a tour de force."[15]

Of this same dance another impression: "Her hair seems to turn into coiling serpents and her eyes turned inward, her fingers changed into long cactuslike projections, and the cataclysmic violence of the demons struck up through her, appearing to rend her cell from cell."[16] In her continuing evolution as an expressionist, the lyrical, ethereal dancer came close to the virtuosic in this dance.

As Isadora approached material of great solemnity, inward contemplation, and thematic grandeur, the light dances of youthful enchantment became less prominent in her repertory. Those that remained were revised, befitting the apparent changes of her body and mental outlook that had evolved through the years. "Isadora brought her own work through dramatic changes in style over the years . . . far from what she danced originally," according to Anita Zahn.[17] Her comment was equally affirmed in the reviews of later Duncan works, when words like "minimal," "immobile," and "stillness" began to characterize her more architecturally designed movements.

Though there was a visible reduction of motion, it was compensated by more intense emotion and stronger, more sustained movements. By paring away the nonessentials and finely honing her gestures, Isadora believed herself to be moving ever closer to unveiling the interior drama, the true essence of her dance's expression. "She dances now with less joy and movement, but what she creates is more human—very profound and moving."[18]

In general, Isadora seemed to be unconcerned with analyzing the mysterious and malevolent. With few exceptions she let no demons disturb her dance revelations. When she penetrated the dark abysses of music, she was striving, with the composer, to extricate the unbearable, to rise into the light of reason, and to depict the promise of renewal—the very ethos of musical romanticism.

From a miscellany of composers—Dvorak, Grieg, Moszkowski, Strauss, Schumann, Schmitt—Isadora arranged shorter dances, lighter in vein, immediately appealing because of their spirit and grace. Johann Strauss' *Blue Danube Waltz* must be mentioned here as the first show-stopper of Isadora's early years. This 1902 choreographic gem, an impromptu creation from all accounts, displayed to perfect advantage some of her stunning technical assets: a disciplined body, superbly supple, with great elasticity and physical endurance. "With a leap of joy like one arisen from some hiding place in the rocks and shaking off the salt fresh spray, she sways and sways 'til the big audience seems scarcely able to restrain itself."[19] In this yielding, undulating, and rhythmic little dance was the very essence of Isadora's compelling performing personality and her bodily grace. She claimed the emotions of her viewers . . . communication was instantaneous.[20]

Brahms, a major figure among late nineteenth-century composers, composed waltzes for piano that particularly attracted Isadora. Though the composer was dismissed among certain of the musical cognoscenti in France and the United States as "a boresome pedagogue," his waltzes for piano, Opus 39, inspired a collection of beautifully crafted, imaginative dances, each a charming contrast to the others.

The absence of certain composers from Isadora's repertory also did not go unnoticed. The fact that no significant musical score by Mozart (minor pieces were composed for her young pupils) had been selected by Isadora elicited comment from Boston's music critic of that time, H. T. Parker, who found a strong similarity between the styles of Mozart and Isadora (as did author Edith Wharton). Parker cited the "long flowing line of Mozart's music," so like the line of Isadora's dance, "ever springing and curling out of itself." Mozart had the same economical and inventive qualities as Isadora and both could do much with little—"and to beauty." Parker concluded his interesting critique: "On occasion Miss Duncan believed she danced to Beethoven. Almost always she was dancing to Mozart."[21] It seems to me that Isadora was neither a Beethoven nor a Mozart stylist, nor did she follow any one composer's idiom. Her movement line, its upward spiralling curve, and the facile forms of her gestures were inherently and inimitably her own.

Within her comparatively short career (just a quarter of a century), Isadora amassed a large inventory of original compositions that represented music's various categories: brief, delicate, informal pieces as well as larger works of commanding proportion. Stimulated by their tonal colors and multipatterned rhythms, she had at her disposal a sophisticated palette of movement nuances and dynamics with which to explore and evoke a diversity of expressive moods. The incidental music for her earliest suite of dances, *Dance Idylls* (1900), was selected from seventeenth-century composers Rameau, Picchi, Couperin and performed by a small, specialized consort of baroque instrumentalists, including Arnold Dolmetsch, who was known for reviving this early music and its instruments.

The more ambitious of Isadora's choreographies demanded a collaborative effort of professionals from the theater and music arts: conductors, choruses and choir masters, full orchestra ensembles, vocalists, and actors and actresses as needed to perform in the Greek dramas and the Gluck operas. The task of assembling and preparing a large cast usually fell to the managers, directors, or conductors, but Isadora all too often suffered the consequences in the inept and under-rehearsed local pick-up ensembles provided her.

She did not experience the support of a superior, *sympathetic* symphony orchestra until 1908. That August she met Walter Damrosch, a central force in the musical life of America and the conductor of the New York Symphony Orchestra. After seeing Isadora dance at the Criterion Theater in New York, he proposed that his orchestra accompany her in a series of engagements.

This came at a time when top-flight conductors would have been demeaned by lending musical assistance to a member of the dancing "profession," still viewed as a minor and frivolous pursuit. But Damrosch was committed to music and to progress in the arts, and Isadora Duncan had profoundly impressed him.

For both Walter Damrosch and Isadora Duncan it proved to be a fruitful collaboration. Described as possessing "the airs and manners of an ambassador to the Court of St. James," Damrosch was exceptional for his avant-garde outlook on music.[22] He shared with Isadora an attitude strongly pro-Wagner, who was then relatively unknown, unliked, and underplayed in the United States. He expressed the opinion, a minority one at that time, "that rhythmic pantomime is the only art which seems to unite legitimately with music." Prominent on their combined programs was the music of Wagner and Beethoven, the latter deeply meaningful for Isadora, while for Damrosch it was "the touchstone by which he judged all music."

Admonished for submitting to the use of Beethoven's symphony for dance purposes, Damrosch countered with: "I have never felt the real joy of life in an almost primitive innocence and glory as in her dance of the *Scherzo*. The finale (Symphony #7) is a Bacchanale of such tremendous intensity that one little figure on a large stage is not sufficient. The stage should be filled with twenty Duncans, but alas, so far our age has produced only one."

In the years that followed, her presentations in Europe were supported by fine orchestras and prestigious conductors: the Lamoureux Concert Orchestra; the Colonne Orchestra, under the baton of the venerated Edouard

Colonne and, after his death, Gabrial Pierné; the London Symphony led by Désiré Défauw; and the Pasdeloup Orchestra with Albert Wolff.

Isadora's most valued musical advisers were her pianists and accompanists. Thorough musicians with a technical mastery of both music and instrument, they advised her on characteristics of the piano, musical structure, phrasing and rhythm, all to guide her development of the choreography. When Arturo Toscanini lamented the fact that composers were at the mercy of interpreters, he was not alone in that wisdom. A persistent concern for Isadora was that she not misrepresent or understate the essential character of the score nor the basic intent of the composer.

Isadora was intent on using pianists of outstanding caliber for those programs which included the piano compositions of Brahms, Chopin, and Schubert; by and large she chose successfully. Certain of them achieved with her an uncommonly blessed rapprochement, however brief the collaboration. Those pianists who worked with her early in her career included Rudolf Zwintscher and Hermann Lafont; Lafont accompanied her in the popular Chopin-Abends and was with her for her eventful debut in St. Petersburg in December 1904. The esteemed Dutch musicologist, composer, and pianist Julius Röntgen contributed handsomely to the conspicuous success of her Netherland appearances in 1906–07, while the gifted pianist Hener Skene was dear to Isadora and her pupils until his death in World War I.

For Isadora's South American tour in 1916, the French conductor/pianist Maurice Dumesnil became her musical director. His musical proficiency produced effective transcriptions of orchestral pieces for the piano when necessary.

An international virtuoso in the earlier decades of this century, Harold Bauer was heralded as a "prince among pianists." Isadora regarded him as her "musical twin soul." He, in turn, remarked on her musical intuition.

The most significant of Isadora's accompanists later in her career was concert pianist Walter Morse Rummel (the "Archangel" of her memoirs). An acclaimed interpreter of the piano music of Liszt and Debussy, Rummel's musicianship was displayed in his powerful transcriptions for piano of the organ and orchestral works of Franck and Wagner, which were prepared specifically to accompany Isadora. Their joint recitals in France, Belgium, and England in the years 1918–1921 earned them rave reviews. On at least one occasion Rummels's superb performance upstaged the "grande artiste" herself.

No longer in dispute is the legitimacy of dance as an art or music as a choreographic inspiration. Isadora Duncan navigated those uncharted waters with confidence and artistry. Her efforts paved the way for others, whose results can be seen today in both contemporary ballet and modern dance.

NOTES

1. "Polemic," *Algemeen Handelsblad* (Amsterdam), January 7, 1906.
2. J. E. Crawford Flitch, *Modern Dancing and Dancers*, p. 108.
3. Maria-Theresa, "Isadora—The Artist," in Abraham Walkowitz, *Isadora Duncan in Her Dances*, p. 4.
4. Francis Steegmuller, *Your Isadora*, p. 175.
5. Isadora Duncan, *My Life*, pp. 223, 224.
6. Maria-Theresa, "As I Saw Isadora," *Dance Magazine*, November 1928.
7. Elsa Wiesenthal, "Die Bedeutung Isadora Duncans als Tanzerin," in *Memoiren* (*My Life*, German edition), p. 397.
8. Edwin Denby, *Looking at the Dance*, p. 337.
9. Friedrich Nietzsche, *The Birth of Tragedy*, p. 23.
10. Isadora Duncan, *My Life*, p. 152.
11. Romain Rolland, *Essays on Music*, p. 205.
12. Isadora Duncan, "The Dance in Relation to Tragedy," *Theatre Arts*, October 1927, p. 756.
13. Louis Untermeyer, "Isadora Duncan Dancing," in E. Dickson, *Poems of the Dance*, p. 246.

ISADORA DUNCAN DANCING

Faint preludings on a flute,
And she swims before us;
Shadows follow in pursuit,
Like a phantom chorus.
Sense and sound are intertwined
Through her necromancy,
Till our dreaming souls are blind
To all things but fancy.

Haunted woods and perfumed nights;
Swift and soft desires;
Roses, violet-colored lights,
And the sound of lyres;
Vague chromatics on a flute—
All are subtly blended
Till the instrument grows mute
And the dance is ended.

14. Shaemus O'Sheel, "Isadora Duncan," *Forum*, February 1911, p. 190.
15. C. and C. Caffin, "Isadora Duncan," in *Dancing and Dancers of Today*, p. 61.
16. Mabel Dodge Luhan, *Movers and Shakers*, p. 333.
17. Anita Zahn in conversation with author, 1984.
18. Dunoyer de Segonzac, Letter in *John Quinn: Man from New York*, p. 399.
19. Gertrude Norman, *The Theater Magazine*, February 1, 1905, p. 36.
20. J. H. Rossing, *Nieuws van der Dag*, April 6, 1906.
Public reaction to the *Blue Danube Waltz*, which was generally reserved for a program encore, caught Isadora by surprise. She believed that too much emphasis had been placed on an incidental piece intended as compensation for those in her audience who didn't fathom her more abstract conceptions. So captivating was this waltz that Isadora was forced to upgrade its status and it became an ever popular staple of her programs for many years.
21. H. T. Parker, "Isadora Duncan," in *Eighth Notes*, p. 237.
22. George Martin, *The Damrosch Dynasty*, pp. 221–223.

PART II

The Isadorables

CHAPTER FOUR

Temples of the Dance

"Art is man's epic song about himself and his environment. It is, all of it, one neverending lyrical and fantastic autobiography of the human species."
ANATOLE LUNACHARSKY

Grunewald

THE DANCE AS PERCEIVED and practiced by Isadora Duncan was the "free, plastic expression of a feeling, the irresistible urge to transmit an emotion strongly experienced." She firmly held that revelations of the inner self, when made manifest in an outer form of natural grace and freedom of bodily movement, would bring meaning and beauty to enrich human existence. Fundamental to her concept of a rational world was education that included the dance as an art and a language of movement to be studied and applied to the experience of daily life. One begins with the child, she said: "Let us first teach little children to breathe, to vibrate, to feel and to become one with the general harmony and movement. Let us first produce a beautiful human being."[1]

With this lofty aim Isadora established her first school of dance near Berlin, in the countrified suburb of Grunewald. Her choice of Germany was as logical as it was desirable, for it was in the centers of German culture— Berlin, Munich, Weimar—that she had been intellectually invigorated and creatively stimulated toward some of her most ambitious inventions in movement. Her unprecedented alliance of dance with musical compositions; the novel technical idiom she employed; and her unorthodox dress and performing style provoked challenging polemics on esthetics within the intellectual community. In Germany she commanded attention as nowhere else and was respected for her innovative approach to dance. The burgher class may have condemned her "barefoot exhibitions," but "she is the idol of the artistic world." Her public appearances rapidly increased and she was showered with tributes of praise.

Although the doors of the villa she purchased in Grunewald opened in December 1904, Isadora had contemplated and articulated plans for this project well in advance of its realization. In 1902 she had assured a Munich correspondent that her artistic intentions went far beyond that of a personal career; she would expand her scope through a school for children where she could fulfill her true aim: "To awaken the will for beauty," and "To make dance a part of life." Small hands would eventually carry the bright torch for the new spirit in dance. Enviably persuasive and convincing, Isadora anticipated that from her institute of education, the dance of the future would spread over the globe.

They came to Grunewald from the slums of German cities, "recruited mercifully from among the poorest," Isadora related.[2] Other children came to her from disadvantaged homes where their fathers were ill, absent, or deceased, and their mothers were the breadwinners, too often earning meager salaries—curious echoes from Isadora's personal childhood memories. It was all too clear why many of these children were brought to Grunewald.

> The children were boarded and educated free of charge; this
> includes clothes and other necessities . . . the pupils will receive
> academic instruction from a competent public school teacher
> and in addition, in order to stimulate their artistic sensibilities,
> there will be regular visits to museums with lectures on art.[3]

Day students ran contrary to her belief that the healthy, mentally and physically alert child must have a holistically regulated environment: fresh air, clean surroundings and personal habits, wholesome, nourishing food, an exercise regimen, rest, medical check-ups, and supervised academic activities. Two governesses would be in charge, Isadora herself would personally see to their training, while the management of the school was to be in the hands of

Isadora's sister, Elizabeth. "This free, non-profit dance school founded by Isadora Duncan and supported by her financially, is not a philanthropic institution in the ordinary sense but an enterprise dedicated to the promotion of health and beauty in mankind. Both physically and spiritually the children will here receive an education providing them with the highest intelligence in the healthiest body."[4]

So read the publicity releases sent ahead of Isadora's arrival in cities where she was scheduled to perform and where she arranged to review the young local applicants. Auditions were most informal. With a piano accompanist (most likely her mother in those years), she gently urged the child to imitate in a "follow me" manner the gestures she demonstrated. This was somehow sufficient for her to detect the glimmer of ability in a child, considering, as she did that almost every child was a natural dancer, given the opportunity to tap her innate abilities.

The Swiss-born Anna Denzler recalled looking like a disaster after her long and sooty train ride; dishevelled and sweaty, she presented herself to Isadora. That she was among those chosen, Anna attributed to Isadora's brother Gus (Augustin). He was charmed by her winning smile. Irma Ehrich-Grimme remembered trailing Isadora's motions to the music of Schumann's *Träumerei*. Only years later did she learn that it was Gordon Craig who called the child to Isadora's attention with: "Take her, she has the eyes!"

Between eighteen and twenty attractive little girls, ages four to ten, were enrolled at the school during the course of its existence, the number fluctuating with the inevitable drop-outs and occasional drop-ins. The six who would become the Isadorables stayed on.

> Six girls to have been the chosen ones, to have stood on the same
> stage with Her, performing Her dances and bringing joy and solace
> to so many . . . to have had the wonderful and privileged
> experience of a life of culture and great adventure with
> Her . . . this wonderful woman and creative artist . . . our Maestra.[5]

Though these sentiments were actually spoken by Anna Denzler (b. Switzerland, 1894, d. New York, 1982), they were shared by the other Isadorables: Theresa Kruger (b. Dresden, 1895, d. New York, 1987); Irma Erich-Grimme (b. Hamburg, 1897, d. California, 1977); Elizabeth (Lisa) Milker (b. Dresden, 1898, d. Dresden, 1976); Margot (Gretel) Jehle (b. Berlin, 1900, d. Paris, 1925); and Erika Lohmann (b. Hamburg, 1901, d. Connecticut, 1984).

Irma, the only one of the official Isadora Duncan Dancers to publish her memoirs (*Duncan Dancer*), described her schoolmates as she met them at Grunewald for the first time in January 1905. Anna—"pretty and dark-haired with round rosy cheeks and small chocolate-brown eyes"; Theresa—"blue eyes, blond hair, and a lot of freckles on her tiny nose"; Lisel—"with the pretty golden curls and the large brown eyes of a startled deer"; Gretel—"with violet eyes, ash-blond hair and the delicate look of a Dresden China-Doll"; and "dark-eyed Erika who at four years of age was the youngest in the school."[6]

Isadora's glowing idealism was reflected throughout the building at Grunewald. Thoughtfully and with great care she introduced an esthetic scheme for fostering the pervasive atmosphere of beauty she desired for the children's learning and living environment. The entrance foyer, Irma wrote, featured a large and imposing statue on a pedestal—a model of Polycletus' *Amazon*, with its strength and heroic spirit filling the area. Luca della Robbia bas-reliefs greeted the children in their dance classroom along with Donatello's sculptures of dancing children.

The child was envisioned by Isadora "as dreamed of by the painters and sculptors of all ages . . . children dancing on Greek vases, tiny figures from Tanagra and Boeatia. . . . the dancing children of Gainsborough. . . . The real children of my school moving and dancing in the midst of these forms would surely grow to resemble them; to reflect unconsciously in their movements and their faces, a little of the joy and the same childlike grace. It would be the first step to their becoming beautiful, the first step toward the new art of the dance."[7] The human body in its most perfect rendering was present everywhere in plaster and bronze reproductions of fleet-footed runners, jumpers, and dancing girls. For one child, a future Isadorable, it was the small statuette of Isadora by the German sculptor Walter Schott, a graceful, dancing Isadora, that did more for her understanding of Isadora's art than all the reproductions of antiquity.

The training and activity taking place within the unusual dancer's equally unusual house of dance soon drew much interest and curiosity from artists, journalists, musicians, and educators who hastened there to inspect the physical premises. All were intent on determining just what it was that was being referred to as a new system of childhood education. One frequent guest, who paid very close attention to demonstrations by the children, was Swiss musician Jaques-Dalcroze. Visitors learned from Isadora, or her sister, that she had no "system." The purpose and effort of her instruction was to lead the children to grow and move in accordance with their nature and their natural responses.

Surveying the unparalleled setting for the Duncan philosophy of the dance, educators were beguiled and amazed by the rare sight of children moving with natural grace and poise, displaying both a physical and spiritual comportment. But was it not beyond the comprehension of such young tots to be subjected to composers like Beethoven and Schumann, whose music they surely could not understand at so tender an age? Very young children could never learn through words alone, they were told. "Children learn though movement . . . They learn from the spirit or from intuition—even the smallest children understand Beethoven and Schumann."[8]

Visitors were impressed by the serenity of mood and the classical tenor that prevailed throughout the house; all were charmed by the children. Their bedrooms, carried out in a blue-and-white motif, were ornamented with the ceramic children of della Robbia figurines of the Madonna and Child. Bathed in light and fresh air, the rooms had an orderliness and cleanliness that conveyed comfort and peace.

A Dutch journalist related a detailed account of a visit to Grunewald where, in Isadora's absence (she was on tour), an interview was conducted with Isadora's sister, Elizabeth.[9] The journalist was taken on a tour of the building, but was somewhat perplexed, almost uncomfortable, when viewing the blue and white of the dormitories. Wasn't this too serene, too harmonious, too controlled? "Little white muslin curtains, little blue satin blankets, little white painted chairs, little blue slippers beside each bed." Then there were the children themselves, who appeared in "little blue tunics, bare little arms and legs shod with little yellow sandals."

In talking with Elizabeth the reporter voiced some skepticism about the wisdom of these "little pioneers in human movements and perception of beauty" being treated as artists at so young an age. Elizabeth explained that, eventually, the dancing youngsters would form a background for her sister's dances; they would become her chorus, so to speak, her willing, intelligent instruments. "None of the children is being brought up to become an independent dancer; each is but a link, a small link in a bewitching chain."

At this stage of her life, Isadora possessed a captivating charm and physical loveliness. Her soft, musical voice and affectionate ways endeared her instantly and deeply to the children. "She was love personified," Anna beamed as she reminisced decades later. "We worshipped her," Theresa added. "She was my 'angel in white' and would always have flowers for us. Upon her return from her concert tours she would kiss us, opening her arms and gathering us to her." Within the night dreams and daytime fantasies of these children dwelled their "fairy queen," "goddess," and "heavenly vision."

The dancer's well-publicized successes in Germany began to spill over with travels extending into Belgium, Holland, Scandinavia, and Russia. The separations from Grunewald lengthened, and the six children, drawn to their charismatic idol, reacted with sadness, longing, and tears. A longer association and gradual maturing would be needed before they could realistically appraise the ofttimes quixotic behavior of the woman they revered. Only then would they admit to their emotions—of the terrible anger and sense of rejection that her departures inflicted upon them.

Isadora's absences were also protracted by a priority of another kind— her intimate relationships. The school, squeezed between the two powerful claims of career and love, was all too often bested by the other two. Love at the peak of passion could eclipse all. But art and children were the only passions that lasted and the ideals for which she repeatedly marshalled her finest energies. And children, above art, she regarded as "the most holy thing in the world."

In her capacity as director and overall supervisor of Grunewald, Elizabeth Duncan demonstrated the qualities in her character for which Isadora, the younger by six years, respected her. Elizabeth was methodical, pragmatic, and business-like. Besides being Isadora's co-planner and co-worker, Elizabeth was already known as a pioneering figure among physical culture educators. She "dreamed of remaking the woman's body through eurythmics," wrote Arsène Alexandre in 1911, " . . . battling against old pedagogical prejudices and false traditions that distort the concept of beauty and natural elegance." Alexandre prophesied that this thinker, enclosed within a frail, small body, would one day be as recognized for her contribution to education as her sister would be for the dance.

The two sisters were embarked on an educational venture. Though initially united philosophically, in practice, there would be divergences in the time to come. Their striking dissimilarities have been likened to those that existed between the early Greek city-states of Sparta and Athens: Elizabeth, the Spartan, emphasized strong physical and mental disciplines; Isadora, the Athenian, was the intellectual visionary and artistic architect of the enterprise, in short, its guiding spirit.

The disparity between the sisters was extreme both in personality and in physical appearance (Elizabeth had a limp and did not dance), in their relationship with the children, and in their approach to training them. To pick up and hug a child could not have been imagined of the reserved and impersonal Elizabeth. The little kindnesses and personalized attentions, the warmth of actual physical contact craved by the children, were seen to only by Isadora. Nevertheless, both women, like separate streams flowing together, fed the developing lives of the chosen six.

Elizabeth provided the dance instruction during Isadora's prolonged absences. Lisa and Irma shared the view that one lesson with their idol made up for all the classes taught by Elizabeth. "Each reunion with her [Isadora] worked miracles . . . we were beings transformed," recalled Anna. More than the teaching itself, according to Theresa, was the inspirational element in their contact with Isadora that proved to be so significant.

The infusion of exuberance and childish glee that the children derived from their bond with her sister did not escape Elizabeth. She had great regard for the artistic merit of her sister's work and could observe the evident gains in the quality of the dancing when the youngsters were in Isadora's hand. "If these girls are to become artists," Elizabeth was overheard to say, "there is only one person who can do it, and that is my sister. If they are to become dancers, only Isadora can accomplish that."[10] And so it was.

Stirred by their adoration for Isadora and their respect for her artistry, the pupils gave fully of themselves in their classes with her. Consciously, happiness was equated by these young girls with time spent dancing with Isadora. Unconsciously, perhaps, they may even have sensed that their destiny lay with her. The dignity and sincerity that characterized Isadora Duncan in her dance was also bestowed on her young pupils. This mutual regard that bound teacher with disciple has been described in its rarity by Irma. "Like members of a religious community, under the benediction of some holy influence, we became an ever more dedicated group as we were further initiated into the secrets of her art. This was a world no outsider could enter, nor could he ever fathom the depths of understanding and spiritual communion that existed among us whenever we worked or danced together."[11]

Not until decades had passed, memory had reshuffled events, and attitudes had been tempered, did some of the Isadorables reconsider their childhood impressions. In reviewing their youth with a more seasoned and balanced perspective, they acknowledged Elizabeth's contribution to their early development and recognized her role in the organization. Not so Irma, however, whose account in her memoirs of her school years, left an unrevised, unsympathetic, and rather damaging portrait of Isadora's sister. As an educator and as a force within the Duncan constellation, Elizabeth Duncan still awaits and merits closer examination.

From its inception, the school at Grunewald faced chronic financial problems that increasingly worsened and threatened its existence. While Isadora's active concert schedule earned her grand sums of money, there were also grand bills she had to meet for the cost of running the school and the sizable retinue of people dependent upon her for support.

Early in 1905, the Society for the Support and Maintenance of the Dance School of Isadora Duncan was organized by a group of influential and enthusiastic citizens who wanted to preserve the fine project begun in Grunewald. The association had two major objectives: to draw the business community and the private sector into membership by subscription and contributions, and to sponsor demonstration performances by the school to encourage those memberships. There were liaison committees formed in Leipzig and Holland, where financial assistance for the Duncan school was considered "a project of international artistic importance," and the beauty of Duncan dance "above nationality."

Locally, German burghers were raising eyebrows and tempers as they witnessed the little Duncanites moving about Grunewald and Berlin clad in their light dresses with bare legs and sandaled feet. Highly unconventional, indeed, and smacking of indecency! The sisters Duncan looked to the benefit performances by their school as the way to best gain credibility among the public for their undertaking.

From 1905 through 1908, the children appeared frequently in theaters and concert auditoriums, propagandizing the worthiness of natural dancing, strong bodies, and self-confidence through self-awareness. Schedule permitting, Isadora joined them, but it was primarily Elizabeth who prepared and presented the children to the public.

Present at the very first appearance of Isadora and her pupils in July 1905 at the Royal (Kroll) Opera House in Berlin, was Isadora's lover, Gordon Craig. "To see her shepherding her little flock, keeping them together and especially looking after one very small one of four [Erika], was a sight no one there had ever seen before and, I suppose, will never see again."[12] Reflecting on that first performance, Anna clarified the extent of the children's participation. "What we did was not really dance but a sort of rhythmic parade to win audience sympathy for the school." Irma concurred. "We were still too young to actually dance with her." They were not, however, too young to enchant their audience. At the end of Isadora's program, the children joined hands with her in a lively round of skip or polka to melodies of the genial composer, Engelbert Humperdinck—especially his "Rosenringel" and "Tanzreigen." Arms filled with flowers, their teacher then beckoned each child to skip toward her to receive a pink rose.

Isadora created dances for the children in keeping with their physical growth and their developing musical responses. Added to Isadora's growing repertory were Schubert's "Ballet Music I and II" from *Rosamunde,* Schumann's *Kinderscenen* (prepared by Elizabeth), Lanner's *Valser,* and the "Andante" from Gluck's *Alceste* (in which the children joined Isadora on stage).

Elizabeth's forte lay in getting the students to visualize music and to discover for themselves the ideas for dance in rhythmic songs, imaginative stories, and poem interpretations. Each child would be encouraged to contribute her own movement patterns through which she could state her ideas. Several of the early dance pieces that arose out of such guided improvisations proved to have an endearing naïveté for audiences.

Using Lanner's *Werber Waltz,* Isadora taught the children to "weave and entwine, to part and unite, in endless rounds and processions."[13] This configuration of movements, with its fluency of motions and superb grace of line would, in the years ahead, be transferred to other choreographic frameworks and remain a spellbinder for spectators. Described by one reviewer, a Lanner waltz performed by the children featured "a fine, silken fabric arched overhead into a triumphal arch beneath which the dancing figures passed in pairs and then scattered to the four winds."[14] The same review extolled the young dancers: "The arms, the hands, the entire body is here awakened into graceful motions and rhythmic life."

By 1906 and 1907, the programs listed the children as the *schulerinnen* (pupils) of Isadora Duncan, their names appearing under the dances they performed. At the New Playhouse on Nollendorf Square, the April 1907 program consisted of rondos and musettes of the twelfth to seventeenth centuries, and dances to the music of Corelli, Couperin, Scarlatti, and old French airs. Anna led the group in *Rondeau* (music by Max Merz).

In July 1907, the city of Mannheim celebrated its Tercentenary Jubilee. Isadora and her performing group had been invited to dance in the exposition's outdoor spectacle, to be held in the huge municipal park, ringed by houses. For the Grunewalders, the moonlit fairy-tale in which they participated was every bit the fantastic event reports have described it to have been.

Colorful balloons and Chinese lanterns dotted the air, while searchlights flooded the central stage with dazzling light. The stage on which the dancers appeared was an improvised platform erected over the illuminated fountain site in the center of the park's lake. (Gordon Craig had come up with this floating stage idea in answer to Isadora's question: "How to dance in the middle of water?") For the festive occasion, the fountain platform was decorated with wreaths entwined with roses.

When dusk deepened on that warm and beautiful summer evening, thousands were seen sitting on the grassy area around the lake. Heads were everywhere, watching from surrounding rooftops and open windows. "It was a people's festival of enormous dimension."[15]

Sounds of Gluck's overture to *Iphigénie in Aulis* came from the orchestra across the lake. That was Isadora's cue. Leaving the water's edge, she sailed in a gondola to the platform. As the orchestra played, a concealed choir sang and she began to dance. At the appropriate time, a second gondola, adorned with lighted lanterns and equipped with costumed oarsmen, bore the children to the spectacular stage. All in white, they were gathered by Isadora around her, she very much resembling the hen in the basket among her chicks. They all danced to the music of *Alceste* while the beams of light playing on their moving forms, and the melodic strains drifting over the water, created a sorcery of sight and sound. Enthralled, the thousands present "never so much as uttered a sound to disturb the illusion." At the very end of the dance, after the white-garbed children and their teacher had sailed back and were safely returned, only then was there an explosive "Long live Isadora!" amid the thunderous applause. In the judgment of Mannheim's mayor, "There had been nothing . . . like it since the days of Louis XIV."[16]

On May 29, 1907, the Dutch newspaper *De Nieuwe Courant*, carried a report of the concert Isadora and the children gave at the Resident Theater in Frankfurt am Main on May 25 of that year.

Perceived in this relatively new art form was its search for an individuality of expression within a collective effort. The pupils "danced in the same spirit as their teacher although each developed individually; the essence of this art was open to convey ideas of personal artistry, rather than sterile imitation." Grace seemed to be second nature to them. When the curtain was raised prematurely, several of the children on stage were caught by surprise. With consummate poise they made for the opposite corner and did so "with such poetry of motion that though not a dance, one cherished the treat of the moment."

Not until their adolescent years would the six Isadorables receive a recognition of their own, but audiences and critics alike were entranced by the young performers. A reviewer's eye might single out one individual child, not by name, but by a particular quality of expression or a physical trait in her manner of moving, but more often than not there were references to the "dancing little fairies," "ethereal beings," and "merry sprites," who brought "the joy to gladden heavy hearts."

As late as 1908, public ordinances and police censorship were still impeding the school's efforts to raise constantly needed funds. Persistent opposition to bare-legged young children seen on stage in unorthodox apparel, under the supervision of a woman of questionable morals (Isadora, who in September 1906 had borne a child out of wedlock) posed formidable obstacles. Under the aegis of a group of prominent women in German royal circles, the children were granted permission to appear in an afternoon performance at the Berlin Kammerspiel on March 25, 1908.

"Children were in the audience, sunk deep in their theater seats, stretching their necks to watch what their contemporaries were doing on stage," a reporter wrote.[17] He goes on to admit his own trepidations about seeing children looking more like miniature Duncans than like their own delightful, unselfconscious selves. Happily, he was later able to report that the little performers danced as though not having been taught, but of having freely uttered the joy of an untroubled soul. "The simpler the dances, the more beautiful they are." On the beat of the music, each of the children danced the polka one time over the stage. "Now they can be seen as they are; some serious, cautious, others freer and still others with a refined elegance and rhythmic abandon."

Isadora availed herself of every opportunity to address her audiences on behalf of her school. Stepping forward to the foot the stage after a performance, she would call out, "*Aidez-moi, aidez-moi.*" Soon, she promised, they could see the youngsters for themselves. She planned to bring them on her tours so that all could see the fruits of her labor, the beauty of body, and the spirit of joyous children. That promise was fulfilled for the Netherlands and other countries during their tour in 1907. Because of child labor law restrictions, only eight girls from Grunewald appeared in The Hague, Rotterdam, and Amsterdam, where critic Simbacher Zynen basked in their glow. "All elegant and endearing . . . for they know that dancing is not just moving. The little bodies danced, the little heads, too, and the innocent features were all alive." After the children and Isadora completed an *air gai*, they danced a minuet and ended with a fantasy to the waltz music of Lanner.

> What lovely freedom of movement, what a good sense of rhythm
> and presence some already manifested . . . A dark-haired child
> attracted much interest with her light, elastic little
> jumps. . . . The live little forms . . . pursued each other dancingly
> with floating little feet . . . arms spread out or high, the . . . faces
> all aglow. One could not get enough of this scene.[18]

A more formal review of the group's short engagement in London at the Duke of York Theater in July 1908, informed readers that the children (the "corps de ballet") did well in Gluck's music but better in a waltz by Lanner, given as an encore at the program's conclusion. "It is hoped that they will carry on the good tradition of their teacher," the *London Times* reporter added.

Novelist John Galsworthy was moved to tears by their faces, "so utterly dear and joyful," by the expression and movement of the "tallest of the children" and her "grave and fiery love"; another child evoked "a strange soft charm," and would move him by her "most magical, sweet passion."[19]

> There was no tiptoeing and posturing, no hopeless muscular
> achievement; all was rhythm, music, light, air, and above all
> things, happiness. Smiles and love had gone to the fashioning of
> their performance; and smiles and love shone from every one of
> their faces and from the clever white turnings of their limbs.[20]

Of one small child he wrote: "She danced as never child danced . . . full of the sacred fire of motion." Of all the children in their dance, "each flight and whirling movement seemed conceived there and then out of the joy of being." Much later in his life, when summing up the rare moments of supreme beauty that had touched him, Galsworthy counted Isadora's young dancers among them.

Little thought did the children themselves have other than the sensation of pleasure that dance brought them and the excitement of being on stage near their idol. Irma treasured her memory of "the gaze of her [Isadora's] little pupils turned towards her as flowers towards the sun." Among themselves lay emotions veiled and dormant until, with humor and introspection much later on, they could laugh at their childish pettiness and competitive antics. Anna, for instance, was amused when retelling how each of them vied for Isadora's attention and affection, and tried to outdo the other in performance to win the coveted approval; Isadora did little to conceal her pleasure when a child performed to her satisfaction. After a performance there was a scramble to find the usual bits of dance paraphernalia left on stage, children's mementos of their beloved teacher—Isadora's hair pins, a scarf, a flower. They were but children, capable of jealousy, mischief, even willfulness, yet utterly unaware of their freshness, charm, and grace, and quite innocent of the beauty of their young bodies as they sprang and circled in space.

The phrase "petites artistes" had already been used by many of the youngsters' enraptured audiences; the children were dazzled as royalty feted them and as luminaries from the European creative community bestowed their admiration upon them. Anna Duncan took pride in a favorite memory of herself being dangled on the knee of the great virtuoso violinist, Joseph Joachim.

Conforming to the original prospectus for the Duncan school were the excursions to museums and concerts, as well as to important buildings and famous sites. When brought to Paris in the spring of 1908, following their concert tour with Isadora, the children were elated by the splendor of the city. That they pursued their study and observation of the French capital's historic art treasures is attested to by E. V. Lucas. In his A Wanderer in Paris, the author wrote of his visit to the then-Palais des Beaux-Arts. Suddenly "the vast spaces of the sculpture gallery were humanized by the gracious and winsome presence of a band of Isadora Duncan's gay little dancers with a kindly companion to tell them all about the pictures: and—what interested them more—the statues. These tiny lissome creatures among the cold marbles I shall not soon forget."[21]

The Isadora Duncan School of the Dance came to a close in 1908, less than four years after it was founded. Insurmountable costs, Isadora's accelerating career, her inability to hold the reins of control and guidance, sundry harassments by patrons and local officials objecting to the theater appearances of young children, and the inevitable reaction to rumors surrounding Isadora's private life—all were factors that brought the curtain down on Grunewald. It was farewell to the tall, yellow stucco house, its large garden, the airy and sunny rooms where singing, dancing, painting, and learning had encouraged its children to understand and explore the movements of life.

The center of the dancer's career activity, along with the changing course of events in her personal life, began to shift away from Germany. France became the new focus. Within the year, her fame would peak in Paris. She purchased a fine property in the Parisian suburb of Neuilly and made plans to bring the six Isadorables to France. Of the children left at the school, many returned to their families while others joined Isadora's sister, Elizabeth, in Darmstadt, Germany, where she continued the training begun at Grunewald, but this time under her own banner.

A familiar trio of events, reminiscent of the Grunewald years—career, love, maternity—delayed Isadora's project for a new dance institute. Several years would elapse before one materialized in Bellevue, France. Until then, the Isadorables were housed and supervised by Elizabeth at her Darmstadt facility. There, the girls instructed the young starters in the rudiments of Duncan dance, all the while awaiting Isadora's call to join her in performance.

Between teacher and disciples a new relationship emerged as an innovative chapter in the dancer's choreographic art unfolded. "From the beginning," Isadora wrote, "I conceived the dance as a chorus or community expression. . . . I so ardently hoped to create an orchestra of dancers that in my imagination they already existed."[22] Isadora now had her chorus in the talented and dedicated sextet. The group had made significant strides and were eager to advance to a higher level in their work. Their teacher deemed them ready for more ambitious participation in her programs. In a radical departure from Isadora's customary stage format, that of soloist, she adapted certain choreographies for them where feasible. Original works, that included them, were also created.

Out of her creative adaptations, Isadora experienced a more ideal and amplified dimension of her artistic conceptions, such as in those dances based on Euripides' drama of *Iphigenia*, where the presence of her disciples was choreographically woven into priestesses and maidens of Calchas, or in the Orpheus tale where blessed Spirits and demonic Furies could fulfill her creator's vision.

First the pupils stepped forth into the lighter Chopin and Schubert repertories. "She took great pleasure in teaching us the lyric Schubert waltzes which were subtle versions of children's games," according to Anna. The

Chopin numbers, as with the dances to Schubert's music, were arranged for them individually, in pairs, trios, or full ensemble. The girls had to be ready for this material both in body and mind, as Isadora would soon learn. When in 1911 she tried to teach them sections of the Bacchanal from the Venusberg music of Wagner's *Tannhäuser,* they could not sense its voluptuous nature. She threw up her hands and turned to her brother Augustin, Anna well remembers, in complete frustration. Wise Gus pacified his sister by pointing out that the girls were just "too inexperienced to grasp it." She continued to dance it alone.

For the disciples, learning the dances from Isadora posed obstacles that troubled Isadora as well. From the Isadorables we obtain an impression of the dancer as teacher.

THERESA. "Most that we learned from her came to us in the form of conversation or through observing her. She had no method, no theory, nor pedantic arrangement of steps, and not the slightest pedagogical idea."[23]

LISA. As adolescents, Isadora taught them in her own way: dancing before them until they had grasped "*l'esprit et la forme de la danse.*"[24]

ANNA. "As is so often the way with genius, she had no patience as a teacher. Though she taught us comparatively little over a long period of time, she made it up in intensity."[25]

IRMA. "Unfortunately, she turned out to be a very impatient teacher. Her method consisted in demonstrating the sequence of a dance perfectly executed by herself . . . [she] then . . . expected her pupils to understand immediately and repeat it."[26]

For Isadora, verbal analysis in conjunction with movement dissection as a teaching method dismayed her. Being the creator, she was never confronted with having to master and interpret the unknown opus of another, as her pupils now faced. The problem was not a verbal one. Certainly she made more than her share of speeches in her spectacular lifetime. Her words in personal letters, conversation, or in writings on the dance, capture the ease and rhythm not unlike the flow of her bodily movements. But she was incapable of fragmenting her fluent dance phrase into static segments for analysis. Furthermore, her "way with genius" personality that brought a bewitchment and brilliance to her stage presentations was an impediment in the studio.

She lacked the qualities of diligence and consistency, traits more generally identified with her sister, Elizabeth.

Anita Zahn, a pupil from the Elizabeth Duncan Darmstadt school, recalls that Elizabeth's teaching took place from a high bench where she sat "instructing by word and arm gesture." Macdougall informs us that Elizabeth conducted her classes by "pedagogical word of mouth . . . her feet always firmly planted on the ground." (However, Elizabeth's sedentary method did not at all prevent her from producing fine dancers and teachers of dance.) Macdougall goes on to say that "Isadora herself moved and ran rhythmically to demonstrate the artistic possibilities of the free and gracious body."[27]

The secret of Isadora Duncan's teaching, Mary Fanton Roberts wrote, "lies in her power to inspire a child's soul, letting that inspiration join by gesture with great music until the response is inevitable."[28] This inevitability of achieving the desired response occurred wherever and whenever she imparted her love and faith in her dance to children. It was noted by the American artist and teacher of painting Robert Henri,[29] "I was tremendously impressed one day in Isadora Duncan's studio, by the look in the faces of the children. As they passed by me in the dance, I saw great dignity, balance, ease." Hener Skene, who as pianist worked closely with her and the girls, found her method perfectly acceptable. It achieved results. It was just "more difficult for the learners."

Enthusiastic and committed, the learners accommodated themselves to Isadora's way. They listened, observed intently, and repeated their teacher's demonstrations until the sequence of movements took hold in their minds. Then the body structured, strengthened, and ultimately refined the forms. Whatever pedagogical deficiency may be attributed to her, the Isadorables were, unequivocally, the skillful and distinctive creation of the less programmed, but inspirational, Isadora.

68 Rue de Chauveau

With no exception I viewed the house that Isadora purchased late in 1908 in Neuilly-sur-Seine as my primary destination during my first trip to France. To read and reread the poignant details of her life is to feel the necessity to return to her "Temple of the dance" where so many critical events took place. The studio-home had been the first and longest held of her properties in France, and it was there that some of the best times—and most of the worst—in her life had taken place.

The Parisian suburb of Neuilly in the late nineteenth century was regarded as a painter's paradise. Situated near the Bois de Boulogne, Neuilly boasted charming villas, gardens that were large, colorful, and peaceful, and parks that were green and lush. In addition to its resort-like atmosphere, leisurely pace, and educated, affluent residents, its proximity to Paris ensured its reputation as *the* place to live.

French royalty in earlier centuries had discovered Neuilly's many virtues. Literary royalty were among its admirers and residents in the nineteenth century: Théophile Gautier, Charles Baudelaire, Anatole France; in the twentieth century, Marcel Proust, King Carol of Roumania, and Robert de Montesquieu all called Neuilly home.

My pilgrimage to Neuilly couldn't have taken place on a more beautiful September day. Approximately five miles from the center of Paris, the lovely suburb sparkled with fine shops, wide elegant avenues, handsome homes and gardens, and parks. A *patissier*, standing in the doorway of his *salon du thé*, gave me excellent directions to rue de Chauveau, easily recognized by the American Hospital on its corner.

The walk was exhilarating, hampered only by my uneasy sense of anticipation and the nagging anxiety that this landmark might no longer exist. The resurgence of interest in Isadora was still several years in the offing. At this point the particulars of the celebrated existence that had highlighted an era were of little curiosity but to a few. Isadora's disciples had had no word of the fate of the many studios, schools, and theaters that figured in their history with her. They, too, awaited my findings.

I carried with me a photograph luckily hunted out of a folio of miscellaneous old prints and papers found on rue de Rivoli a few days before. Though taken at the time of the much-publicized auction in 1926, the still sharp photo would help identify the building. It showed a good-sized, three-story structure with clover-shaped attic windows, set back deep on grounds that had large trees, a garden area, and some small buildings adjacent to it.

The pleasant, residential rue de Chauveau is situated between the boulevard Victor Hugo with its famous American Hospital at one end and the boulevard Bourdon along the Seine River at the opposite end. Turning the corner on rue de Chauveau, I calculated the Duncan residence to be within a short distance from the hospital and began watching closely for stone walls densely topped with ivy, a black iron grille gate, and what appeared in my photograph to be an enamelled plate with the number sixty-eight on the upper right wall.

I first spotted the stone walls (*Could this really be it?*); then an iron grille gate (*This must be it!*); and on the upper corner of the right side wall, an enamel plate marked 68 (*This was it!*). But that's all there was. Looking through the gate, I could see two young women laughing and playing badminton in front of a modern structure that was clearly not Isadora's Temple of the Dance. I learned from one of the women that the current house had been built a few years back. She was not familiar with the history of the famous property.

The tension of the day had caught up with me. In a small and quiet neighborhood cafe across the street, I rallied with a cognac while the young bartender, who could not have been born when the dancer died in 1927, rattled off everything he knew about the once-famous house on his block.

Isadora purchased number 68 rue de Chauveau from the French painter-muralist Henri Gervex. The most prominent feature of the main building on the property was its huge studio, purposely constructed by Gervex to execute a large-scale work commissioned by the Russian Czar Nicholas II in celebration of his coronation. (The mural is supposed to have been shipped to the Grand Palace in St. Petersburg.)

The studio was vast, measuring some twenty by thirty meters. When at work in this great space, alone or with an accompanist, Isadora maintained a rule of strict privacy. An open stairway at one end of the studio led to her private apartment on the high balcony that had been remodeled in a striking, somewhat bizarre mode by the Parisian lion of haute couture, Paul Poiret. Isadora's two children were housed with their governess in a small building on the grounds, where they enjoyed the garden and the more normal routines of childhood, undistracted by activities in the main house.

Many came to the rue de Chauveau residence. Those who recorded their impressions of their visit were all strongly affected by its exterior park-like setting and the pervasive, mystical aura of the interior. Irma Duncan, one of Isadora's disciples, compared "entering her [Isadora's] beautiful three storey [sic] studio . . . to entering a cathedral. The long blue drapes covering the walls and hanging down from the ceiling in heavy folds suggested a Gothic interior. The mystical mood was further deepened by the effect of soft lights filtering through overhead alabaster lamps."[30]

French journalist Maurice Bazelgette reporting on the Neuilly house compared it to an annex of an ancient temple. He was awed by its distinctive serenity and atmosphere of a "fine intellectuality." The splendid reproductions of Grecian urns on the walls and the pieces of classical statuary were especially impressive. There was mention of a portrait in oil of the dancer by Eugène Carrière that she preferred above all other studies of her. "Flowers were everywhere . . . filling the veranda were blue hydrangeas. The artist herself, who on stage evoked the image of a tenth muse, was in her home, a graceful Tanagra."[31]

Isadora's return from a cruise on the Nile in 1912 was an occasion for the inimitable reporter Michel Georges-Michel to interview her at Neuilly. His article appeared in *Gil Blas*, prefaced with self-doubts about his ability to recount his chilling experience there. It was a splendid day, he wrote. The country all about him "smelled sweet . . . chestnut tree blossoms spotted the roses." Then came the house. "A gloomy, dark park, large trees concealing a high dwelling—strange and without windows. Up above, where ivy no longer reached, were three clover-shaped attic windows." Georges-Michel approached the entrance: "Dante before the seventh portal of Hell met a distress less woebegone no doubt, than yours truly did in front of the dancer's abode." A small doorway led him into "this mystery . . . the songs of the birds, the scent of the shrubs, the light from the sky, ceased."[32]

Once inside the "lair," there were deep shadows, "the height of gloom." He noticed a reddish glow filtering down from high above. The length of the walls hung with curtains was "damp as from tears." A marble, melancholy-looking statue, reflected in an unframed mirror, stood at the foot of a stairway that wound around eleven times toward the upper level where, "the perfume vapors waft and whirl and from where, unexpected, like a glittering divinity from this nightmarish heaven, appears the dancer. A spot of gold, then azure, she grows taller descending the winding stairway. . . . "

The years between 1909 and 1913 belonged to the Neuilly of an Isadora Duncan in full stride as a woman, an artist, and a renovator in the dance. Both at home in Neuilly and abroad she was admired as a superb performer, recognized as a daring crusader for dance reform, and showered with personal affections from countless friends and supporters. She was a party-goer and a lavish party-giver. The popular Isadora hosted many galas at 68 rue de Chauveau, inviting the elite from the worlds of art, music, and literature.

The year 1909 was a memorable one for the "dancer of the future" and her small band of pupils. Isadora was reappearing in Paris after an absence of almost five years, having engaged the large Théâtre de la Gaîté-Lyrique for two series: January into February, and May into June. The house sold out immediately upon public notice. On the inside the audience crowded "up to the rafters," while on the outside, in front of the theater, stretched "a queue of equipages and luxurious motorcars."

For the children this was their debut in the world capital of art! Their teacher presented them at a matinée performance at the Gaîté for the benefit of earthquake victims in Italy. They danced incidental pieces including Mozart's *Turkish March*. "The little girls she has trained to dance like her are charming. They have seduced the public by their youth alone. But they are not Isadora. They will never be this, without doubt. . . . Isadora can only excite their intelligence, show them how to create. As for imitating her, nothing would be more disastrous," reported Pierre Mille.[33] The February 1909 issue of *Comoedia Illustré* carried André Marty's comments: "Here art consists not in having children perform beyond their level, but to the contrary, in utilizing the child's full range of natural ability . . . and what is admirable . . . these little girls dance as though each of them dances for herself, her own pleasure. All these little single dances combined to form one harmonious whole so that people began to wonder where they were—on the Elysian Fields or in Paradise. . . . "

Coinciding with the second of the Gaîté-Lyrique series that began in May was the auspicious debut of Diaghilev's Ballets-Russes at the Châtelet across town. There was much tumult in Paris surrounding the amazing, sensational Russians, but "for all its atmosphere and social import, the Ballets-Russes had less direct influence on painters than the quieter message of Isadora Duncan and the reinstatement of the more natural movements of the human body."[34] Isadora and her small group continued to draw admiring audiences to their own art at the Gaîté-Lyrique. Appreciation for the children was demonstrated at the end of their programs in the masses of flowers that rained down upon the platform from the auditorium or were brought to the elated young performers. Placed in the center of the stage, the flowers were encircled by the grateful teacher and her radiant pupils who then joined hands to encore with the *Rosenringel* (*Ring Around the Roses*), by now a Duncan tradition.

> I shall always remember her dancing one day with a basket of
> violets she had just received, holding it high above her head, her
> arm stretched like a delicate alabaster pedestal to the basket and
> all her little pupils following her like young fauns . . . all the
> Botticellian freshness of the *Allegory of Spring*.[35]

Fernand Divoire, who originated the term by which the six dancers became identified—the Isadorables—exclaimed: "Oh, garden of happy spirits!"

A second child, a son, was born to Isadora in 1910 in Beaulieu, France. After a short period of domesticity, the dancer resumed creating new choreographies and renewed her concert appearances in France and the United States. At the start of 1913 she was off on tour in Russia with her pianist Hener Skene, returning to Paris in time for her gala season of dance at the Trocadero in March and the Châtelet in April 1913. The Isadorables were brought from Darmstadt by Elizabeth to join her in several dances during this engagement. They rehearsed with Isadora in the huge studio of her Neuilly residence.

The program for the Trocadero featured the enlarged score of Gluck's *Orpheus* and was distinguished by the participation of the noted dramatic actor Mounet-Sully of the Comédie-Française, Rudolphe Plamondon of the Opéra, and the chorus and orchestra of the Concerts Colonne, directed by Gabriel Pierné. A scholarly dissertation by Joseph Peladan on Greek art, ancient tragedy, and the role of the Greek chorus preceded the concert. The second half of the program was almost exclusively devoted to the children who danced to the music of Beethoven's *King Stephen*, Schubert's waltzes and his *Marche Militaire*, and Brahms' waltzes.

The most coveted and cherished reward for the aspiring and competitive disciples was to be offered the rare gift of performing a solo. This honor fell to Irma during this engagement at the Trocadero. Of the Isadorables' performance, Georges Ploch, in his March 29, 1913, review wrote: "The flowing grace of the Grecian tunics, the naked robust and rhythmic legs, supple flashing arms . . . an animating vigor . . . form a sight ever perfect, rejuvenating in us the awareness of beauty . . . The air that bathes them, the silence they stir, the ground they tread share in their gaiety. They discharge with admirable credulity and completely, a vital function of life."

Fernand Divoire, who had been avidly charting the progress of these special youngsters over the years, had this to say "They are grown up now. Tall, supple and graceful . . . no painting of Botticelli or Angelico or Greek fresco . . . expresses as much beauty, chastity and artlessness as these youthful dancers."[36]

Whether this year was "dark with omen" or "turbulent and moody" as described in memoirs of the period, for Isadora it would be all this and more.[37] Albert Flament, a reviewer for *Excelsior*, was at the Châtelet Theatre on Friday evening, April 18, 1913.[38] It was a night to excite warmth and admiration when, as Agamemnon's daughter Iphigenia, Isadora recreated impressions from Euripides' drama. With her bounding leaps and Bacchic grace, Isadora as Iphigenia, a victim, was a vision in white, "moving forward, serene and touching, with the calm of the saints of the Christian martyrdom." When later reliving the evening for his forthcoming review, it was this indelible image of Isadora that haunted Flament. As he prepared his notes, he already knew that within the twenty-four hours after the performance Isadora had experienced the greatest disaster of her own life—the death of both her children. With this in mind, Flament knew these recollections of the "purest evocation of art" would be the last for some time to come. The final vision that remained for Flament came at the concert's end. The clamor in the auditorium had not subsided, and Isadora, in her long, soft cloak kept reappearing from the wings to acknowledge the outpouring of affection and pleasure. She was smiling, opening and offering her hands as though to touch the audience; her eyes seeming to rest on each face before her. She stood there, the saddened Flament wrote, generous and loving and unaware of the bitter destiny awaiting her. The curtain was still raised, but the orchestra members had departed, leaving their empty music stands behind. Isadora stood with her arms outstretched to her public, theirs stretching toward the stage to reach her, and in the semi-darkness of the hall the clamor went on.[39]

On Saturday, April 19, Isadora's two children (Patrick, age three, son of Paris Singer, and Deirdre, age seven, daughter of Gordon Craig) with their governess, Annie Sims, left the Neuilly house so that "Mama" could attend an appointment. Moments later, not far from the house, their black chauffeur-driven car was confronted with an oncoming vehicle. Braking to avert a collision, the Duncan car stalled. Leaving the car in reverse gear as a safety precaution, Morverand, the chauffeur, emerged to re-crank the motor. At the moment combustion was achieved, the vehicle shot backward, jolting the chauffeur from the running board as it quickly plunged into the Seine at the intersection of rue de Chauveau and boulevard Bourdon. Large-scale rescue operations involved the resources of Neuilly and nearby Paris; firemen, police, river engineers, private boatmen, divers, all helped but to no avail. The children and their governess perished.

Within hours, the magnitude of the catastrophe stunned all of Paris. A Neuilly priest hurried to offer consolation to the stricken mother only to be told: "It isn't in your heaven that I shall see my children again . . . I want no church; the heart of a mother is deeper than all temples."[40] Among the crowds to arrive at number 68 rue de Chauveau was the composer Maurice Ravel, who in a few written lines to Igor Stravinsky echoed the lament felt by all: "I am going tomorrow to that unfortunate house. . . . I tremble in anticipation of it. It is too frightful and so unfair!"[41] In the days to come the world seemed to tender its heart to the afflicted Isadora.

In one single stroke of devastating proportions, the Temple of the Dance was transformed into the *maison en deuil* (the house in mourning), and the happy Neuilly years were over. The grieving Isadora fled, leaving the building virtually empty until 1914, when upon request, she allowed the children of wounded soldiers to be housed there.

Interviewed for the February 29, 1919, issue of *Vie Parisienne* Isadora related how she had given her house in Neuilly expecting to help young victims of the war. "I gave them the keys so that they could do what in their judgment was to them the most useful. Instead of the children of the wounded, they put refugees from Compiègne there. Nothing more remained of my house. Even toilet plumbing they took away with them."

The generosity and trust so characteristic of Isadora and all too often given without measure, proved ruinous in this philanthropic instance. By the end of the war, Isadora's house was in a shambles. Possessing neither the heart nor the funds for the staggering cost of restoration and maintenance, she leased it to a manufacturer.

Resuming her career, Isadora travelled and performed extensively throughout Europe, the United States, and South America. She founded a school of dance in Moscow in 1921, a project that eventually required her private financing. Too concerned with the precarious situation in Russia and too removed from her responsibilities in Paris, the property in Neuilly became a court matter. By this time, Isadora had returned to France.

The French court placed the Neuilly house up for sale in the Palais de Justice, on November 26, 1926 as a result of long-overdue taxes and several mortgages. There was nothing Isadora could do about it. Her life was at its lowest ebb since 1913. She was penniless, prematurely worn and aged, and adrift in the changing currents of post-war France. The epoch in which she had brought her artistic ideals to fruition had ended, and Europe had yet to find its footing in the uncertain ground of the future. Isadora's predicament seemed almost salvageable when she became the beneficiary of the estate of Sergei Essenin, the Russian poet she had married in 1922, who died in 1925. But she refused the money, preferring that Sergei's mother and sister in the Soviet Union be considered the heirs.

Were her critical financial difficulties and the loss of her Neuilly home not enough to sap Isadora's incentive to live, the serious decline in her artistic life since returning from Russia in 1924 threatened to be the final straw. It was a case of both moral and material failure. The welfare of children became her single concentration. Only they could effect a refocus of her life; they could heal her. She wanted children to teach and to bring joy into their lives through her dance. "It is this I live for—without hope of realizing this, my life would no longer have meaning."

A call-to-arms sounded to her friends and loyal fans to snatch Neuilly from under the auctioneer's hammer and reclaim it for Isadora. A "Committee to Save Neuilly" was organized. More than Neuilly, it was, for many, an attempt to save a way of life that Isadora epitomized. In her studio could be found the antidote for the indifferent and pleasure-seeking society of Parisian life. Referring to the house in Neuilly, one journalist wrote: "Everything here is fragrance . . . luxury . . . calm. All that the world of today still allows of beauty is here."[42]

The English-language newspaper, the *Paris Herald*, and its sympathetic editor, Eric Hawkins, published Isadora's personal appeal for contributions.

By December 1926, enough private donations had been received to forestall the final sale of the property. The committee was granted additional time to come up with the balance of the debt.

To assure a broad base for the fund drive, a public subscription was instituted and an appeal printed in *Comoedia* on February 25, 1927 by Lotte Yorska, who considered the cause of Neuilly, "the cause of France." She asked the "dear public" never to forget the artist who brought an esthetic revolution to the art of the dance, and whose dance realizations had served their country throughout its agony of the war years; how in 1914 her villa at Bellevue with all its furnishings was unstintingly offered to house and rehabilitate the Allied wounded; her memorable 1916 performance at the Trocadero to benefit the "Armoire Lorraine"; and the benefit concert on behalf of French war orphans that she gave in the United States at the Metropolitan Opera House. Not omitting the public's most vivid memory of Isadora, Yorska cited the powerful message of *La Marseillaise* that the dancer had dramatized throughout the world.

Accompanying Yorska's plea was a series of declarations by Isadora herself. She enumerated the efforts of her early years to found schools and to maintain them, with no tuition, for children, all at great personal and financial sacrifice. When no longer able to support her center for art and after all her pleas for assistance had failed, "I was forced to accept a proposal from the Soviet government." She then asked: "Should I not have gone there, where I could exercise my true mission?"[43]

Isadora, in her declarations—forthright as they were—appeared to be offering an explanation for her unpopular sojourn in Russia from 1921–1924. Rarely one to retreat from a firing line she was, however, perfectly aware that her stay in a communist country, her subsequent marriage to a Russian poet, and most damaging of all, her interviews with correspondents in which she lauded the Soviets, had antagonized many and brought her heavy criticism—undissipated and still lingering in the discernible apathy to her Neuilly crisis.

In keeping with Isadora's own wish, the house in Neuilly, if successfully reclaimed, was to be given to the French government; she reserved the right to its use only during her lifetime, after which the studio would become a school commemorating the dance of Isadora Duncan. Again, she envisioned a broad scheme for her institute were it to come to pass. Studios and an auditorium were to be set up and equipped for use by artists, dramatic producers who lacked their own means of financial backing, and other creative individuals who had little support from the established commercial theater.

If in principle Isadora was receptive to the objectives of the committee's campaign and presented a cooperating image for the public, to close friends she did not conceal her vexation and impatience. She was urgently in need of money for daily subsistence and could not get the committee to release any of the funds to her. While in the south of France where she struggled on her own to emerge from her straits, she was kept minimally informed about the committee's efforts in Paris.

Comoedia, generous in its press coverage of the Neuilly project, further extended its support to the cause by allowing the use of its auditorium for a large exhibition entitled, "Hommage à Isadora Duncan," on Thursday, April 28, 1927. Donated works of sculpture, paintings, jewelry, and miscellaneous objects would be sold. Artists represented on the list of submitted contributions included Marie Laurencin, Henri Matisse, Tsugouharv Foujita, Van Saanen Algi, Dunoyer de Segonzac, André Messager, Jules Grandjouan, Francis Picabia, José Clara, and Emile Antoine Bourdelle. (The latter had sent the dancer a letter urging her not to let his donated sculpture, *Bacchante Dancing the Grape Harvest*, sell for less than 30,000 francs.) This tremendous outpouring of labor, time, money, and spirit came too late, however. By the time this mammoth effort could reach fruition, Isadora Duncan was dead.

Dionysion

The principal mission for another of my trips to France was to delay no further in locating the most splendid of Isadora's properties. I had come too late for the residence in Neuilly. Her small wood-frame house in the rue de la Pompe in Paris, with its exterior and interior alterations, left little traceable to the days of her occupancy there. I anticipated, however, a successful outcome for my search for the Bellevue mansion, the last grand gesture of Paris Singer to the dancer and mother of his son, Patrick.

My optimistic expectations were encouraged by the fact that so splendid was this palatial house in Bellevue that its distinguished architectural style and structural beauty (as revealed by photographs and anecdotal accounts) seemed destined for preservation and survival; further buoying my spirits was my awareness of France's dedication to the rescue of its centuries-old buildings. The well-known Paillard Pavillon, once Isadora's home and school of the dance, would certainly deserve no less, I was certain.

In the environs of Paris the village of Meudon runs into its sister town of Bellevue-sur-Seine. On the main thoroughfare of this attractive suburb, my inquiries on the location of the Pavillon encountered blank stares and shrugs. The banks were closed and the lone gendarme leisurely walking along the quiet avenue shook a *non* with his young head. I came upon no one who knew of my grand edifice, not the *boucher* (butcher), the *boulanger* (baker), nor the *chandelier* (candlestick) maker.

After a frustrating morning I found the *Mairie*—the Town Hall— shared by both Meudon and Bellevue. To a young woman in a large private office, I outlined the purpose of my quest. She listened courteously as I delivered my carefully worded tale in slow French. When I finished she expressed her doubts that such a place still existed. But a building of renown does not disappear that easily in France, I persisted. Oh, no, things were always changing, she added. Perhaps the medical college built in more recent times was constructed on the property I sought, she conjectured. It was evident that she arrived at this hypothesis as a plausible response to my inquiry. With a "*C'est ça!*" ("That's that!") expression on her face, she re-enforced her masterful resolution. It was quite clear. The building I was looking for was obviously destroyed and replaced by the present medical school. She offered a wan smile and briskly went to the door, opened it, looked back at me, encouraging me to depart. Our business was apparently at an end. I remained standing where I was as though nailed to the floor.

Closing the door she approached me to ask if there was something else that I wanted. Yes, there was. Would she kindly phone that college and confirm what she had just told me. Her telephone conversation with the school personnel did not support her hypothesis. The medical school was not erected on land once deeded to the Paillard Pavillon. The mystery of the Duncan residence now began to pique her curiosity. She pressed on with three more phone calls, each one yielding a piece of heartening news. After the last one, there was a wide grin on her face. Isadora's house existed! It was reported to be alive and well, entirely intact on the exterior, but with a remodelled interior that now housed the *Centre National de la Recherche Scientifique* (the National Center for Scientific Research). The original address, #1 Place de la Lune, was now #1 Place Aristide Briand. Phone call number five that afternoon made by the now most eager and aroused clerk, resulted in an appointment for me with the administrator of CNRS and a tour of the premises. I was provided with a letter of introduction, promptly and efficiently typed to take with me. When the clerk opened the door this time, I followed. We regarded each other momentarily with an air of mutual triumph, both of us beaming with satisfaction.

At nine thirty the next morning I arrived at CNRS, immediately recalling having passed it the day before on my entrance into the town of Bellevue. It was not the building I expected to see. CNRS, a vast laboratory facility, was a modern structure jutting onto the main street. I drove through a wide passageway that led into a large courtyard and there, set back along the rear, completely eclipsed from outside view, stood Isadora's "Dionysion" as I had dreamed it and as she had known it, save for certain differences. The nondescript CNRS facility and Isadora's Italian/French Renaissance architectural treasure sat parallel to each other, separated by the courtyard and connected with armlike extensions on the right and left sides.

The facade of Dionysion appeared mercifully unchanged. Victims, however, of the auto age were the lush lawns and flowers, now given way to concrete parking spaces blooming solely with Peugeots, Renaults, and Citroëns. Close to the house one can recognize another survivor (by its rams' heads), the large Romanesque urn against which Isadora had been photographed some seventy years earlier. It was now filled with bright red geraniums.

Two strong impressions of Paris Singer sprang to mind while standing before his magnificent and magnanimous offering to the woman he had loved. This man that Isadora described in her memoirs as having been more attuned to the state of his family fortune (derived from the Singer Sewing Machine), to which he was, in part, heir, than to the state of the arts (her dance mission in particular), appears to have had more understanding and sensitivity than was credited to him and to have unstintingly expressed it with abundant generosity. To assess the gift of Dionysion as a gesture by Singer calculated merely to resume a sundered relationship would do him a disservice. It was, more likely, a genuinely compassionate response to aid the great artist by restoring her will to live and to resume her purposeful work after the loss of her children.

This splendid mansion purchased by Singer late in 1913 was known to French "high society" as the Restaurant and Hôtel Paillard. A white, regal structure, the Pavillon Paillard crowned the elevation of Bellevue as it overlooked the Seine below and the French capital in the distance.

The Bellevue property claimed a royal pedigree, according to Monsieur Poussier who met me on my arrival. Allegedly, the original and first owner was Madame Pompadour; the house a gift to her from King Louis XV. It was passed on to three of her children and after a time moved into private ownerships. Since 1938 the handsome building had undergone architectural modifications and additions as the property of CNRS.

A group of photographs in the possession of Monsieur Poussier revealed the stages of transformation from the time of Isadora to the present day. The building interior on the first level had retained most of the earlier features. The long *salle de danse* that Isadora had converted from the dining hall of the Paillard restaurant was essentially unchanged; its use reserved for company conferences and for screenings of technical films for employees. Still hanging were several mirrors that Isadora had never reclaimed. Recognizable from photographs were the high, arched, Palladian window doors along the length of the wall. The opposite wall that once had window doors opening onto Isadora's rear gardens was now solid space. Above, the quaint balcony overlooking the conference tables and seats seemed misplaced and a bit incongruous without an instrumental ensemble and the lilt of a courtly gavotte for which it had been intended.

A side doorway led us up the carpeted marble staircase with an iron balustrade that wound to the second-floor landing flanked by Corinthian columns. White-smocked men and women, CNRS technicians, stepped quickly and noiselessly in and out of rooms off a long corridor where once Isadora and her children had slept.

From the roof (a turfed terrace in 1914) the panorama was unsurpassed. Here Isadora watched the variable skies of Paris. On clear days she could see the Bois de Boulogne and the Arc de Triomphe.

In the direction of Neuilly, she could follow the graceful interlacing of the serpentine Seine. Closer were the streets of Meudon and below, the surrounding woods with flowering paths and gardens that so strikingly framed her white house. There were factories on the nearby small island that later became the headquarters of the Renault car industry.

Indulgently, my amiable guide, with his charming Maurice Chevalier English, escorted me once more around the conference room. I envisioned glass doors opening out from the *salle de danse* to the rear gardens where children once playfully chased each other on the green lawn, amid flowering shrubs and into the woods beyond; now there were just additional employee parking spaces. Walking back to the entrance courtyard, I turned to view the classic beauty of Isadora's home, its evocation of *le temps perdu* inhabiting my thoughts. For two hours Dionysion had been real, eclipsing CNRS. As I parted from Monsieur Poussier I wondered if in some future tour of the building, he too might see lightly clad young bodies swaying gracefully to the music of Schubert and Chopin.

Isadora named Paris Singer's gift to her *Dionysion*. First to arrive at the new temple of the dance were the Isadorables. The six girls, reunited with Isadora, were elated by the magnificence and spaciousness of their Bellevue home. Larger than Grunewald, and more suitable than the house in Neuilly as a residence and educational facility for many children, Dionysion was sufficiently capacious to accommodate in its sixty or so rooms the fifty boys and girls that Isadora planned to receive there. The chosen ones, with their young energies and easy laughters, enlivened the enormous house and gave heart to their melancholy teacher, still mourning the deaths of her children.

While the new mistress busied herself with preparations necessary for housing a new generation of pupils and making esthetic touches throughout the interiors, several of the girls and their chaperons left for Russia in April to recruit youngsters for Dionysion. They combined their stay with demonstration-performances for artists and royalty before returning to Bellevue with the new recruits. However, the anticipated number of children to inhabit this unusual school ultimately fell short of expectation.

The school policy for Dionysion remained consistent with that of its predecessor. Isadora asked nothing of the parents for the years of study and training of their children, only for the "loan of their souls and expanding minds." The favored disciples, young adults now, became her assistant teachers, a boon to Isadora who was now pregnant with her third child.

Toward five o'clock in the afternoon the Isadorables usually took tea with Isadora in the large hall. Here, in an all-blue decor was the main dance studio—the *salon bleu*. Blue velvet draperies (that left only the window arcs exposed to the light) lined the exceptionally long wall (said to measure about forty meters), and a blue velvet carpet covered the floor. At the end of this room Isadora had built a raised dais. There were seats and couches and tables with flowers. Tea was served to the guest observers. On occasion, visitors wrote impressions of this most unusual interior with its "music cabinets, musical instruments of many kinds, and the statuary replicas."[44] Never failing to elicit comment from Dionysion's guests was the "cloister-like atmosphere and the classical serenity"[45] that pervaded the studio.

Down the rear steps one entered a smaller dance studio—the *salon blanc*—used for daily classwork. The walls of the all-white room were completely covered with a soft material hung from cornice to floor. Above the suspended fabric the moldings were decorated with reproduction fragments of the frieze from the Parthenon. Beneath a bay window and between two divans, on a stone pedestal, stood the white sculpture of the Greek *Danseuse*. Atop a table rested a miniature plaster model that the dancer prized highly. Architect Louis Sue had designed this model when Paris Singer and Isadora were selecting a suitable site for their cultural center to be constructed in Paris. "We will play the tragedies as in ancient Greece with a dancing chorus. I hope, oh, I hope that Mounet-Sully would want to appear there—the greatest actor since before Jesus Christ . . . all in him is dance."[46] Personal differences and temperamental squabbles kept derailing the plans. Dooming the effort, finally, was the children's death in 1913.

At Bellevue, the Isadorables knew of their mentor's renewed plans to build the theater of her dreams. Talk was revived and construction plans for the festival art center, to be built this time on the grounds of the school, were promising. A visionary of broad strokes, Isadora's blueprint indicated an ambitious structure with grand scale objectives that would harmoniously fuse all the arts in a celebration of life. Greek tragedies would be presented, played by the leading exponents of the dramatic stage, while a full symphonic orchestra of major musical rank would support the dance performances. This theater of her dreams would bring a new impetus to the intellectual life of France. To quote an enthusiast of Isadora's vision: "It would have given France a Bayreuth."[47]

Dionysion's second level housed the dormitories with their rather spartan furnishings: a bed, a chair, a chest of drawers, and one or two inspirational reproductions on the walls, reminiscent of the children's rooms in Grunewald. The beauty of these rooms lay entirely in the light and spectacular vista of the Seine and beyond. A large, well-stocked library for the children's educational studies and esthetic development had been expanded by merging several of the rooms into one.

During the late afternoon in the *salon bleu,* the Isadorables might dance informally, with Hener Skene at the piano, or would listen to the lively conversations that spoke of the "harmony and magnitude of things." Rodin was a frequent visitor at this hour as he lived in Meudon—an easy stroll away. As his arrival was announced to Isadora, she would remark: "There's a great joy, a great blessing in my house. A god has come down to us,"[48] referring to the Olympian gods of old who condescended to visit the homes of mortals. The disciples would bring a comfortable upholstered chair for the "god" and Rodin, after kissing Isadora's hand, would settle back in his chair and begin to converse with them. Placing a divan cushion at his feet, Isadora, wrote André Arnyvelde, was heard to comment: "As Brunhilde at the feet of Wotan." He added, "She listened to him like the believer receiving the eucharist."[49] Friday afternoons were reserved for guests who regarded Isadora as the "enchantress who awoke this palace from its lethargy and decided to radically change its destiny." Seated on the platform of the large dance salon, they were eager to see the "nymphs" and the new works in progress. A typical gathering might consist of the actor Mounet-Sully, the violinist Jacques Thibaud, the Italian poet D'Annunzio, the actress Eleanora Duse, and the Belgian virtuoso Eugene Isaye.

Through velvet draperies the "nymphs" entered the serene and reverent ambience of the blue-draped hall; the enchanting music, the gentle rhythms and dynamics of the dancers in motion gave credence to Isadora's image of the dance as a music of moving lines. For the visitors it was a unique exposition of the dancer's philosophy: "That beauty is latent in every human body and that it can be realized only by developing the spirit to an understanding of it."[50]

Isadora made the Bellevue house accessible to artists. She encouraged the intellectual interchange between them and her young, maturing disciples, sensing the mutual value to be gained from such a rich and stimulating artistic experience. The freedom to sketch the children as they danced or ran about the gardens of Dionysion intrigued the artists. The children, in turn, listened with adoration to the words of Bourdelle or Rodin, inspired by the communication. "Indeed," said Mary Fanton Roberts, "it is not enough that they learn to move with the ecstasy of all free creatures. . . . The art of the world is poured into the spirits of these children, flooding their minds and flowing back again into the world through expression and gesture, to enrich and renew life."[51]

Saturday morning was set aside for the artists. The day would include a fine lunch and a lesson in the garden, weather permitting. When not dancing, the children ran through the woods, laughing and shouting, their capes bright bits of color as they darted among the trees. As they ran, Rodin sketched. Finding excitement in the expressive human body, he loved his visits to Dionysion: "If only I had such models when I was young—models who understood the science of movement as Isadora's pupils."[52] André Arnyvelde who witnessed this rare community of art and spirit, exclaimed: "How advantaged are the painters, sculptors and musicians . . . by the generous hospitality of this sacred house."[53]

The new enterprise at Bellevue afforded the French press a fresh round of publicity since the death of Isadora's two children. The existence of the school delighted the friendly and provoked the curious to cynicism—in some instances, to worse. If Isadora was powerless to impede the oncoming threat of war that in a few months would contribute to the dissolution of her school, she could and did create a minor skirmish when she became a central target for criticism and ridicule.

Such was the case of her suit against the cafe-theater, La Cigale, where in a tableau entitled *In Bellevue*, she and her school were the subjects of a satirical revue. On stage, in parody, was "The School of Miss Isadora Duncan." The fact that the literary genre of mocking the contemporary famous had been going on since the days of Aristophanes did little to lessen her humiliation and anger. "The limits of satire have been greatly exceeded in this instance,"[54] she insisted. The theatrical caricature perverted her art, she said, and inflicted serious injury on her, her pupils, and her school.

At the hearing, the dancer's attorney read the letter she had addressed to the plea judge.

> My own career has collapsed. . . . I am trying to give my art to others—to fifty little children I am seeking as pupils in forming a school of dance . . . a school that will have an effect on its period, by creating a dance art that will be the purest, most noble expression of human aspiration. This parody . . . can to an extreme degree, be detrimental to the founding of this school in that it gives the public a completely false idea of my work. . . . In the name of my grief, in the name of mothers who now are entrusting to me their children, I am requesting that this theater caricature . . . be stopped.[55]

La Cigale was ordered to remove the name of Isadora Duncan from the set. The tableau itself, however, continued.

One prominent politician, Paul Boncour, Jr., wrote of cafe-concert parodies that vilify and slander. He defended the high scholastic quality of the educational program at Bellevue by calling attention to the staff and their numerous university degrees and to the cultural emphasis of the teaching content. "Ah! How beautiful verse takes wing with ease in the bright room where sculpture reproductions and antique prints re-enforce . . . our great classics."[56] He guaranteed his readers that having once witnessed the youngsters at Bellevue in their comfortable, sensible dress as they consulted their assignment schedules and attended to their lessons in a wholly organized manner, "the most skeptical will bow before the generous-hearted 'danseuse' who has renewed her desire to live in order to raise the children of others in beauty."

The second Isadora Duncan School of the Dance was officially inaugurated with a performance by all the children at the Trocadéro Theater on June 28, 1914. More than a herald of the continuing future of Isadora's art, the affair signalled to the thousands of Duncanphiles who came to celebrate and honor the much-admired woman, her emergence from behind the veil of mourning. Homage was paid to a grand artist on the occasion of her return to the intellectual world. "There would be no further withholding of her genius and powers that bring into our hearts joy, and into the world, beauty."[57]

Isadora did not dance that evening, a fact that visibly stunned her audience and the critics who were unaware of her advanced pregnancy. Their attention was captured, however, by the irresistible charm of the Isadorables. Here was Isadora's solid evidence of the seriousness of her undertaking and the worthiness of its result. It was they who now filled the tremendous theater stage and carried the program on their youthful shoulders.

"Long ago Isadora had trained them, had taken their soft, childish arms in her divine hands, curved their tender necks, straightened their shoulders and aligned the heads, and finally, by the caressing touch of her grace through their yielding bodies, initiated these virgins into the mysteries of rhythm."[58] This time it was Anna who was, in her own words, "so specially honored to have danced the middle part [central figure] of the Schubert Marche Héroïque. This dance was Isadora's memorial tribute to her children."

But it was Isadora, usually seen with her graceful cortège of young girls, who was missed. "When the younger and newer children came on barefoot, with small steps and tender arms, shy and sweet like cherubs and lacking only wings to make them angels, it was she among the cherubs who was missing— the big sister Isadora—and the endearing sight of the little ones running behind her under her spreading scarves."[59]

The Isadorables danced, the first recipients of an artistic credo that prepared their bodies and minds not only "in the intelligence of the dance but in the intelligence and practice of life."[60] Their dancing that June day was compared to their remarkable season at the Gaîté-Lyrique in 1909. "They now were taller, like slender stalks, displaying more confidence in their gestures, more authority and greater fullness of the rhythmic form."[61] Their loveliness captivated the audience. As their dancing flowered into an ensemble more artistically mature and esthetically defined, critics began to take note of their separateness of personality and performing character. "The children are purely Isadorian but each retains an individuality. . . . Lisa, the light butterfly in contrast with Teresa [sic], the wild. Irma, the technician, Anna, the graceful. . . . Erika shy . . . with a richness of intimate ecstasy . . . Margot . . . a fragile grace . . . seized by the large virile rhythm of the Schubert Marche Militaire."[62]

Only weeks away from the birth of her child, Isadora was very much present in the Trocadero but seated in the back of a loge to the left of the stage. Her eyes were focused on her young school. She was overheard commenting: "In two years, it will be quite good." For many Duncan partisans in the audience, the concert held great import. The art of Isadora's dance was not deemed solely a passing phenomenon. There was at last visible assurance of what "her long effort and genius" had borne into fruition: a dance art whose beauty could be preserved and transmitted. The Isadorables had become the tangible threads of a new tradition.

Shortly after the Trocadero performance in early July, the children left their temple of the dance for a holiday in England—presumably just for the summer months. But by August 1914 France had already entered the war, which erupted one month earlier, a war that political optimists speculated would surely be of short duration. The Isadorables and eleven of the younger children remained with Paris Singer at his Devon estate while Isadora, nearing confinement kept close to her Bellevue home.

But 1914 was not fated to be the time for Dionysion. The war escalated. In early August, the son born to Isadora lived but a few hours. And the children's dispersal from Bellevue was to be a permanent one.

The second Isadora Duncan School of Dance lasted little more than seven months—a slim shaft of brilliant light between dark crags. On one side, the tragic loss of the dancer's two children had lengthened its grim shadow with the death of her third child. It was "as if the others had died again," Isadora said. On the other side, the pulse of life and art she sought to revive through the dance had become incongruous with the monumental cataclysm of war.

The ironic, incalculable waste of it all! A grand-scale residence and school in a setting of such natural beauty, security in the certainty of financial backing, the arduous preparations and buoyant aspirations for many children—gone up in smoke along with the plaster model of Isadora's festival theater—her symbol of hope reborn—that burned when a fire damaged the white salon that summer. A half century later, Irma Duncan expressed her regret that Isadora had not made more of an effort—war or no war—to keep Dionysion. "Wars have come and gone, and life is short, but art lives forever."[63]

England in that August of 1914 allied itself with France against Germany. With the exception of the Swiss Anna, the Isadorables were German. It was considered prudent to send the children in September to the still-neutral United States. Paris Singer's estate at Paignton, in Devon, was to be used as a war-time hospital, and Isadora turned her mansion at Bellevue and its furnishings over to Les Dames de France as a hospital center for the rehabilitation of the Allied wounded. She joined her disciples in the United States in November 1914.

The following month, on December 3, 1914, the proud American dancer led her small troupe of dancers in their American debut in Carnegie Hall. The program for that first appearance of the Isadorables would read, "At which time Miss Duncan will present six young dancers." Erika remembered the occasion of her American debut as the climax of her dancing career. Decades later, spectators present on that day remembered how deeply stirred they were by the première of a new work by Isadora—Schubert's *Ave Maria*.

The children danced? No, one writer answered. They

> throbbed and lived, and magic breathed from their living. Here was the breath of God, yes, the beatific vision was in these little ordinary human souls. These wands of simple average childhood struck the rock,

and the waters of life gushed, the heavens of beauty unveiled. This art, this hope, this way of life could be our own! They were Isadora Duncan's "children."64

An interview with the Isadorables in 1915 elicited the following observations:

> The little girls of the early blue-and-white stage have grown up into miniature Isadora Duncans . . . the six star pupils who appear with Isadora Duncan in her exhibitions [Spring of 1915 at the Century Theater] form an interesting group. . . . Anna . . . the eldest is actively concerned with the affairs of the world about her. . . . Therese and Irma come next, an impulsive and spirited pair. Lisel is long-haired and long-legged, physically the best dancer of any of them. Gretel [Margot] is a thoughtful child, filled with a sense of her dignity and somewhat mystified with the American manner of doing things; Erica, the youngest, is also the most serious.65

American writer-poet Witter Bynner paid poetic tribute to the American dancer and her artistic progeny:66

ISADORA (TO HER SIX DANCERS)
Beauty came out of the early world,
Her hyacinthine hair still curled,
Her robe still white on auroral limbs;
And her body sang the self-same hymns
It long ago had sung to the morn
When death gave birth and love was born.

And once again her presence proved,
As most immortally she moved,
That in her meditative eye
The child of death can never die
But dances with inspired feet
On every hill, in every street.

She raised her hand—and Irma came,
Theresa, Lisel, each like a flame,
Anna, Erica, Gretel: the tread
Of life still dying, never dead . . .
And like a bird-song in a wood,
Within their very heart she stood.

Photographer Arnold Genthe's studies of the group in ensemble, in pairs, trios, and individually, eloquently revealed their physical maturity into young womanhood and their developed personal grace. According to the impresario Sol Hurok, they were "the loveliest children imaginable." The six chosen ones were hardly children at this time and they had little humor for being so regarded. Especially did they bristle at Isadora's persistence in calling them her "little pupils." The Isadorables had come of age.

NOTES

1. Isadora Duncan, *The Art of the Dance*, p. 77.
2. Isadora Duncan interview in *Excelsior*, December 28, 1910.
3. Irma Duncan, *Duncan Dancer*, p. 6.
4. *Ibid.*
5. Anna Duncan interview with the author, 1966.
6. Irma Duncan, *Duncan Dancer*, p. 17.
7. Isadora Duncan, *My Life*, pp. 173–174.
8. Isadora Duncan, *The Art of the Dance*, p. 124.
9. *Algemeen Handelsblad* (Amsterdam), August 4, 1906.
10. Anna Duncan in *Ballet Review*, Volume 3, #1, October 1969, p. 25.
11. Irma Duncan, *Duncan Dancer*, pp. 33–34.
12. E. Gordon Craig, *Index to the Story of My Days*, p. 263.
13. Isadora Duncan, *My Life*, p. 214.
14. Irma Duncan, *Duncan Dancer*, pp. 74–75.
15. "Als Isadora Danst," *De Telgraaf* (Holland), August 2, 1907.
16. *Ibid.*
17. *Nieuwe Rotterdammer Courant* (Rotterdam), March 27, 1908.
18. Sibmacher Zynen, *Algemeen Handelsblad* (Amsterdam), December 14, 1907.
19. John Galsworthy, *A Motley*, pp. 254–255.
20. *Ibid.*
21. E. V. Lucas, *A Wanderer in Paris*, p. 153.
22. Isadora Duncan, *My Life*, p. 140.
23. Maria-Theresa, "As I Saw Isadora Duncan," *Dance Magazine*, November 1928, pp. 23, 49.
24. Odile Pyros, a pupil of Lisa Duncan, in conversation with author, 1984.
25. Anna Duncan in conversation with author, 1967.
26. Irma Duncan, *Duncan Dancer*, p. 127.
27. Allan Ross Macdougall, *Isadora Duncan: A Revolutionary in Art and Love*, p. 109.
28. Mary Fanton Roberts, "Isadora—The Dancer," *Denishawn Magazine*, May 1925, p. 12.
29. Robert Henri, "Toward the New Education," in *Dionysion*, Volume 1, Number 1.
30. Irma Duncan, *Duncan Dancer*, p. 125.
31. Maurice Bazelgette, "Miss Isadora Duncan," *Renaissance Romantique*, July 1909, p. 50.
32. Michel Georges-Michel, "Isadora—Isadora," *Gil-Blas*, September 6, 1912.
33. Pierre Mille, "Isadora Duncan," *Le Théâtre*, February 1909.
34. John Drummond, *Colour, Rhythm and Dance—Paintings and Drawings of J. D. Ferguson and His Circle*, p. 23.
35. Gaspard Etscher, "Renaissance of the Dance," *Forum*, September 1911, p. 328.
36. Fernand Divoire in Irma Duncan, *Duncan Dancer*, pp. 128–129.
37. Virginia Cowles, *1913—An End and a Beginning*; Poinecaré, *Memoirs: Dark with Omen*.
38. Albert Flament, "Une automobile tombe dans la Seine," *Excelsior*, April 21, 1913.
39. *Ibid.*

40. Michel Georges-Michel, "La Mort sous les Fleurs," *Comoedia*, April 23, 1913.

41. Maurice Ravel in Eric White, *Stravinsky: The Composer and His Works*, p. 548.

42. Henriette Sauret, "Chez Isadora Duncan," *Chanticler*, July 23, 1927.

43. "Declaration d'Isadora Duncan," *Comoedia*, February 28, 1927.

44. Mary Fanton Roberts, "The Dance: By Isadora Duncan," *Touchstone*, October 1917, p. 4.

45. *Ibid.*

46. Michel Georges-Michel, "Les Ennuis et les rêves d'Isadora Duncan," *Gil Blas*, December 3, 1911.

47. André Arnyvelde, "Isadora Duncan va rouvrir son école sous le patronage de l'Etat," unidentified source, May 5, 1920.

48. André Arnyvelde, "L'Ecole de danse gratuite d'Isadora Duncan," *Le Temps*, April 12, 1914.

49. *Ibid.*

50. Mary Fanton Roberts, "The Dance: By Isadora Duncan," *Touchstone*, October 1917, p. 4.

51. Mary Fanton Roberts, "Isadora Duncan's School," *Dionysion*, Volume 1, Number 1, 1915.

52. Auguste Rodin in Anne Leslie, *Immortal Peasant*, p. 321.

53. André Arnyvelde, "L'Ecole de danse gratuite d'Isadora Duncan," *Le Temps*, April 12, 1914.

54. Georges Claretie, "Procès de la Cigale," unidentified source, May or June 4, 1914.

55. *Ibid.*

56. Paul Boncour, Jr., "Une Oeuvre," unidentified source, June 23, 1914.

57. *Ibid.*

58. Maurice Montabré, "Les Nymphs ont danse," unidentified source, June 29, 1914.

59. *Ibid.*

60. André Arnyvelde, "L'Ecole de danse est ouverte depuis aujourd'hui," unidentified source, February 19, 1914.

61. Maurice Montabré, "Les Nymphs ont danse," unidentified source, June 29, 1914.

62. Fernand Divoire, "Les Elèves d'Isadora," *Decouvertes sur la danse*, pp. 91–92.

63. Irma Duncan, *Duncan Dancer*, p. 149.

64. John Collier, *Survey*, June 3, 1916, p. 251.

65. *Literary Digest*, May 1, 1915, p. 1019.

66. Witter Bynner, "Isadora (To Her Six Dancers)," in E. Dickson, *Poems of the Dance*, p. 84.

CHAPTER FIVE

The Isadora Duncan Dancers

"If we are waiting for a renaissance of the dance, its inspiration will not come from an erudite professor but rather from joyful movements of children leading the flute of the great god Pan."

ISADORA DUNCAN

THE YEAR 1917 SAW the United States enter the European conflict. It also found Isadora's young dancers engaged in a private battle of their own—a generational confrontation with their mentor. Pressing for greater personal and professional independence from their venerated mother figure, the disciples could not avoid the resulting discord and bitterness that affected their relationship with her. In stereotypical fashion Isadora, in her parental role, protested what she considered to be their audacious and unreasonable demands, insisting that they were not yet ready to appear without her.

To ensure that her work survive her own contribution to her art, Isadora had founded her schools. She once drew a parallel between herself and Rodin: "Rodin surrounds himself in his studio with slabs of marble. I want to surround myself, also; my block of marble—my pupils." Obsessive on the subject of perpetuating her ideas through trained disciples, Isadora must have been profoundly threatened by her pupils' rebellion. Without a current school and new pupils to train, these girls were all she had as testimony to her life in dance, yet they were determined to emerge from the chrysalis fully winged for flight.

Complementing the young women's youth, beauty, and talent was a secure technique, a physical pliancy, professional poise, and a substantial repertory of dances they could perform with musicality, grace, and conviction of interpretation. When in motion, their magnificent young bodies seemed to flash silhouettes of an earlier Isadora. How understandable if their elasticity, elevation, and verve caused her more than a twinge of envy, even jealousy. Yet how plainly lay her signature on their gesture's curve; the integrity of her artistic credo disclosed in their animated forms.

The girls stood their ground (some more boldly than others), unrelenting in their strike for artistic independence and a theatrical limelight of their own. To avoid complications for her disciples (who were now regarded as enemy aliens since the United States had entered the war against Germany), Isadora set in motion the process for their legal adoption (reported as finalized in 1920). Irma, Lisa, and Anna would permanently assume the name of Duncan. Newly named "The Isadora Duncan Dancers," the ambitious sextette took off on a series of tours across the country between 1918 and 1920, with the assistance of pianist George Copeland, and later, Beryl Rubinstein, under the management of Sol Hurok. With a half-hearted, grudging consent for this career-launching undertaking of her protégées, Isadora returned to France.

Across the country audiences greeted the young dancers as "the offerings of Isadora Duncan's spirit."[1] Not only, as one reviewer put it, were they "making their first large venture unguided by her," but they left no doubt as to "the fitness of the Duncan Dancers to carry on the unique art created by Isadora Duncan."[2] The auspicious beginning brought other reactions: "From under the protecting wing of genius, they emerge to test themselves, to feel their own weight and space about them. . . . Each one begins to measure her lot and fame alone."[3] Indeed, there was a restlessness within them, each desiring to present her personal art and to articulate a private inspiration without in any way lessening the collective harmony of the ensemble effort. It was as Isadora had predicted during the Grunewald years: "while forming part of a whole, they will preserve a creative individuality."

All matters were now in the girls' own hands. They alone were responsible for selecting the dance numbers, arranging the program content, working with accompanists and backstage technicians, and resolving the unexpected snags of weather, travel, schedules, and other trials that imperil a touring company. With the exception of a few of their own dances, the programs consisted primarily of Isadora's choreography.

Unlike Isadora's programs, theirs were performances of interpretation and of recreation, not of innovation. (Gordon Craig contrasted Isadora Duncan with the actresses Ellen Terry, Mme. Rachel, and Eleanora Duse, by designating her the greater artist. They, he explained, were "remarkable interpreters of the literary giants, but Isadora "interpreted no one at all—she positively created.")

The six young dancers were now the headlining attraction upon whom audiences focused their full attention. "I see them now, circling on the immense stage, six girls, the light falling yellow over their young heads and along their arms so gently linked. Something idyllic, something innocent, tender, something indefinitely grave was the slow movement of these young people together."[4] More personal recognition came their way as each performance revealed their individuality. There was "Anna's interpretive art . . . Anna, the black-eyed, the black-haired . . . the leader in their lives as in their dancing and she is very beautiful, beautifully made, with a most exquisite modeling of chin and neck and shoulders. Though she is not tall there is something heroic in her structure."[5] Lisa was singled out for her famous leapings, "Lisa of the golden locks . . . kin to Undine of romantic legend."[6] Margot's fragile beauty seemed

> more delicate in repose than in motion. . . . Erica, dark-eyed
> and of a quiet manner looks upon the world with great
> solemnity. . . . Irma . . . perhaps the most distinctive member of
> the group in whose mocking grey-eyed face there is mingled
> wisdom with a mischievous gaiety. She has an amusing wit. She
> is gifted. . . . Theresa is the loveliest of all—a simple maiden with
> long blond braids wound around her head. She is complete in her
> response to music and when she dances her face, alight with joy,
> gives . . . great pleasure. Waltzing, she is more than anyone like
> Isadora, lost, ecstatic, whirling through an immense quiet. . . .[7]

Included in the girls' itinerary during 1919–1920 was San Francisco, Isadora's birth place. They demonstrated to those who came to see them that Isadora's art was "pulsating and young in another generation." A young Martha Graham reacted to the six dancing Duncans: "I saw something that was of natural quality, yet had a certain formalism. It spoke to me emotionally. It did not excite the senses, it spoke deeper than that."[8] Writing many years later, critic Carl Van Vechten considered Isadora's "children" "but pale reflections of her thrilling performances." It was his opinion that the group did not "capture one iota of the great woman's spirit." Music critic Sigmund Spaeth wrote of the Isadorables: "It may truthfully be claimed that no dancing in the world today has more of truth and sincerity in its appeal than has the dancing of these six adopted daughters of Isadora Duncan."[9]

The two-year concert circuit had unquestionably earned the six young women enough successes to satisfy their immediate ambitions: warm public reception, favorable critical recognition, professional status as a performing group, and socially, an enjoyable celebrity. Their appearance in May 1920 concluded their auspicious career start while simultaneously signalling the beginning of the end for them as the Isadorables.

Only five of the girls returned in June to Europe in response to Isadora's cable that they join her to work on important repertory. Erika broke the chain. She had made an irreversible decision to leave the group and her life in dance, and devote herself to the study of painting. (Artist Van Deering Perrine, in his frequent visits to the Elizabeth Duncan school in Tarrytown, New York, sketched the young dancers and knew Isadora's girls during their temporary residence there. He knew Erika best and thought her a remarkable artist in creative design.)

Isadora, reunited with her girls, took them to Greece where they studied more advanced and complete dance scores to the Beethoven, Tchaikovsky, and Schubert symphonies in the Duncan repertory. They could now conceive the larger range and dramatic import of the music as visualized by their teacher, and contribute their own interpretive insights. These dances, Isadora stressed, had to be learned to a "state of perfection, or as near to it as possible, before dancing it in a theatre." "We girls had particular love for the great Schubert Seventh Symphony in E major with its Apollonian spirit and special Dionysion character of the 'Scherzo,'" Anna told me. "We were taught the last two movements of this work that Isadora called her hymn to the goddess Diana."

The sojourn in Greece was also intended by Isadora as an attempt to reestablish a vital relationship with her disciples. Instead, it took a serious and unfortunate turn that would eliminate yet another Isadorable—the beautiful and talented Anna—further fragmenting the group. Anna and Isadora's lover and accompanist, Walter Rummel, had fallen in love. To stem Isadora's increasing suspicions, resentments, and uncontrolled jealousy, Anna planned to leave the ensemble after the upcoming engagements with Isadora at the Trocadéro, starting in late November 1920, and at the Théâtre des Champs-Elysées, in January 1921.

Ornaments (above and below) *from a* Comoedia Illustré *article on Isadora. (Collection of the author)*

*Isadora and her children,
drawing by José Clará
(Collection of Museo Clará,
Barcelona)*

A Tragic Fate, *drawing
by José Clará. (Collection
of Museo Clará, Barcelona)*

Isadora on the grounds of her home, "Dionysion," in Bellevue.
(Roger Viollet Collection)

Isadora and her pupils in Rye, New York, c. 1914-1915.

Lisa Duncan, poster for Second Christmas Roll Call, by Arnold Genthe for the American Red Cross, 1918. (Collection of the author)

THE

ISADORA DUNCAN DANCERS
AND
BERYL RUBINSTEIN
Pianist
Management: LOUDON CHARLTON, Carnegie Hall, New York
MASON & HAMLIN PIANO

The Isadora Duncan Dancers on tour of the U.S., 1918-1920. (Collection of the author)

Isadora and her group in her rue de la Pompe studio, Paris, taken during the dance season, 1920-1921. Lisa (standing), *Theresa* (to Lisa's left), *Anna* (seated on platform, left), *Irma* (center), *Margot [Gretel]* (right). (Roger Viollet Collection)

Irma Duncan, c. 1932. (Collection of Hortense Kooluris)

Margot, Anna, and Lisa.
(Courtesy of Hortense Kooluris)

Margot, Anna, and Lisa as the
Three Graces, c. 1922.
(Courtesy Hortense Kooluris)

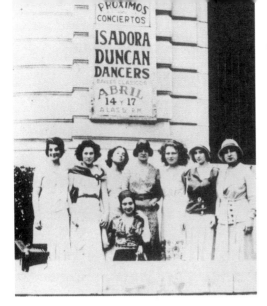

American Duncan dancers in Havana, Cuba, 1931. (left to right) Mignon, Ruth Kramberg, Julia Levien, Irma, Sima Borisovana, Bela, Sonia, and (below) Hortense Kooluris. (Collection of the author)

American Duncan dancers. (Photograph by Soichi Sunami. Courtesy of Julia Levien)

American Duncan dancers (left to right) *Ruth Kramberg, Sima Borisovana, Hortense Kooluris. (Photograph by Arnold Genthe.)*

American Duncan dancer Mignon Garland, 1944. (Photograph by Lotte Jacoby.)

American Duncan dancer Hortense Kooluris (Photograph by Kirby Kooluris)

American Duncan dancer Julia Levien, 1980. (Photograph by Leo Loewenthal)

The disciple who claimed to have been in awe of her mentor and who never quite lost the sense of attachment and reverence for her, recalled with sadness the last choreography that Isadora taught her famous pupils for their Paris engagement. "It was the lofty and grand Flower Maiden scene from *Parsifal* and took place in the studio of Isadora's house in rue de la Pompe in Paris. This is where we last worked with her all together and where the big separation occurred. It gives me quite a pang,"[10] Anna recalled.

"She [Isadora] talked of these scenes from *Parsifal* as frescoes in movement and light. At our first rehearsal we had two or three great upsweeping gestures with which to cross the entire studio. After we girls performed the movements just once, she went over to a couch and broke into a loud, sobbing cry." It was a cry of gratitude for her wonderful pupils, for their intuitive grasp of her creative intentions, Anna believed. Afterward, Isadora approached Anna and enfolded the pupil in her arms. To be able to comprehend and dance as she, Anna, had done, was what really mattered after all, Isadora sobbed. Forty-five years after the unrepaired estrangement, Anna Duncan could speak of her foster mother: "Even her malice would be made good by a kindness afterward."

Days before Isadora and her disciples opened their grand Festival of Music and Dance at the Trocadéro on November 27, 1920, a select group attended their rehearsal at the rue de la Pompe address. Throughout this house, as with all the dancer's residences, were books, engravings, and drawings by José Maria Sert, Léon Bakst, Auguste Rodin, and sculptures by Charles Despiau and Emile-Antoine Bourdelle. On the walls hung photographs of the Parthenon. The spacious blue drapes in the large, rectangular studio plunged the room in shadow; a thick carpet softened the tread. "In the studio of Mme. Duncan, as in a temple, you proceed slowly and speak in a soft voice," reads Michel Georges-Michel's account of that evening.[11]

On a platform were deep armchairs and divans for the invitees—journalists, poets, and painters. Tall candelabra on each side threw a diffuse and flickering light onto the incense-laden atmosphere that was enough to "cause mystics to swoon and the godless to sneeze," reporter Michel Georges-Michel wrote with his customary puckish impudence.[12] The flame of one taper cast an awkward light at the foot of the stage while an "hebraic" candlestick illuminated the white narcissus on the table. A golden punch, a light tea, some mousses and crèmes were served, and then the "nymph" herself appeared.

Looking like an apparition in the dim light, clad in her gray tunic with its soft, billowing fabric, Isadora placed herself in front of the Parthenon photographs to address her guests. She spoke of the dance as fundamental to the interpretation of tragic expression in ancient poetry and drama. She then mentioned her young dancers who were no strangers to most of the assembled audience (among them Henriette Sauret, Gabriel Astruc, Cecile Sorel); the girls would soon dance for them. And then, she closed her remarks by saying "The dance is the noblest of the arts; everything beautiful is the dance; a lovely poem, a flower, the horses of the Parthenon—that is dance; Rodin's *The Thinker*, is dance."[13]

Moments later, from the shadows, four dancers rushed out—Theresa, Irma, Anna, and Lisa; Margot was ailing and did not participate that evening or in the subsequent performances.

> One has a small head, narrow shoulders and hips rounded like a vase; another, serious eyes beneath heavy eye brows and one sees only that about her; the third is mist, sweetness and charm and even when directly in front of us, we cannot retain the lines of her moving form for more than an instant . . . and the last—this one leaps like a crystal waterfall striking a clear rock. . . . From the first gesture they blended one into the other, harmony created with each step.[14]

To Schubert's funeral march (*Marche Héroïque*), played by Walter Rummel at the piano, Isadora and her pupils developed through their movements a fresco of mourning women; other dances that followed brought "new visions and shapes, creating new enchantments," a journalist commented.[15] He described the dead silence that ensued when the music ceased. "The antique vision had disappeared and everyone, as though in a stupor, struggled back to reality and the immediate surroundings. One spectator whispered to another: Greece did well to send us a magician."[16]

It was a gala season at the Trocadéro. From the first to the last performance, the cavernous theater was sold out. The press simply had to announce that Isadora Duncan and her garlanded pupils were to appear in the French capital for the vast hall to resound with the public's fervor.

At the première, Isadora and her Isadorables presented an all-Wagner program. Once again, the bold American offered a spectacle unknown and unthought of in the world of art: dance united with music in excerpts from *Parsifal*, *Tristan and Isolde*, *Die Walküre*, and *Tannhaüser*, with the esteemed conductor George Rabani (a pupil of D'Indy and Franck) and the Colonne Orchestra. The music of Schubert and Gluck supplemented the Wagner programs.

The reviews from that time attest to the performers' success:

The four Isadorables . . . pupils dignified by a teacher such as Isadora Duncan . . . seem to perpetuate the art of the inspired one. She has delivered to them the sacred flame.[17]

Once they were likenesses of Luca della Robbia's children. Now they have become, in spite of their Greek souls and Helvetic bodies, fluent Botticellian beings.[18]

Young children today have become young goddesses, having learned the secrets of a dance . . . which are . . . the glorification of energy, courage, joy and love.[19]

Because of Isadora's genius, these inspired young girls offer us a revelation of beauty which, to quote Milton, "men will not let die willingly!" These young girls . . . are the only pupils of the great dancer and their art is more of the spirit than the flesh. . . . Gluck, Chopin, Schubert is the lyre with three chords from which they draw their inspiration. The program . . . Orpheus, the suites of Schubert Waltzes, is one of the most beautiful that can exist. Not to see Isadora Duncan and the pupils of her school is a misfortune; failure through thoughtlessness would be a crime.[20]

Anna, who would soon leave the group, Theresa, Irma, and Lisa were the core of Isadora's ensemble work. These four young women, the most accomplished of the group, provided the dynamic spark of the action on stage. Strong in dance technique and performing energy, their assertive personalities and physical beauty made for an attractive presence in the theater. With their exuberance and exquisitely shaped gestures, they brightened the stage with an unforgettable luster.

Upon completion of their immensely successful season at the Trocadéro, Isadora and her small ensemble had a brief interlude before their scheduled appearances at the Champs-Elysées, beginning January 25, 1921. All that day the performers rehearsed at the theater, where the blue curtains encircled the stage and Isadora, from the hall, supervised her dancers. The program featured works from their Schubert, Wagner, and Tchaikovsky repertory and the dancers were assisted by Albert Van Raalte (a pupil of the legendary conductor, Arthur Nikisch) and the Orchestra of the Champs-Elysées.

During the weeklong event, the Isadorables danced with distinction and excited the critics. In the annals of theater, their performances would "forever remain . . . as one of the most precious and glorious of presentations."[21]

> The four young girls she presents to us are admirable: in their groupings we rediscover the true dance; their poses, forms, their bearing, recall those figures. . . . that evoke Pompeii, Rome, Naples. In the Schubert waltzes they display a grace of delightful charm.
>
> The little Isadorian dancers . . . for whom nothing is more natural than this art seemingly inborn in their soul and flesh, and for whom life, since the most tender age, has been one harmonious tableau. . . . offer truly symbolic ideals for a superior humanity.
>
> An exquisite ray of sun came forth . . . when four adorable young girls brought . . . the dazzle of their grace, their talent and their youth. . . .[22]

The reviewer's "exquisite ray of sun" followed his lengthy negative evaluation of Isadora's own performance.

While commenting that Isadora herself was no longer supple and lithe, one observer applauded her achievement in transferring to her disciples "elegance of line, agility in movement and harmony of gesture."[23] The evening's high point was "the appearance of the lissome . . . girls, hair loose and tunics fluttering, who created before our eyes, intertwinings and flights of incomparable refinement."[24]

The countdown continued for the Isadorables once the engagement at the Champs-Elysées ended. Anna left the group; only Lisa, Theresa, and Irma remained. Later that spring they appeared with Isadora and Rummel in Belgium and in London. All but Irma of the remaining trio rejected their teacher's invitation and urgings to accompany her to Russia to establish a new school, to "teach all the little ones . . . how to dance as they know how to read: there will be joy for all." The usual powers of persuasion were ineffective. Lisa and Theresa anticipated no joy from the proposed venture. Chary of the recently proclaimed Bolshevik regime and equally wary of Isadora's impulsive moves, they chose to pursue their own private plans.

Isadora's need to have a school and her obsession to leave successors increased as she aged and witnessed her group shrink before her eyes. Her pleas for a subsidized school of dance had reverberated over the years through czarist Russia, the United States, Greece, and France. She had banked heavily on France and on her strong supporters in the Ministry of Fine Arts. Salvaging the Bellevue property after the war and refurbishing it for use as a dance center was a leviathan task overwhelmingly beyond her means.[25] The sympathetic posturing of the French government toward her pleas momentarily lifted her spirits, but the restoration of Bellevue would have been a project of pure folly for a country facing critical postwar shortages. They debated, and Isadora dangled, while the public reacted.

Among the articulate spokesmen for Isadora's plight, Arsène Alexandre spoke of her long-time efforts to develop her art and her tenacious desire to teach the young. Recalling to his readers the beautiful young disciples, he asked: "Who dares to say this is an idle fancy?" For Alexandre, it was France that should recognize Isadora's contribution to the world of art and her own aid of French causes especially in wartime. France must now be the one to aid, shelter, and realize in Isadora "one of the precious and most genuine riches of mankind." This said, Alexandre put it straight to his government: "The State itself should consider this woman of Irish origin, this American from Athens, this living work of Art to be the concern solely of France."[26]

In late 1919 Bellevue was sold for a pathetic fraction of its value. Had an offer to assist the desperate Isadora come from another planet, she would not have turned it down. When it came from Russia, long cordial to her ideas, she accepted it. So with Isadorable Irma—her school of one—she departed for Russia in July 1921, with high expectations for her unflagging dream of a dancing humanity.

Apart from Irma, whose life and career remained interwoven with her teacher's until Isadora's death in 1927, the years with Isadora ended for the "Isadora Duncan Dancers." The nest was abandoned. Except for a brief round of appearances made jointly by Lisa, Anna, and Margot in 1922, the dancers went their separate ways—Lisa and Margot to France, Anna and Theresa (and the already defected Erika) to the United States. All chose to pursue independent careers. No further collaborative ventures took place among them; not even for the tributes to their foster mother's memory.

The cultural heritage held in common by the Isadorables throughout their childhood and adolescence became channeled in adulthood into a personal urgency for self-fulfillment to which each was singlemindedly committed. But though they no longer lived or worked together, they continued to share a friendship and concern for one another, and a formidable emotional tie to the woman who had created an extraordinary life for them and whose art gave special value to that life.

Theresa, Lisa, Irma, and Anna—the principal Isadorables—were determined to carry the Duncan banner wherever their private destinies led in the years ahead. That was only appropriate. Were they not the most perfect exemplars of an art form that had resulted in what the French termed a *bouleversement* (overturning or commotion) in Western dance spectacle? Were not the movements Isadora conceived—summaries of the ideal human forms found in nature—also their movements?

Who but they could so definitively demonstrate, teach, and reinforce the crucial changes their mentor had secured and made basic for the dancer of the future: her challenging perception of the human body as a vehicle for intelligent, enlightened communication; the unhinging of the body apparatus from restricting practices adhered to by older, more entrenched dance traditions, the yielding to a physical release and liberated movement that psychologically was analogous to freedom of the psyche; the concept that without emotion, the dance would have craftsmanship, but not art. They, the disciples, and the future of dance, took their measure from Isadora. These four women, distinguished artists in their own right, assumed the responsibility of perpetuating the tenets of Isadorism, each in her own sphere of professional activity.

MARGOT
(GRETEL)

IN THE WAKE OF Irma and Isadora's departure for Russia, in July 1921 Margot joined Lisa and Anna for an American tour. After several months the lovely but delicate Gretel returned to Paris where she opened a studio for dance. Little is known about her from the time of her return until her fatal illness and death in January 1925. She was twenty-five years old. Isadora, in Paris at the time of Gretel's last illness, hurried to her. She survived her pupil by just two years.

Life in Two Worlds, published in 1962, is the autobiography of Marevna Vorobëv, a talented and beautiful young girl who left Russia to study art in Paris in 1912. There, she met and fell in love with the Mexican muralist, Diego Rivera, and bore him a child. Marika was three years of age when Christine Dallies, a friend and former secretary of Isadora's, suggested Margot, "the great dancer's best pupil," as a dance instructor for the child.

In her memoirs Vorobëv describes Margot in 1923 as "a fragile, airy being, showing her pupils plastic, rhythmic movements." Marika was asked by Margot to improvise a story of a child walking in the woods. With some shyness, the three-year-old performed a brief representation of a child walking among flowers and butterflies, then, growing tired, lying down to sleep. So graceful and true to life was this depiction that Margot agreed to teach her without compensation. "Perhaps," wrote Vorobëv, "it is thanks to Margot that all her child's life she kept the lightness and suppleness, the harmony of movement."

ERIKA
LOHMANN

I DIDN'T BEGIN TO gather information on Erika, the youngest of Isadora's special disciples, until the 1970s. My efforts were unproductive and I soon discontinued them. Those in Isadora's circles could relate only slim strands of hearsay concerning Erika's life from the time she left the Isadorables to pursue her art studies and a private life. What sporadic news drifted down the grapevine to Manhattan—the center of Duncan dance activity—from Connecticut where Erika was assumed to be living, was sparse: the death of Erika's lover, Erika's retreat to a convent, Erika's fragile emotional health. It was presumed that these circumstances contributed to her apparent elusiveness and estrangement from her past. As the years went on, the continuing lack of information about Erika only strengthened the aura of mystery that already surrounded her.

It was much later, at the home of a book designer in Connecticut, that I again picked up Erika's trail. Her name had slipped into the conversation. My host had met her at a small gathering. She had been introduced by a mutual acquaintance, Marguerite Harris, a woman who had given sanctuary and extended friendship to Erika during the crises of her life. My host recalled the particular discomfort that he experienced while in the presence of the socially awkward Erika on that occasion. I left Connecticut with Erika Lohmann's address.

Cautioned not to be optimistic by those who already had attempted to communicate with Erika, I nevertheless sent a letter to her, proposing an informal meeting to talk of her years as one of the Isadorables. As predicted, the letter was ignored. Some months later a second letter was sent. It, too, failed to elicit a response. She had patently registered her disinterest. I considered the matter closed.

When in the spring of 1984 Erika's brief obituary appeared in a local Connecticut newspaper, I became conscious once more of the solemn child at the Grunewald school, "often frightened and unhappy" during Isadora's absences, who looked for reassurance from an older and protective Irma and Temple, Isadora's niece.

Thoughts of the mysterious Erika persisted. In my box of filed items a photograph of her girlish face stared up at me. The short, dark, stylish haircut with the audacious bangs, popular in the early twenties, and her huge, round, laughing eyes held me captive. Erika Lohmann could not be left in obscurity.

Marguerite Harris, the woman who had made Erika's life her concern, was most cooperative and gracious in agreeing to see me the very day I phoned her. Arriving hours later at her house on a peaceful, scenic cove of Long Island Sound, I met the very pretty, intelligent, and lively octogenarian. Her home perfectly and attractively represented the values of her active life: literature, horticulture, religion, and art.

In preparation for this visit, Harris had brought out a portfolio of photos, clippings, and letters of many years' accumulation, all pertaining to Erika. Before our discussion began, though, I was introduced to the artist, Erika Lohmann, through her paintings. Marguerite Harris was particularly partial, and with justification, to the unusual *The Last Supper*. In oils, the painting had the appearance of an illuminated manuscript. Erika, she pointed out, had effectively used "gold tones and gold leaf to create an icon-like type of face and devotional image."

In a less conventional representation of this biblical episode, Erika had placed Christ and his disciples in close formation around a circular table. The human forms had the flat perspective of the primitive school of painting, but the composition of the figures, the concentrated colors and stark expressions, especially that of the conspicuous and discordant Judas, were perceptive of the psychological and narrative elements in the intense spiritual drama.

Three passions, according to Harris, dominated Erika's long life after Isadora and the dancing years. And to each she gave herself fully. The first— her love for her artist/teacher and the love of her life, Wienhold Reiss. Together they had traveled to the American West where they had studied and sketched Indian life and artifacts. Erika had painted independently while also assisting Reiss with his distinguished murals that brought him renown for his unusual depictions of the Blackfoot Indians.

"Reiss," Harris remarked with an appreciative smile, "was a romantic and dashing figure. He attracted attention whether wearing flowing ties more associated with the nineteenth-century poet and musician, or looking just splendid in tweed suits. Dressed for the opera in his short, black cape, he was roguishly handsome, and with the lovely Erika on his arm, they were a striking couple."

A temperament most at ease with the tranquility and beauty of a rural landscape, Erika found studios to live and work in that were never far from ponds and woods. Her last house "stood at the edge of woodland leading down to a small stream." The natural world that Erika loved was shared with friends who came up from the city to visit on week-ends, and with Wienhold Reiss who was there frequently.

The subject matter for the second passion of her life—painting—was suggested by nature's riches. The young artist painted the flowers, fruits, plants, and animals that surrounded her. How artfully and lovingly she incorporated these early stylistic and exquisitely drawn objects into the design and ornamentation of the art of her maturity, would soon be apparent to me at the St. Birgitta Convent.

Quite suddenly and prematurely, Reiss fell ill and died. The shock of his death had shattering consequences for Erika. The long, painful ordeal of her internal devastation was detailed by the woman who knew the history well. Ultimately, what brought Erika through her lengthy siege was the support of close friends, and their infinite understanding and endless patience. Erika found solace and gradual healing in a retreat within "the shadow of the monastery with its pure Gregorian chant." In time, she gathered both strength and peace of mind to live the remainder of her life in "beauty and serenity."

It was after Reiss's death that the German-born Erika, the daughter of a Jewish mother, converted to Catholicism. From this point on, Marguerite Harris said, Erika discovered the third passion of her life in religion—the deepest source of her well-being and creative inspiration. Her paintings of devotional themes reflected the fervor and paramount influence of the religious experience in her existence. Evolving her own highly individual style, her unique "sense of perspective and space," she brought to her art a profoundly mystical perception illuminated by a childlike wonder and sincerity.

Rural Connecticut continued to offer Erika the desired refuge and calm she sought for her almost reclusive existence. Limited and select in her social relationships, she insisted on and obtained the quiet and privacy she required for her painting. Her work was the result of a slow, careful, and precise treatment of her subject.

To Marguerite Harris I addressed the question of Erika's past and its relevance to the life of her mature years: the dance, the memories of the great moments in her youth, her former relationships? Like the other Isadorables, Erika was regarded as remarkably intelligent, capable of brisk temper, and stubborn—an interesting personality. Despite a life almost exclusively devoted to other interests, Harris said, "Music always remained a special part of it. Many of our discussions revolved around her fascinating life as a dancer. I had seen her and the other Isadorables several times when they appeared in New York. Although she had minimal contact with her former colleagues as the years went by, she continued to maintain friendship with Irma for whom she had great admiration. Erika took great pride in her close association with Isadora Duncan." But for the Isadorable of the serious manner and introspective nature, true fulfillment was attained, Harris astutely observed, "when Erika transmuted her art into another form and brought it to fruition." In this regard, one could say that she, of the six pupils, albeit in a medium other than dance, possessed true creativity.

One can only speculate, based on the oils and pen and ink drawings now in the St. Birgitta Convent in Darien and on those canvasses now in private collections, libraries, and churches, that Erika was a productive artist. Being by nature reserved and preferring to live a sheltered existence, exhibitions of Erika's work were largely the result of efforts by others. She would "seldom travel to see her own exhibitions," Harris commented. At the time of her death at the age of 83, the balance of her paintings were sold at auction.

But the collection at St. Birgitta's is an unusual one. It could well represent the finest work of her life as a painter. It most surely reveals how deeply painting had penetrated into her consciousness and artistic being—as had dance before it. *Days of Creation* is a series of biblical episodes in which pen and ink has been utilized with striking effect in a scratchboard technique. The sketches have a dramatic urgency and a rhythmic power. Her imagination makes forceful the religious conception; the design originality—meticulously executed—adds to the intrigue of the overall composition. Neatly printed in the lower right corners can be found the name ERIKA.

Harris spoke of the study of the Gospels that went into Erika's preparations. Manifested in all the canvasses on view are her obvious patience, thematic integrity, and spiritual joyousness. Most appealing for the charming, yet formal arrangement of the religious narrative elements, is her version of the *Nativity*, hanging in the music room. The careful, clean brush strokes and gentle tone make lucid all her forms, be they tree, person, the Virgin, the lamb. While standing before these intense and sensitive renditions, this viewer concluded that painting, for Erika, was the gift of a soul's liberation.

Fourteen paintings that depict the "Stations of the Cross" decorate a wall in the chapel at St. Birgitta. The art of the Italian Renaissance comes alive in Erika's vivid and brilliant oil colors. Clarity of detail accents the iconographic piety and a chorus of mournful, robed figures portray in their light, slender grace, the refined gestures so ingrained in Erika, the Duncan Dancer.

Long ago, the French poet and critic, Fernand Divoire, discovered that Erika "possessed the richness of intimate ecstasy." At St. Birgitta, the ecstasy still lives. Isadora Duncan's precepts of self-revelation and self-realization through a synthesis of the arts, eventually led Erika Lohmann to a personal expression in her passion for religion and its exaltation in the pictorial image.

LISA
DUNCAN

BECOMING ANOTHER ISADORA DUNCAN was not an ambition Lisa entertained. She had already declared to her teacher: "Isadora, you are a genius. We are not."[27] That exchange resulted after Isadora criticized Lisa's independent venture as a dancer. "Lisa is doing idiotic things here," Isadora had written to Irma in 1926. (Equally critical was she of her other disciples, Anna and Theresa, whose New York performances prompted her to refer to them as "quite absurd.") "Of course," Lisa recalled, "she wanted us to continue her tradition, but it was a little like a woman desiring her children to resemble her. Children must become themselves."[28]

Isadora's death assigned the Isadorables their mandate. They automatically became the custodians of the Duncan heritage to enlighten and teach the young in her ideological image. Only by conscientious and diligent training, along with esthetic development, could the valuable legacy be transmitted to others. Irma, Theresa, and Anna were performing and teaching in the United States. Lisa did the same in France.

Odile Pyros, one of Lisa's pupils, was teaching dance in Paris when our conversations took place. Though preoccupied with preparations for an upcoming recital of her own students, the pleasant and bright Pyros discussed the teacher and friend who had profoundly influenced her life both personally and professionally. Our exchange of questions, replies, and viewpoints continued later via correspondence.

Lisa, according to Pyros, started her first dance class in the studio of the Champs-Elysées Comœdie Théâtre. Pyros began her studies there in 1932. Some time later she became Lisa's class assistant and then a member of her teacher's performing company. Because of this long and close association, Pyros was able to share with me the nature of the complexities that faced Lisa in her transition from the school of Isadora's dance to that of her own.

As Isadora's disciple, Lisa had imposed a dual commitment upon herself. In one instance, she was in possession of a magnificent art form she desired to perpetuate and was a striking and finished performer in that medium. In the second instance, she had a strong drive towards seeking a means of expression that could affirm her own personality and creative gifts, apart from Isadora.

Attempting to synthesize the two raised a host of questions. How does one contain the essence of Duncanism, reveal its essential meaning, and then proceed from there? Can the new be advanced without compromising the old? "Lisa," Pyros told me, "strove for an originality in her own choreography that would define her personal esthetic statement, which is as it should be for any creative artist."[29] Actually, all her work, according to Pyros, made use of the full, flexible Duncan range of the body, and she always conveyed in her movements the intent of the motivating spirit. This was equally true of her teaching methods. They were based on total body development in order to ensure a plasticity and ease of movement in response to the music.

Witnessing Lisa's wrestle with conscience was Fernand Divoire. "To have known the finest dance expression . . . and to wish for its integration within the modern sensibility without departing from Isadora's premise, was an onerous task and was accomplished only after years of search and anguish."[30] Divoire credits Lisa with ultimately preserving the pure Isadorian dances while simultaneously creating her own. This is confirmed by Lady Madeleine Lytton, a prominent exponent of Lisa Duncan's teachings, who as a third-generation Duncan dancer in Paris, today retains the "pure tradition" taught her by Lisa. Lytton has also made mention of how her teacher "started creating her own dances—*very* different from Isadora."[31]

Additionally confronting Lisa as she endeavored to survive both economically and professionally were the signs of social change in the French capital. To those, like Irma, who saw her in Paris in the late 1920s and admonished her for the liberties she had taken with Isadora's original dances, as well as to others displeased with her newer trends, she replied that Paris had become disinterested in the simple and the unadorned; Parisians wanted more spectacle and visually stimulating theater. She was attempting to adapt and suit the modern vogue by effecting an esthetic mixture.

A significant assistant toward her "esthetic mixture" was Lisa's personal affiliation and artistic collaboration with the young charismatic dancer, Georges Pomiès. Described by Lady Lytton as "the first modern dancer of France," and, by other accounts, as a major dance talent, Pomiès undoubtedly was instrumental in directing Lisa to be creatively daring in her evolving style. She adopted a more technical and stylized manner of dancing, making use of more elaborate costuming and theatrical lighting.

The choreography that reflects the period of Georges Pomiès' direct influence did incorporate the outstanding skills that had brought Lisa her distinction as an Isadorable. Her highly developed and controlled arm movements were uncannily utilized in her dance *Apparition*, set to the music of Chopin. It was an imaginative simulation of a winged creature in flight. The rapid motions of her flexible arms, suggestive of subtle and undulating wings, were so magical and descriptive that audiences visually conceived a soaring, celestial bird. Almost producing a *trompe l'oeil* effect, the movements of Lisa's feet kept audiences spellbound watching to verify, if indeed, they were touching the floor.

To the music of Auric, Lisa created a tango for herself and Pomiès that had great appeal. But Lisa's pupils resented the dance, *La Dernière Nymphe* (*The Last Nymph*), in which Pomiès seemed to be mocking the Duncan style.

Attracted to the impressionist composers, Lisa also composed a dance to Ravel's music, *Imperatrice des Pagodes* (*Empress of the Pagodas*) and to several of Debussy's piano scores—his 1907 *Poissons d'Or* (*Golden Fish*) and the 1910 *Danseuses de Delphes* (*Dancers from Delphos*). (Debussy in particular, was a composer strongly disliked by Isadora Duncan.)

With her *Blue Danube* waltz, Lisa artfully created a river that laughed, splashed, and coursed merrily along between flowering banks. "She released the Danube," wrote Divoire. "The double rhythm of the dance and the pulsing current of the blue water carried us along with it." In her *Valse Triste* of Sibelius, her versatility was even more apparent when she appeared as a woman engulfed by grief. "Not an art of mime, but of dance, she produces a single gesture as might Isadora before her—slow, magisterial, indelibly memorable—a living fresco of human sorrow."[32]

Moonlight on the Alster found Lisa and her partner, Pomiès, enveloped in a blue-tinged atmosphere. With his powerful technique, Pomiès leapt with astonishing agility and elevation. Supple and swift, he sustained the flight of the dancer he was carrying. In this dance, Pomiès was a puckish figure, mischievous and frolicsome, cavorting with his entrancing sprite.

Eighteen months after the sudden death of Georges Pomiès (which caused Lisa's first bout with depression), she staged her version of Gluck's *Orphée* at the Opéra Comique in Paris in 1935. She addressed the inevitable critical comparison with Isadora's own rendering of this music. "Those who saw Isadora reproach me, perhaps, for not having completely respected her interpretation and for having dared to treat this well-known music in another manner. I retained the Isadorian dances of the Blessed Spirits and their gentle and serene happiness, because they were as unique an interpretation as one could humanly conceive. But for Orpheus' tragic despair, I felt the urgent need for my personal interpretation."[33]

Pyros spoke of this work, in which she participated, as possessing a demonic character. Lisa had specially designed masks made to make the Furies more monstrous, and in their dances she had them roll around and around over themselves in a never-ending wheel of motion. They formed a ten-headed monster which agitated its legs like darting flames. "Orphée was her apogee," Divoire believed. "There was a richness of invention and a dynamic fury which spectators of the Opéra Comique acclaimed. . . . Her perfect control, perfect comprehension of the music, her perfect interpretation of the rhythm, Lisa made of them living instruments of her inspiration."[34]

The dances of Lisa's invention were considered more than movement constructions. Each was a creative entity composed of original ideas, well-marked rhythmic focus, a sense of form, and discipline. Gestures, as elements, were selected and arranged as themes in a musical poem. "Some of her creations are worthy to rank with those of her foster mother," assessed one writer.[35] Still, Lisa continued to be reproached for her modernism and what was perceived by many to be her deviant Duncanism.

Two decades earlier, Jean Laurent had reviewed Isadora Duncan's performances in Paris. Judging by his critique of Lisa's recital at Théâtre Hébertot in 1941, he was not yet able to cast off the lingering spell of Isadora. While the program photograph illustrated Lisa as she was best known—barefoot and clad in a light Grecian costume and in every way reflecting the Duncan mystique—on stage the critic recognized her only in those dances of Isadora, like "that adorable 'Knucklebones' from Gluck's *Iphigénie* and in *Les Petits Riens* of Mozart." Otherwise, Laurent found the dance slippers she wore, the technique and virtuosic perfection she emphasized, a travesty. Laurent presented his grievances: "How could an artist, an exceptional interpreter of a beloved school that had altered the art of choreography . . . submit to being half-rate in a different genre so as to give the illusion of renewing her esthetic?" For Laurent who considered this disciple "the most qualified . . . to receive the doctrine and ideal of the great Isadorian vision," it was a disappointment too great to conceal. "Lisa, blond one, are you going to remove the garland that bound us to her who gave you her name, her art and her heart? Or will you rightly pass on the torch to those who never knew her but who dance barefoot in her shadow?"[36]

Laurent's emotionally pitched critique was at the crux of Lisa's old battle with conscience, when her "esthetic mixture" theory was to resolve the plaguing issues of her allegiance to Isadora. Obviously, no decision could be the right one nor satisfy her quandary. Had she chosen for example, to suppress her own innovative talents and devote herself solely to performing in the style of her predecessor, she would, at best, have been derivative, and repetitive. Lacking, as did her colleagues, Isadora's genius for artistic creativity and her powerful performing flair, Lisa would have endured almost certain comparisons with Isadora which could only have diminished her. By choosing, instead, to explore and tap inner reserves unique to herself, she did make manifest a new voice—her own—but she was to continually risk, from those who remembered, their cry of "heresy."

Whatever distinctiveness or artistry Lisa displayed in her original choreography and in her performances, in her treatment of Isadora's dances, or in the intermeshing of dance styles, it brought her years of success and popularity in France until World War II began. Her school of dance brought admiration from her students who considered the able dancer an equally able teacher. With an easy, direct manner and clean, precise instruction, she commanded respect and affectionate rapport with them, Odile Pyros recalled.

Lisa's teachings were in many respects firmly related and rooted in Duncan movement concepts; she retained and utilized much of the technique and stylistic qualities that are Duncan hallmarks. In her technical work with pupils, she placed strong emphasis on developing bodily suppleness and lightness, "preparing and shaping our bodies to fully serve our expressive intentions," according to Pyros. The legs had strength and the arms and hands were made especially flexible. Lisa's musical sense was true and solid and always she conveyed to her students that sense of beauty with which Isadora had imbued her in her childhood, and that "joy of being" that Divoire identified as one of the principal characteristics of Isadorism. Reflecting on her years of training with Lisa, Odile Pyros discovered what every serious student of Duncan dance learns: "What seems so simple and natural, in reality, required a long apprenticeship."

What of the dances from Isadora's own repertory? Did Lisa pass any of them on to her disciples? "Lisa taught us those dances that Isadora had created for the young children of her school, then those that she taught them in their adolescence," Pyros recalled. "It was Lisa," said Anita Zahn, "who knew these wonderful dances and taught them to us so beautifully."[37] Zahn, a student of Elizabeth Duncan, appeared as one of thirty students brought by Elizabeth in a week-long tribute to the recently deceased Isadora in June 1928 in Paris.

According to Odile Pyros, practically none of the compositions from Isadora's solo repertory was taught them since Lisa did not truly know them. Isadora's "catch-as-catch-can" method of instruction and the abbreviated glimpses of her on stage that her girls caught from the theater wings left incomplete and unreliable impressions. Still more to the point, Isadora would forbid the group from watching her from the wings because, with her pixieish sense of humor, the temptation to stick her tongue out at them would be too great, and after all, that would hardly be in keeping with the spirit of her performance.

> From the suite of Brahms waltzes [Isadora's *Waltzes of Love*], only
> one did Lisa teach us and taught it with great concern for
> accuracy. She was scrupulous about properly designating those
> numbers danced which were hers, those of Isadora, and even
> those of her students.

Lisa had her own arrangement of the waltzes which she taught along with Isadora's work, always respecting the separateness. On tour in France and abroad, Lisa and her performing company observed this formality in programs featuring the mixed choreographies.

Though German by birth, Lisa was hostile to the Nazis and discontinued dancing and teaching once Paris was under German siege. Preferring to share the next fateful years with the French, she found refuge with friends in a small village in France for the duration of the war. Returning to Paris afterwards was traumatic for her; her studio was gone and many of her pupils had scattered. Lisa nevertheless began to reassemble the pieces of her life, her dance, and her teaching. She did manage to re-form a group of dancers and to give performances. But the disruption of her career by a brutal war was too painful, and the years of struggle and stress that ensued overtook her in the form of illness and frequent hospitalizations. She spent her last years in her native Dresden, in the care of her sister, until her death in 1976.

Odile Pyros spoke to me of Lisa's love for the dance. "It never left her. To the last, she held precious her memory of a life given to the furtherance of beauty." In a letter to Pyros, Lisa herself wrote: "To dance is a great happiness—like every wonder of art—and to communicate one's belief to others is the purest joy."

ANNA DUNCAN

IN THE MID-SIXTIES I began a closer connection with the Isadorables in the New York metropolitan area. There were interviews, tapings, encounters at dance recitals, letters, and phone calls. A student in Anna Duncan's dance class, held in an old studio on East 57th Street off Fifth Avenue suggested I attend one evening to meet for myself the seventy-year-old Anna.

Nondescript in her dark, well-worn winter cloth coat with its small fur collar, Anna arrived at her studio that evening directly from her job as a sales clerk at Brentano's book store. She entered the studio and greeted her students—a group of women, some young, others much older. They were costumed in variations of the Duncan tunic (Anna detested leotards). Her dyed black hair effectively concealed the gray, and her aging body, trimmed down from heavier proportions, had been the result of efforts by devoted former pupils who were determined to bring Anna, after too long a hiatus, back to her life's primary goal—teaching the technique and dance of Isadora Duncan.

The women moved about in preliminary work-out, stretching, limbering, and whirling with one another. They showed evidence of previous training in Duncan method, either with Anna in earlier years, or with other Duncan exponents. While Anna adjusted her skirt and smoothed back her hair, I noticed the deep blue varicose veins on her ankles and legs that prompted me to wonder if she could still dance.

93

The accompanist arrived and took his place at the piano. Like a torrent, his fingers rippled up and down the keyboard. He struck several chords, tossed off fragments of Schubert waltzes and then looked up to await his cue from Anna. A few words of instruction to the women, a nod of her head to the pianist, and the class began with a review of familiar movements. There were no organized calisthenics. Gymnastics would have to be done elsewhere as there was too little class time, Anna advised them.

Several times Anna interrupted the women, displeased with a particular execution; she corrected their technique by simply raising her skirt above the knee and, in place, producing the desired leg position and action. Again the class began a sequence of gestures and once again these were not to her liking; the students were not sustaining the music's phrase and not making fully finished movements. Stepping to the center of the floor as the women moved back, she signalled her pianist.

That was my first close-up view of the dancer Anna Duncan (I had last seen her dance from the bleachers at New York's Lewisohn Stadium decades earlier), and I experienced some suspenseful anticipation as she started her demonstration. She confined her movements to a small area, and within moments, all sense of her physical, material reality—the varicose veins, the aging body—vanished. Lighter than air, her torso and her right arm moved upward, the left arm rising for counter-balance. The chest was beautifully expanded, the back but slightly arched; her small, well-poised head was lifted up and tilted back. As the arm overhead continued its outward motion, it propelled the body to turn her slowly in its direction. All the while, she sustained the quality of the motion and the viewer was conscious of a mind subtly calculating and in control. She completed one full turn without ever interrupting the smooth current of her motions and then she floated her movements upward, repeating the turn. As she completed the turn, she allowed her gestures to drift into a soft descent to starting position.

That's all there was but it was all; the very heart of a movement's life—from its inception to its expressive completeness. In her brief demonstration (more aptly, a mini-performance), Anna had made visible her teacher's concept of "movement that mounts, spreads and ends with a promise of rebirth."

Anna stepped back alongside the piano, obviously oblivious to the effect she had produced on all of us. Her somewhat reluctant students resumed their positions to repeat after her. Simple as it had looked, it would be a tough act to follow, I thought. Close to me, one of them whispered: "She can't really expect us to do *that?*"

Among the intimates in Isadora's circle were those who held that it was the dark-eyed Anna who was "so like Isadora when she danced, so like her in her charisma and rapport with the audience."[38] Friends in Europe have recalled her as "an exceptional being who touched all with her kindness, joie de vivre, and unswerving dedication to art and beauty."[39] Within the Isadorable ensemble it was Anna who received the respect of the others, who was relied upon for her level-headedness, and who was entrusted with what had to be organized, supervised, and resolved.

Anna impressed everyone who met her. She was beautiful, strong-willed, and alert. It was remarked that she had an "intellectual clarity rare among dancers." Photographs of Isadora's attractive disciple reveal her elegance in a Fortuny gown of luxurious but classic simplicity, or her striking demeanor in an Art Deco couture outfit. Enhancing her dramatic physical appeal was a personality distinguished for its wit, down-to-earth humor, and gift for storytelling. Audiences who attended her lectures early on in her career were delighted with her vivid anecdotes and enthusiasms when reminiscing about twentieth-century dance, opera, and theater stars she had known. "Anna had a sexy, full laugh," her pupil Julia Levien once mentioned to me. "If Irma's laughter rose on high, Anna's resonated in the lower register." It was a deep and musically rich voice which, given Anna's authoritarian manner, brought a theatrical color to her conversation.

By the late twenties, young Anna was at the peak of her dance form and activity, plunging into teaching and performing. The excitement of interest her appearances stimulated convinced her that "talent, adequate preparation and loyalty to a purpose . . . always bring their proper rewards."[40] And rewards came her way in the comments of reviewers, most of whom responded to the simpler and more tender pieces to which she brought a brightness and "exquisiteness of person," and in the large, responsive following she attracted to her concerts.

The "Heiress of Isadora Duncan" review singled out her "exotic features . . . lithe dancer's body—leopard-like in her swift, suave gestures."[41] She drew a full house at Carnegie Hall in 1927 with the Philadelphia Symphony Orchestra and Eugene Ormandy, in a program of Schubert, Chopin, Gluck. Her "dance individualism blossomed in the *Moment Musicale* but she was found less effective in choreography calling for broad, vigorous or elemental expressions."

Dance Magazine of July 1927 mentions the pure Duncan spirit of the Brahms and Schubert waltzes, but it was in an encore of fragile beauty that "young Anna was her flowerlike self; about all her movements there is a fine caressing quality, a feminine tenderness in every gesture. Her hands are like petals, unfolding, her arms like the swaying branches of very young trees . . . she flashes forth a smile so precious, so gay and girlish that she touches in you a chord that vibrates like a lute string."

The Lewisohn Stadium performance in 1929 prompted a critic to rec-
ommend for her the ensemble, rather than the solo dance expression, since
she lacked intensity. "Elusive, abstract art promulgated by Isadora requires
above everything a titan personality to conceive and project it to advantage."[42] The following year, Anna's appearance enchanted the multitudes. "It
seemed that she winged closer to perfection and deeper into the hearts of her
willing subjects." Anna's ideal of dancing was found to be "utterly removed
from the whole fabric of modernism . . . aloof from the principles of the exponents of other schools."[43]

Both theater and music were passionate interests of Anna's but because
the dance as a viable profession held dim prospects for her economic future,
she considered becoming an actress—on stage or in motion pictures. In the
Theater Review Index one can follow the small trail of plays in which she
briefly figured: *Arabesque* (1925), Philip Barry's *John* (1927), in which she
appeared as Salome, *Ladies All* (1930), and *Elektra* (1932), as leader and director of the chorus, with Blanche Yurka and Mrs. Patrick Campbell.

Seduced by the promise of a possible career in Hollywood, Anna ventured there. What materialized was a bit part as a maid in George Cukor's
film, *Dinner at Eight*, released in 1933, but then, nothing more. For the serious
Anna false hopes brought quick disillusionment with the "moving picture"
mecca.

At the start of the thirties Anna generously sent her most talented pupils
to bolster Irma Duncan's dance company, hastily assembled to fulfill a contract
with Sol Hurok. In mid-decade she performed with her own group at the
Lewisohn Stadium in a program enthusiastically received by crowds of dance
devotees. She was assisted by symphony orchestra and conductor Hans Lange.

Now mature and professionally more experienced, Anna's best pupils
moved on to pursue their own independent dance ambitions and to find means
of surviving the economic depression of the thirties. By the end of the decade,
Anna was viewing with distress and indignation the inroad of experimental
modernism in dance, and with it, the gradual decline of Duncanism—the art
that had shed so bright a glow over preceding decades and of which she had
been part.

Desiring nothing more than to perpetuate the dance as conceived by
her foster mother, Anna, in contrast to Lisa, developed no distinct identity of
her own. Obvious to all who came in contact with this Isadorable was her
total commitment to Isadora's teachings and the sharing of her repertoire.
She spoke often of her plans to preserve on film those dances that comprised
Isadora's visible legacy, and indeed, rehearsed several of Isadora's dances with
two of her former pupils, Julia Levien and Hortense Kooluris. After having

the dances filmed, however, Anna was displeased with technical flaws and saw to it that the film was never released. The dances Anna had dreamed of recording for posterity remained unfilmed and she left no true visual history of herself.

Shortly before the United States entered World War II in 1941, Anna appeared in performance at Jacob's Pillow where she represented the dance of Isadora Duncan. At the close of the war, she arranged to teach dance in her native Switzerland, but the venture was unsuccessful and she was forced to return to New York, earning a modest livelihood with such jobs as a stock clerk for S. Klein-on-the-Square, a shopper's consultant for Saks Fifth Avenue, or a saleswoman at Brentano's. She lived in a one-room furnished apartment to which I drove her one night after attending a lecture on dance. She laughed as she said, "It's a small space that can't even accommodate one Duncanesque fling of the arm."

The hard realities of Anna's life in her advancing years only increased her repeated references to the past. She gloried in the wonderful fairyland of her privileged youth and in her intimate relationship with one of the "great women of all time." Indelible were the adultations from the public when, as a child, she and the others had danced in many of Europe's finest theaters, feasted at the tables of aristocratic society in villas and castles, and later, as an Isadorable, moved in an elitist environment of music, art, and literary notables: Marcel Duchamp, Francis Picabia, Eugene Isaye, Max Eastman, Edgard Varèse, Fritz Kreisler. For Anna, it was not easy to reconcile this brilliant past with the lackluster present. Difficult, indeed, to see this image fade.

That the past manifested a palpitating presence for Anna was acutely evident during a taped-interview conducted at my home. For hours our talk together traversed cultures, distances, and time, as we moved steadily back to the years with Isadora. Anna began her tale with the death of Isadora's children. She and the other child dancers had been in Neuilly when the tragedy occurred. They were participating in Isadora's performances at the Châtelet in April 1913. Her voice faltered as she re-visited the city, street, house, the very room, reliving every detail and each emotionally charged moment. When the terror-stricken child Anna had to confront her adored teacher in her bereavement, Anna, the narrator, was sobbing heavily. It was grief recollected but grief nonetheless. I switched off the tape recorder. Suddenly, it seemed an intrusion, a privacy disturbed. This segment was left incomplete. Always when speaking of Isadora and her art, Anna's heart and soul were involved. Her reaction to the filmed biography, *Loves of Isadora,* in the late sixties, could produce fresh pain and distressing emotion. "So gross a distortion," she cried. "I *knew* that woman and lived part of that great life with her."

For many years Anna's career had stagnated. According to one of her pupils, Sylvia Garson Doner, "Anna adopted ultra-conservative attitudes and looked frowningly on much she saw happening around her."[44] She found in Christian Science a means to better cope with her life's disappointments. Toward her married colleagues, Irma and Theresa, she was resentful. (Despite her numerous romances, the exquisite Anna never married.) She would insinuate that her colleagues enjoyed a career advantage denied her, in the moral and economic support they received from their spouses. The bond forged in youth among these Grunewalders showed strain. Though in geographical proximity to one another, in attitude they had become distanced.

Anna's pique over her own adverse circumstances may have accounted for the carping criticism she frequently levelled at students of the other Duncans who, from time to time, sought her expertise. Putting her best authoritarian voice forward, she would insist that she alone taught Isadora's dances authentically. "I don't know where you learned to do that," she lashed out at them, "but this is the way Isadora did it!" It would, however, be erroneous to assume that the frustrations and disillusionments of later life eclipsed all the charm of personality and outgoing nature that characterized the more promising years of her youth.

There remained in Anna a sweetness and thoughtfulness that prevailed throughout the span of years in her unbroken correspondence with friends in Europe. Anna's was one of the first calls of concern for my welfare received in the days immediately following the 1967 race riots in Newark where I then lived. Nor could I fail to appreciate the genuine delight and interest she displayed in guiding my first Isadora Duncan research expeditions. For my trip to Isadora's native city, San Francisco, Anna equipped me with a list of Duncan-related names and addresses. For Paris there were still more recommendations, foremost among them a list of people who might still be there to tell me about Isadora firsthand. (Mischievously, she couldn't resist adding some spicy details about a few of them.) Then, for my creature comfort, there was a certain hotel in rue Casimir Delavigne on the Left Bank, and not to be missed, her favorite drink—a vermouth cassis—but only at le Dôme Café in Montparnasse, her favorite hang-out. All instructions were obeyed with gratifying results.

Considering Anna as teacher, one could readily cite her faults: the impatience, the inability to explain her instructions, the acid criticisms. But it was her undiminished love for dance, her enormous talent, and her rich inheritance that "made brilliant her teaching," as Mignon Garland, a pupil and teacher of Duncan Dance, expressed. Julia Levien told of Anna's effective use of literary and art allusion to heighten the students' own conceptions of their dances. "When working on the dances from *Orpheus*, Anna insisted that we *read* Dante's *Inferno*, *look* at Blake's drawings for this subject. For the conception of the Blessed Spirits, for example, she referred us specifically to Blake's "Morning Stars" from his *Job* series, and to the Botticelli *Primavera* for the ethereal, lyrical image of the Three Graces."[45] Anna sent her young pupils to the museums to study the Greek vases and the terra cotta Tanagras. Intellectual comprehension was a prerequisite for intelligent interpretation. Libraries and museums became adjuncts to the learning of repertory.

No less than the musician striving to re-create in his playing both the technical fidelity and emotional content of the composer's score, Anna was valued for the thorough study and understanding of the dance tradition she had preserved. Taking into the account the fallibility of memory in the hands of time, she nevertheless appears to have insulated her impressions of the compositions taught her by her teacher with exceptional retentiveness. Zealous as she was in her teaching of these dances, she demanded of others no less than technical competence and artistic integrity. Always on guard was Anna, lest the irresponsible and the inept adulterate Isadora's work. Well did she know how easily it could be misunderstood, distorted, diluted, and trivialized.

For Anna Duncan there was no equivocation when it came to the fundamentals governing Duncan dance: sensitivity to details of music's rhythm and implied spirit; explicitness and clarity of movements; and genuine feelings without which the substance of the form would disintegrate. Particularly annoying to her was the sight of unessential, superfluous motions. "Isadora screamed at us if we added extraneous movements to destroy simplicity," she would remind her dancers.

"It was something of an extraordinary opportunity to work with her," Hortense Kooluris explained, "in that she insisted on nothing less than pulling every bit of artistic ability out of you. I am especially grateful to her for teaching me from Isadora's Chopin repertoire, the *Butterfly Etude* [#9 in G flat op. 25] and the little *Prelude in A* [#7, op. 28] which she made so poetical and personal an interpretation."[46] Reflecting on her teacher, Kooluris' perspective, in retrospect, is one of appreciation. Anna's high standards, her exasperating, almost impossible demands for perfection were, in the end, the true preservatives by which Isadora's dances survived for the succeeding generation with a minimum of erosion.

In the seventies, dance in America edged its way closer to center stage in the cultural life of this country. There ensued a ground-swell of aroused interest and avid curiosity concerning Isadora Duncan as the founder of the modern dance movement. Isadora was re-surfacing, tunic and all. Contemporary young dancers trained in the newer disciplines became intrigued with Duncanism and desired to supplement the range of their dance experience with the freer, refreshing, and elegant Duncan style.

They sought out the bearers of the tradition, Irma and Maria-Theresa among them. And they also came to Anna who responded to this re-awakening by teaching a select few for the all-too-brief period that remained before chronic illness and blindness forced her retirement. By the time the Isadora Duncan centenary celebrations began in New York in 1977 and 1978, Anna was unable to attend. For the première presentation of the Centenary Dance Company (organized by Levien and Kooluris) at the Theater of the Riverside Church, she sent a personal message of greeting and encouragement to the youngest generation of Duncan dancers and to the audience. It was read from the stage of the theater.

On the occasion of Anna's last birthday, Louise Craig Gerber and Julia Levien visited their teacher and friend of many years. They spoke of that which had united them in a long and meaningful bond of relationship—their joy and love for the dance they had shared together. At one point, quite suddenly, Anna moved an arm up over her head and out—"so poised, so perfect," Julia wept. The ever-musical Anna told them: "When I die, I want Fischer-Dieskau's recording of *An die Musik* played." It was done.

MARIA-
THERESA

"THE RE-INCARNATION OF A Grecian nymph" described Isadorable Theresa for the photographer, Edward Steichen, who did many superb studies of her. She was "grave and scholarly" to the writer Shaemas O'Sheel, and Lin Yutang, Chinese author and philosopher, compared her dancing to " . . . Chinese caligraphy—free fluid, flame-like, eloquent and symbolic. . . . "

Maria-Theresa, as she preferred to be identified professionally, moved quickly to plant her individual roots in American soil and leave her personal imprint. She brought Isadora's dances and her own creations to the American college campus and concert hall in the twenties. They were years of vitality and self-confidence for the beautifully finished Duncan dancer. Her special qualities of musicality, serenity, and endless enthusiasm for her art enjoyed a harmonious unity when she danced. And Theresa always wanted to dance. "Not to dance, is to die a little everyday," she expressed in correspondence to me.

Examining concert programs of her Carnegie Hall appearances in this period, one notices immediately that she expanded into new and large musical territories unassociated with her illustrious forebear. She explored more Mozart and Bach, composing dances to the latter's Brandenburg Concerto and his Organ Concerto in B minor; more Beethoven—piano sonatas, his *Pastorale* and *Eroica* symphonies. She continued to widen her spectrum of musical source material. There were the *Ballades* and *Rhapsodies* of Brahms, the full suite of *Moments Musicaux* of Schubert, more Gluck, and Saint-Saëns.

At her all-Chopin recital in Carnegie Hall, Theresa captured a critic's pleasure and admiration. "Sparkle, gaiety and allurement. . . . [She] gathered up murmurings of the sea, the rush of wind . . . and flung them to her audience in magnificent abandon."[47] For her Dance Festival in Memory of Isadora Duncan in 1929, reviewer Mary Watkins found that Maria-Theresa spared no pains in the preparation of her major scale program effort. The *Eroica* symphony (if one danced such music, Watkins added) was an "effort . . . of extraordinary beauty and significance. This dance bore an artistic burden of quite superhuman proportions and bore it with fine dignity."[48] Elsewhere, the critic commented on Theresa's own program notes for her interpretation of the *Eroica* how they "testified to her intellectual and metaphysical grasp." In other ways, the reviewer found that the concert demonstrated "more intellectual understanding than physical expansion." In the area of a creativity and technique of her own, the dancer displayed "little resource." But in the Bach "Aria" from the Orchestral Suite in D, the "Beautiful plastic quality of its presentation was almost the most lustrous moment of the entire program."[49]

Theresa's fine physical coordination and sensitivity to music and its rhythmic structure were all the more exceptional in the light of a hearing defect that, as a child, posed certain problems for her. Maria-Theresa would be the first to sit at Isadora's feet when she addressed them, always the one to inquire more frequently and observe more intently while being instructed. At a far later period in her life, her pianist would accompany her with an accentuated musical beat so that the increasingly hearing-impaired Theresa would be guided to an appropriate rhythmic response to the music.

Articulate and voluble, Maria-Theresa contributed numerous articles on themes related to dance, music, and teaching, but above all, on the subject of her teacher. Printed in *Dance Magazine*, November 1928, her article "As I Saw Isadora Duncan," commented on the dancer's fundamental law interrelating art and life; her concept of life itself as a great dance; and her art as "a purely intellectual vision carried through with the spontaneity of a primeval force." Isadora's "great secrets of success," Theresa wrote "were her gifts of concentration and her extraordinary gift of expression," both heightened by "the fluidity of her personality." Isadora, Maria-Theresa contended, "went before people to rouse them from lethargy and lead them to a deeper comprehension of life."

The decade of the thirties presented dramatically different patterns in the visual landscape of industrial America that changed the state of the arts and with it, the artist's expressive focus. Filtering through the visual and performing arts were manifested the developing technologies that heightened the pace of industrialization and created a drastically transformed art image. The painter's landscape caught the new urban sight of hard and solid lines of factories; photographers played with the light and dark forms of the coiled and angled machineries; architecture reflected the materials of steel and concrete in its geometric constructions; the dance boasted its own modernism of harsh outline, a more strident voice, in its preoccupation with angles, thrusts, and staccato rhythms.

The process of change in American society and culture took its toll on the Duncan tradition with its belief in eternal beauty, its motions of fluency and grace, its aspects of love and dignity, and its humanistic goal of universal fraternity. The new trend, in its youthful proclamation and clamor, seemed to sweep aside all else in its wake. In the period ahead, the dance-conscious audience—a small one—gravitated towards the modern experiments in dance. For the few performing in the Duncan idiom, the audiences dwindled. Recitals were attended, in part, by the curious, those seeking an esthetic alternative to the advancing modern schools of dance, and those veterans of the Duncan era who took refuge in a familiar ambiance, away from the abstractions of modernism and the cacophonies of the new music. In Maria-Theresa, Isadorism still lived.

In the thirties and forties, Maria-Theresa found time for her private family life and her career in dance, not at all a common feat for a woman (and a "classical dancer," at that!) almost a half century before the era of easy acceptance of working women. Married to the erudite art historian Stephen Bourgeois, whose gallery of art was one of the first to show modern sculpture, she was also mother to two sons. Her recitals were fewer, but there was the addition of a dance company who performed with her briefly before disbanding. Her young Greek-American pupils, the Heliconiades, were included in the concerts at the Guild Theatre on May 23, 1937, and January 1938.

Maria-Theresa, in her intermittent role as teacher, had been reported as lacking in consistency and organization; her emphasis on technique lax. But for the serious few, out to plumb the depths of this dance idiom, Theresa, in her private sessions, with them, could not but excite their sensibilities with her intellectual vitality and expressive spirituality. The cardinal message of her art that became the single most reiterated piece of advice to dancers seeking a truth and conviction of expression was absolute fidelity to the spirit and the dictates of the music.

By the forties and fifties, the auburn-haired Theresa, with her feminine, womanly body, was alone among her dancemates still appearing before the public. Strikingly handsome in her maturity, she would, on occasion, be accompanied at the piano by her tall, friendly husband.

In the forties, critic Edwin Denby attended Maria-Theresa's recitals of dances to the music of Chopin. Through her movements he found the rare opportunity to discern the ways in which Isadora Duncan's style and plasticity of gesture had influenced twentieth-century ballet. Denby viewed the historic renovations of Russian ballet by Fokine not as an outgrowth of the classical Marie Taglioni or Carlotta Grisi, but of Isadora Duncan. Through the perspective of Maria-Theresa's "sensitiveness of extended phrases, in the stress it gives to contrasts in space . . . in the yielding quality of many arm gestures and back bends," Fokine's *Sylphides* became full of Duncanisms. Again, in Denby's reference to "the rose-petal hands, the loosely drooping fingers" of the Fokine and of Nijinsky's *Spectre de la Rose*, there was allusion to details of gesture that were characteristic of Duncan.[50]

A master performer, Theresa could invest minimal motion with maximal emotional statement—especially as she matured. Artfully she manipulated her costume draperies. Her outer fabrics could become architectural structures in themselves, with rhythms in their folds that moved in parallel or contrapuntal motion to her body. With her eloquent arms upstretched, the garment folds formed vertical-like flutings of Doric columns, elongating her body lines and directing her skyward reach. On the floor, a somber-colored cloak could enfold her like a bastion shielding and cradling her deep rhythms of grief. Striding with her arms flung wide open, Theresa could fill the stage with her scarves and set them to flutter like banners in a parade.

Because her span of dance activity bridged the decades longer and more fully than any of the other Isadorables, Theresa escaped, to a large extent, the "celebrated-disciple-of" complex that shadowed the "six" in previous years. Still, she took every occasion to impress upon others that "I was not just a pupil of Isadora. . . . I had a long and independent career as a creative artist in my own right."[51] And it was during the centennial celebrations of Isadora Duncan's birth that her statement was so dramatically realized. At that time (1977–1980) a schedule of festivities began that brought together the youngest and oldest of Isadora's dance descendants honoring her in exhibitions, demonstration/lectures, and in performances of her choreography. Maria-Theresa, then in her eighties, was the last of her colleagues able to participate in this commemoration of their eminent teacher and her living dance legacy. She did so by dancing.

During the winter season of 1979–80, there were several evenings when Theresa appeared with her Heritage Dance Company and presented works of Schubert and Brahms, as well as her own conceptions and adaptations of

Isadora's dances to scores by Liszt and Beethoven. The dances of simplicity and brevity, youthfulness and gaiety, or physical energy were assigned, properly, to the young dancers. The eighty-four-year-old Theresa was a study in human will and heroism, maneuvering her less than steady way across a plain platform that she made live with her personal visions of the music. No longer the "reincarnation of a Grecian nymph," she was profoundly effective in the slower rhythms and the broad, sustained phrases of Liszt's *Les Funérailles*, creating moods of solemnity and poignance. With every tread and expressive posture, she projected a magisterial presence on stage.

An occurrence of an extraordinary kind took place on the theater stage at the State University of New York (SUNY) at Purchase, in the spring of 1981. Climaxing a four-day conference on the early years in American modern dance, laymen, professionals, young dancers and choreographers, and those themselves who pioneered the new experience in dance several decades earlier, saw Maria-Theresa, at eight-six, cast a spell over the densely packed auditorium. With a grand simplicity and dignity of bearing, her gestures were luminous and eloquent in their enunciation of the wonder of the dance. To have seen her then was to realize how splendidly she was kin to the legendary Isadora. And if, in the tumultuous ovation she received, there was homage to Isadora Duncan as well, it was Maria-Theresa, "the creative artist" in her own right, who extended her teacher's art and spiritual presence into the contemporary consciousness.

IRMA
DUNCAN

IRMA DUNCAN ROGERS NEVER wavered in her regard of herself as "the foremost disciple" and successor to Isadora Duncan. Her history tends to substantiate this regard. She assumed and never relinquished a tight rein of attitude and responsible guardianship concerning the art of the dance entrusted to her by the woman she called "the greatest genius of dance the world has ever known."

When the disciple who accompanied Isadora to Moscow in 1921 returned to the United States to open the first official Isadora Duncan school of the dance in the early thirties, she referred to herself as its "titular head." That center of dance she directed did not survive the thirties; the young dancers under her artistic tutelage went on to careers in and out of dance, and Irma Duncan remained a self-appointed monarch without a kingdom for the rest of her life. Less than two years before her death in 1977 at the age of eighty, the authoritative Irma could still decline to "lend my name to any artistic public performance in Duncan dance over which I have no personal control."[52]

Irma was tough and persevering, a strong dancer, and perhaps the best teacher from among the Isadorables. And she emerges the disciple who most affected the course of Isadora's dance in the post-Duncan era in significant ways. To understand the circumstances and events that would shape her later role of pre-eminence in the Duncan hierarchy and public image, one needs to look back at the years spent in Russia.

106

While appearing in London in 1921 with her pianist, Walter Rummel, Isadora was approached by an official Soviet representative. He was favorably impressed by what he saw and was already familiar with her philosophy of the child and dance education. A cable from London dated February 24, 1921, was sent to the first Soviet People's Commissar of Education, Anatole Lunacharsky, informing him that the renowned Isadora Duncan requested admittance to Russia on condition she be allowed to teach many children— "one thousand to begin with. Reward not requested."

Six months later, fully expecting a government-sponsored and supported school for the dance education of Russian children, Isadora and Irma arrived in Moscow. A phone call to Lunacharsky apprised him that the two women were at the railroad station, sitting on their suitcases. What should they do next? This was the beginning of Isadora's Russian years. Her decision to embark on this adventure astonished and horrified almost everyone in her private and public life. Russia was in ideologic and economic chaos, just emerging from World War I and an internal revolution. Beyond Russian borders watched a world with belligerence, fear, and ignorance of the newly established regime. Those friendly to the new system were regarded with suspicion and hostility. Isadora well knew that her sojourn in Russia could seriously jeopardize her prestige in the rest of the world.

As for the Russians, they wondered what had made this world famous dancer agree to come there—a country in ruins. "We are poverty stricken and hungry, with Lenin in our heads and a revolver in our hands."[53] Who could think of art at a time such as this? Apparently Isadora could and did. Physical hunger to her was less a threat to mankind's survival than spiritual hunger. With prospects for a school of dance having failed everywhere else, she took on the challenge. She could put up with the poverty and other material wants. "I shall never hear of money in exchange for my work. I want a studio workshop, a house for myself and pupils, simple food, simple tunics, and the opportunity to give our best work."[54] Politics had no true meaning for her. She had long established friendly ties with Russia and Russians from her previous concert tours before the war. Children and the future of her work in dance were her life's imperatives.

The palatial mansion at 20 Prechistenka with its many spacious (and unheated) rooms housed the two women and the Duncan school that had its formal opening toward the end of 1921. A young Russian journalist with interest in theater and dance was assigned to oversee and assist in the management and administrative duties of the project. Ilya Schneider would remain a central figure, along with Isadora and Irma, in the early years and would continue a leading role right on through to the school's closing year (1949), some twenty years after its founders had departed.

In preparation for her 1975 monograph on the Isadora Duncan School in Moscow, Russian dance historian Natalia Roslavleva met with a group of women who, fifty years earlier, had been among the first children to enroll in the school. They reminisced about their childhood experiences as pupils of both Isadora and her disciple, the attractive, dark-haired twenty-four-year-old Irma. Of Isadora their words rang with evident warmth and adoration; they spoke fondly of her maternal tenderness, and of her kindness. Still sharp was their memory of the beauty of her dancing and the magical world of music she opened to them. Young ears and impressionable minds were captivated by Isadora as she spoke to them of dance as a flight of birds, the playful flutterings of butterflies, and swaying grasses. They would learn, she assured them, to "breathe as freely as the clouds, to jump as quietly and lightly as a grey cat."[55]

Teaching was Irma's forte, an ability recognized by both Elizabeth and Isadora during the Darmstadt years and later at Bellevue, where Irma assisted in instructing the young children. From the beginning it was she who demonstrated and led them in gymnastics. As they progressed she discussed and illustrated Isadora's choreographic ideas with clear, well thought out instructions; she was able to articulate her intentions, and analyze specific movements. Her former pupils remembered her well for the honesty "beneath her severe character," her musicality and talent, and the sincerity she displayed in her relationship with the children.

The resourceful Irma, with her firm qualities of leadership, was almost unanimously considered by these pupils a "born teacher." She pulled, stretched, and bent their bodies every which way to produce the flexibility and technical sureness required of a dancer. If she drove them hard, she gave in good measure of herself, taking every pain to explain the objectives of a dance in terms the children could visualize and comprehend. In praise of Irma, the Russian women credited her with their own subsequent mastery of a dance form deceptively simple to the eye, but as they learned soon enough, subtly tricky to perform. Only after having achieved this mastery did they regard themselves as dancers. And why not, they asked. Irma "could teach a chair to dance." That the Russian school owed much to her, they were in full accord. That Irma "gained much from her stay in Soviet Russia," could hardly be contested.

When six months had passed, both Isadora and Irma were made aware that the funding for the school and the materials essential for its function would be severely curtailed. The government would be responsible for the building alone. This meant reducing the number of children Isadora had hoped to accommodate and limiting their food and clothing rations.

Lunacharsky later wrote of this period: "When Isadora Duncan wanted to give us all her forces, all her life, and tried to assemble thousands of workers' children to teach them freedom of movement, grace, and the expression of exalted human feelings—all we could do . . . in the end, sadly shrugging our shoulders, just tell her that our circumstances were too severe for us."[56] Reviewing her situation, Isadora had two options open to her. She either had to bolster the sagging Moscow project with additional personal revenues or pull out altogether. Less than one year after her arrival, Isadora and the Russian poet she had married, Sergei Essenin, combined their honeymoon trip with a tour of concert appearances, designed in large part to ease the school's financial crisis.

The couple left Russia, traveling through Germany, Belgium, and France, but not before Isadora encountered the first major rebuff to her Russian venture. France, in view of her marriage to a Russian and her new status as a citizen of the Soviet Union, kept snarling her in bureaucratic red tape in order to impede her entry into France. Ultimately, the tangle was resolved through top-level personal connections in the French government. Isadora was allowed to enter France but with the warning of close surveillance during her visit. Communist propaganda would not be tolerated, she was told with due emphasis. The authorities were informed by the unflinching, but nettled Isadora, that her dances had long preceded Bolshevism.

Underscoring the ludicrous incident, the French periodical, *La Danse*, printed the following in its December 1922 issue: "Isadora's secretary, sent to Paris to negotiate passports for her, meets with an immigration official."

Off:	The government agrees to give Mme. Duncan authorization to return to France. But you will be obliged to advise Mme. Duncan that if she reappears before the Parisian public, to abstain, in her own interest, from any manifestation that might smack of politics. Do you know what her plans are?
Sec:	No politics at all. Isadora Duncan wants to rent the Trocadero Hall [for a 1923 performance]. She will present there an altogether new dance.
Off:	Isn't she at least going to dance the *International?*
Sec:	Oh, no! It's not political, I tell you. It's a new creation, revolutionizing, superb; the motionless dance!
Off:	A motionless dance?
Sec:	Yes, she doesn't stir. Everything is, how do you say it, from the eyes up.

Off: The eyebrows?

Sec: That's it, the eyebrows. They lift up, then down. They express a
         lot.

Off: Well then, it isn't the motionless dance; it's the dance of the
         eyebrows. If she dances that at the Trocadero she'll have to
         supply her audience with binoculars. Ah, well! That's her
         problem. Inform Mme. Duncan that she will have her passports.

The dance curriculum at the Moscow school during the year of Isadora's absence abroad remained in Irma's hands, fully assisted by Ilya Schneider. But Isadora's expedition failed to appreciably relieve the pressing needs for funds. Upon her return she arranged yet other tours, within Russia this time. Her travels through the Volga and the Urals in 1924 were, in every sense, a disaster, never rising above the levels of "ordeal," "nightmare," "catastrophe," and a "calvary," as her letters to Irma bemoaned.

Upon Isadora's return from the Crimea, a letter written to her brother Augustin sang the praises of the children in the school. They are, she wrote, "simply a Miracle. The first school [Grunewald] was nothing in comparison but Hélas, How shall we feed them. The government gives *nothing*. . . . It will be a crime for such Beauty of Movement and Expression I have never imagined could come true."[57] A letter of September 2, 1924, to Allan Ross Macdougall glowed with pride in the progress of the school: "They dance beautifully, but they are almost always hungry. However, they have great spirit. They live on Kasha [groats] and black bread, but when they dance you would swear that they live on ambrosia."[58]

The school, plagued by its ongoing financial and material shortages, took its toll on the weary Isadora. Disillusioned, physically and psychologically exhausted, she left Russia in late September 1924 and returned to France. There was talk and there were plans for again raising money abroad through her dance recitals and returning, but Isadora never returned to Russia and Irma remained at the helm.

Life in the Moscow school after Isadora's departure continued as before. Irma, as artistic director, was called upon to handle all the dance-related programming of the institute. She conducted all the dance classes and saw to the separate levels of instruction in keeping with the advancing technical progress of the students. She adapted dance material suitable to these levels of proficiency and created new choreographies on Russian-based themes, using the music of native composers.

In her autobiography, *Duncan Dancer*, Irma didn't mince words concerning Isadora's departure. "I had the entire field to myself now that my foster-mother had left." The coming-of-age feud of 1918, when the Isadorables chafed at their teacher's overprotectiveness, had only partially been addressed. For Irma, the long-standing grievance against being in the background had never dissipated. What sufficed in 1907, when a Dutch critic exclaimed how "the sight of Isadora encircled by her dancing children was a joy to behold," was no longer adequate compensation for Irma. Fluttering around Isadora and never having the opportunity to give personal voice to her own dance interpretations distressed her. "The artist in me longed for self-expression."

Irma now freely moved into the principal dance roles she had long known and cherished, dances in which the focal figure had been Isadora's sole preserve. Ranging from small to large-scale compositions, from the light to the dramatic, the Duncan repertory was the artful manifestation of a single creative intelligence—creations that bore the imprint and energy of one individual, of one prodigious spirit.

Being in possession of "the entire field" had even broader implications for Irma than did the availability of an expanded dance range for herself. At her fingertips also lay the makings of a company with whom she could travel and perform and contribute to the financial stability of the school. The more advanced pupils under her direction were already dancing beautifully, both in form and in spirit. Ilya Schneider's expertise would see to the successful management of such an enterprise. And so it came to pass.

"None of the tours was designed solely to earn the wherewithal on which the school depended," Roslavleva wrote in her monograph. "Propaganda for the lofty ideals set before them by Isadora was carried out on all possible occasions."[59] In advance of the concerts, Schneider spoke to the Russian audiences about Isadora Duncan and the objectives of her school.

Hundreds of performances in 1925 and 1926 were given throughout Russian provinces and cities by Irma and a select group of young dancers. It was Irma now, not Isadora, who had become, in one reviewer's words, "the light, love and animating flame of her encircling young students." Emboldened by the enthusiastic audience responses, Irma pushed for a far more ambitious promotional tour.

In what constituted a transcontinental sweep, Irma and her travelling troupe of approximately twenty dancers moved eastward through towns in Siberia and across to the coastal cities along the Pacific during 1926–1927, climaxing in the unprecedented debut of Isadora Duncan's dance art in parts of China. Thousands in Asia saw for the first time a new cultural form and force in the youthful Russians and sensed its implications. "For our children . . . there open new . . . horizons."[60] As principal dancer, group leader, and director, Irma had won her hard-earned laurels.

Critiques on her interpretations showered her with tributes from the "lyrical and flowing," to the "power and ecstasy," to the "immeasurable diapason of a great artist" and to "being the master of her art." She was described "as true as only a fanatic can be to the ideals of her foster mother."[61]

The foster mother, in the interim, had had no response to the many letters she kept sending from France to Irma. Eventually, to her extreme displeasure, Isadora learned of the Siberian tour and registered her protest against such commercialization of her school to Russian officials. To private sources—according to information Irma later obtained—Isadora poured out a "j'accuse" indictment against Irma for treachery and for absconding with her school.

Explained by Irma, who felt perfectly justified in her decision to strike out on her own with the Moscow dancers, there was no behind-the-back maneuver intended on her part. The misunderstanding with Isadora was one of logistics; a complicated itinerary, the vast distances, compounded by the lengthy duration of the journey, had disrupted communications. Interpreted by Victor Seroff in his book *The Real Isadora*, the incident between the teacher *in absentia* and the pupil at the helm was not at all benign nor accidental. That Isadora's letters were received by Irma, he had no doubt. Nor did he doubt that Irma's indifference to them was a calculated action. She had finally gotten out from under, and intended to keep it that way. Seroff was also convinced that until the very end, Isadora could not conceive of Irma as having usurped her position. Rather, she continued to believe that the Russian school was still hers.

Irma's brief reunion with Isadora in Paris, late in the spring of 1927, removed any doubt that the bond between student and teacher was still in force, as was the love of Isadora for her adopted child. In this meeting—their last—they aired and put to rest their bitterness and misunderstandings and, in an emotional farewell, re-affirmed their love and loyalty.

These events took place more than six decades ago. Looking across the years, one can see that the judgments and decisions made by Irma in Russia proved to have been sound and even providential. The great concert trek through Russia and Siberia afforded her a private triumph of great dimension. The years of preparation for a career in dance had culminated in public recognition of her own identity. She had gained an impressive authority in the dances of the Duncan repertory, bringing to their basic structures an individuality of conception, both personal and powerful. The larger sphere of her achievement must include the young dancers she had trained who plainly revealed, in their bearing and motions on stage, their promise as heirs to Isadora's philosophical and artistic objectives.

The Moscow school offers, in retrospect, interesting comparisons to earlier Duncan dance schools. To begin with, it had an unbroken continuity of program and survived the longest of any school, anywhere, under Isadora Duncan's banner. Irma was the constant factor in that continuity and, for the latter four years, was unaided by Isadora. In the security and stability of relationship between teacher and pupils, and in the sustained supervision and quality of their dance instruction, Irma had achieved with the Russian children what Isadora had failed to do with her Grunewalders twenty years earlier. For sheer number of performances with a supporting company, Irma had exceeded the record of Isadora and her Isadorables.

Months before her death in 1927, Isadora met with impresario Sol Hurok in Paris. There was an urgency to her request that he consider an American tour for her Russian pupils. "I want American to see my work. Promise me only one thing; you will take the children to America." In 1928 a contract was negotiated between Hurok and Irma Duncan, posthumously honoring Isadora's request.

Having been granted approval by the Russian government, Irma and the second generation of Isadora Duncan dancers were set for a grand tour of the United States—a memorial tribute to the American dancer. (Hurok, who believed "Isadora did more than anyone else . . . for the dance in America,"[62] has surprisingly little to say of this venture in either of his books—*S. Hurok Presents* or *Impresario*.) The Russian dance historian Roslavleva wrote that the tour comprised seventy-eight cities and four hundred concerts from December 1928 to January 1930. The dancers debuted in New York City on December 28, 1928 at the Manhattan Opera House; this writer was there.

Oh, those Russians! The event that lit many flames! Like arrows shot from quivering bows they darted out from behind the stage curtains—young, lithe bodies in a fury of exuberant motion; white flesh, short red costumes, they were all beautiful, or so it seemed. One in particular had the audience searching her out in each dance. Short, silky blond hair in bangs that tossed about in rhythm with her movements, she looked to be the youngest of the group. A slender, boyish figure, Tamara was her name. Her motions were zephyr-light and her rapid but incisive skips across stage were like short streaks of lightning that sent electric currents throughout the hall. During their program that one wished would never end, the young artists, in their graceful dance groupings, presented unending visual delights. In their numbers of more persuasive rhythms and strong, resolute gestures, they stirred emotions almost too much for this viewer to bear. When their voices, open and free, sang out as they danced, the joy it induced took on a physical force. I fell from my seat.

Irma Duncan had assembled a series of first-rate programs bound to win the young dancers instant audience favor. They performed the early and familiar choreographies of Isadora for which she was admired and best remembered. Chopin was represented in most of the keyboard forms she had interpreted. Included were popular items from the Schubert repertory that had always enchanted spectators when previously danced by the Isadorables, and Isadora before them. Scores by Schumann, Beethoven, Strauss, and Tchaikovsky added to the glitter and variety of the programs.

The American tour offered Irma the strategic opportunity to première the last dance works that Isadora had created for her Moscow children—dances that spoke the meaning and momentum of their new life in their country. Irma spoke of this final creative phase of Isadora's life in dance as having produced "choreographic chef d'oeuvres [sic] that . . . rank with the . . . compositions to the waltzes of Schubert and Brahms and the various choral dances . . . of Gluck's *Orpheus* and his *Iphigénie.*"[63]

In debut was the large suite of group dances that Isadora had composed in 1924, *Impressions of Modern Revolutionary Russia*, several accompanied by the singing of the performers. Irma, in solo, presented the evocative études by Scriabin that her teacher had completed in late 1921 or early 1922, and introduced her own choreography—a group of charming Russian songs by the composer Gretchaninoff, and a more serious work entitled *Trilogy: Labor-Famine-Harvest.*

When explaining the public's enthusiastic response to his latest theatrical coup, Hurok contended that the Russian dancers "had as a background their great heritage, Isadora. They came with the way already prepared by the fame of their teacher."

The critics were no less enthusiastic. The *New York American* wrote: "Isadora must have smiled benignly at the fascinating artistry of her young disciples of a second generation . . . not in her most fruitful and successful epoch did the great Californian dancer produce any more delightful or captivating pupils than those seen last night."

The New York *Herald Tribune* said: "She [Irma] has so successfully instilled . . . that devotion which is deeper than outward gesture . . . sufficient evidence of her artistic worthiness in her capacity as heiress and guardian of the Duncan formulae."

Literary Digest wrote: "The lamp which was lighted by this bright genius that America produced is kept brightly burning."

Mary F. Watkins, a critic for *Dance Magazine*, said: "The idea by which the valiant and incomparable Isadora lived and breathed and worked was as present on that stage as if that genius herself stood in the wings and urged her followers on. . . . "

Another critical observer found " . . . a thorough discipline of mind and muscle," " . . . not a meaningless or confused idea present," and " . . . technique which deals with broad planes, wide gestures . . . eloquent stillness." Irma's interpretation of Chopin's *Funeral Sonata* had sincerity and dedication but was "without the kindling touch of genius," while Chopin's Mazurka in B by the ensemble was a "marvel of fleetness and high spirits;" his *Polonaise* "aroused the usual enthusiasm." Schubert and Brahms waltzes by the young dancers were "most enchanting" and [Schubert's] *Funeral March* " . . . one of the most beautiful of ensemble conceptions . . . dignified, sincere."

The *Warshavianka*, Isadora's commemoration of the 1905 Russian uprising, "sustained the note of ecstasy and heroic sacrifice. The abandon and fierce, released, almost fanatic fervor of Irma Duncan and her girls, is stirring to the blood."[64]

And in Paris, during the summer hiatus, Irma and her company gave one performance at Salle Pleyel on July 2, 1929. From the many friends and devotees of Isadora, she garnered additional testimony on her exceptional attainment. "The great spirit of Isadora hovered over you all. . . . At moments her breath seemed to pass through you, and the children were beautiful . . . Be proud of yourself, you have done a great work and you have Isadora's school."[65]

Connoisseur of dance and champion of Duncanism, Fernand Divoire wrote in his *Pour la Danse* of the impact of the Russians.

> We found again the same youthfulness, freshness—a grace, less subtle perhaps, less fine, but almost as harmonious and more live yet, more ardent, more lyrical. Isadora's roses had been well-grafted onto the wild shoot.
>
> But the greatest revelation of the performance was the group of sung dances that the little Moscow devils brought us. To dance while singing, yes, that was really the dream of Isadora—and happy to see it so magnificently realized! It mattered little that the words were not understood.
>
> Ah! How we applauded, for instance, the circle of Russian girl-scouts in their merry whirlings—and how we loved that old man who, standing, frenetically cried out "Viva Isadora!" In these glorious sung dances, Isadora had only just begun the realization of her grand plan to revitalize theatrical spectacle.[66]

The enjoyable summer hiatus had no sooner ended when the resumption of the Russian tour was put in doubt. There were serious contract discrepancies at issue between Irma and her concert agent. Then, quite abruptly, the tour came to an end. Immediate return of its young citizens was requested by the Soviet government. Roslavleva's otherwise valuable insights and fresh data on the Moscow school lack mention of this incident.[67] And despite Irma's presentation of her view of the facts surrounding this turn of events, it remains rather strange and ambiguous. For Irma, however, the years in Moscow only strengthened her Orwellian estimate of the "Big Brother" atmosphere. However unlikely the circumstances were, in light of the political climate of the period, when no official diplomatic channels were open between Moscow and Washington, anything was possible. The incredible became credible.

In cloak-and-dagger fashion, an "unofficial" representative of the Soviet government in Washington, reacting to rumors of trouble with the tour, appeared on the scene. He applied coercive tactics against the young and inexperienced dancers and threatened them with reprisals against their family members back home should they not comply with orders to return. Despite the dancers' desires to remain with Irma and Irma's own "strenuous protests," the harassed group submitted under pressure. The second genera-tion of Duncan dancers left for their homeland but without their teacher. Irma Duncan had terminated her affiliations with Moscow.

With her ties to Russia severed, Irma had let slip from her grasp the only school preserving the "purest legacy of Isadora Duncan." It was an onerous position to have been in and she rationalized to others that she had been re-assessing the Russian connection for some time before the crisis forced her hand.

The Duncan school and the position Irma occupied there were already marked for an administrative re-organization that would have reduced her status from artistic director to routine instructor: decisionmaking and artistic policy would have become the responsibility of others. Collectivism, Irma feared, would only subvert the creative independence of the individual; the pervasive bureaucracies would constitute an on-going threat to the spirit of Isadora's teachings—to her "free spirit in a free body."

What then was the fate of Isadora and Irma's school? Ilya Schneider con-tinued in his capacity as manager, advisor, and kindly counselor for the twenty years remaining of the school's existence. The professional company went on giving performances in Russia, the more experienced and older dancers became instructors, the more competent teachers graduated to directors, and the most talented pupils assumed the principal dance roles for as long as the original choreography remained intact. Historian Roslavleva assures readers that the school policy kept Isadora's dances in performance on a high level of artistic standard, as was the choice of music, costumes, and lighting.

In the forties, Ilya Schneider turned his attention toward making the Duncan repertory "more consonant with the times." His approach to the modernization of Isadora's ideas was achieved by commissioning noted choreographers, sensitive to the Duncan idiom, to create new dances that would retain the Duncan character and technique "intact." Actual movements were lifted out of some traditional pieces and reset into the new structures. The traditional dances ultimately fell into disuse and were replaced by the new "more consonant" creations. At the final recital of the much-altered school, a lone survivor of the original repertory was presented in performance— Isadora's *Irish Jig*, danced in green tunics to the music of Schubert.

A decade after the demise of the school, Sophia Golovkina, director of the Bolshoi Ballet School, spoke of Isadora Duncan and the influence her teachings had spawned in Russia. "In Moscow alone there are thirty Palaces of Culture, recreation centers at every one of which some kind of dance is taught. In most of them it is a form of plastique based on Duncan dancing."

Attributed to the Duncan plastique influence is the sport of "artistic gymnastics." Several of the Russian Duncan pupils became teachers of this acrobatic form that today is an internationally regarded branch of competitive sports—a fusion of the science of acrobatic systems and the more refined motions of dance art. "Artistic gymnasts," Natalia Roslavleva wrote, "maintain the pliancy, grace and expressiveness that can be traced straight back to Isadora Duncan."[68] An odd legacy, considering that Isadora held no regard for what she considered the sterile body movements of gymnastics!

Irma conducted a sporadic correspondence with Ilya Schneider in the years that followed her departure. Her disinclination to contact her former pupils exhibited the extent of her chagrin that none of these disciples had shown a spark of loyalty to "throw in her lot" with her as she had done with Isadora in 1921. However, in the 1960s, Irma's letters to Schneider, sent along with current photographs of herself, were shared with several of the women, now retired and with grandchildren of their own. His reply to Irma gave a touching account of how her news and her photographs caused them much excitement and happiness.

The Russian experience behind her, Irma, with her customary resourcefulness set up a studio for dance, declared the international Duncan base of operations transferred from Moscow to New York City, and proceeded to assemble "a group of young American girls who had—more or less—some training in the Duncan dance, and worked with them. By magic and sheer hard work I soon shaped them into a group that could appear with me professionally."[69] (Still hanging was the matter of an unfulfilled contract with Hurok, aborted by the sudden departure of the Russians.) It was January 1930.

By what magic did this nameless group of Americans from unstated origins materialize for her, Irma does not say. Particularly regrettable is this omission on her part, since the American contingency that salvaged her contract and furthered her successes in the period ahead came to her through the generosity and sympathetic cooperation of her colleagues, Anna and Theresa.

While her artistic faculties, teaching expertise, and proven organization skills were not to be undervalued, Irma was not the sole legatee furthering the dance objectives of Isadora Duncan. From the studios of Anna and Theresa came their ablest pupils to join Irma, while others were of mixed Duncan backgrounds, their training stemming from Anita Zahn and the school of Isadora's sister, Elizabeth. Several had originally started in ballet and the Dalcroze system before moving on to Duncan technique. There were, as to be expected, differences among them: unevenness in technical and physical development, and in basic aptitudes and sensitivities. All were professionally inexperienced but brought a conscientiousness and quick responsiveness to the undertaking for which they had been chosen.

This, then, was the material from which Irma worked to create a reasonable homogeneity of line and style, to raise and strengthen technical levels, and to achieve an overall, unified "Duncan" look. She produced wonders. Only months later, in April 1930, she and her American wing of the second generation of Duncan dancers debuted in Minneapolis with a performance of distinguished effort and poise for so young a company. The *Minneapolis Tribune* reviewer extolled Irma for her "magnificent art," in that "whatever group she leads . . . the result can be but the same, and that is—perfection of the art of interpretive dance . . . " The reviewer singled out the Schubert *Ave Maria:* "It is to be doubted that those who saw Miss Irma Duncan and her ensemble in this exquisite number will ever hear the music again without seeing in visionary form the dancers." One member of this first American company was Julia Levien. She compared the new group with the Russians she had seen several times during their American tour the previous year. "The Americans lacked the years of performing experience of their Russian counterparts." The Muscovites had "a special vitality and a sustained physical power; moreover, they were more facile than the newer company in technical range—their backs more flexible, their leaps, higher."

The relentless demands on the group to learn a large repertoire for their scheduled appearances quickly matured the fledgling Americans. Two years of work, travel, and performances in the United States and Cuba had created a fine troupe of proficient Duncans, a few of whom would carry on this tradition in the years ahead.

For their trip to Havana in 1931, Irma and her group rehearsed in her large studio temporarily located in the Broadway Central Hotel in SoHo. Informal recitals ("rent parties") were held on Sunday afternoon in the weeks preceding their departure. On one particular Sunday afternoon, this adolescent worshipper paid her first visit to the "temple of the dance" on an upper floor of the hotel. In a small foyer on a table lay stationery with the letterhead, "Studio of Isadora Duncan." How the powerful aura and mystique of the name intoxicated!

Within the studio a small gathering of visitors was seated on folding chairs at one end of the room. Facing them, on the same level at the opposite end, was a soft, green, felt-like carpet illuminated by a central light that defined the dance space. Walled around the three sides of this stage were, I presumed, Isadora's curtains—those famous blue curtains. The ecstasy of illusion lasted fifty years until I learned that the blue curtains used in the Broadway Central Hotel were not Isadora's, but an exact copy given Irma as a gift by Chinese officials during her 1927 tour in China.

Anticipating the start of the program, the visitors quieted down, their attention focused on the empty amber-lit stage. Two shapely nymphs in sheer pastel tunics appeared; they glided gracefully across the carpet and vanished into the darkened area behind the curtains. Another soon followed, entering from the far corner. As she raised her arms, it was obvious to all that she held an ordinary household spray gun. She began to move along the draperies in a delightful, bouncy step—the spray gun with her. Every few steps she aimed her gun upwards, and gently, rhythmically, discharged some mist, her costume billowing with the rise and fall of her walk. While all this clearing and scenting of the atmosphere took place, there was a numbing stillness in the room. Each of us looked on unable to divert our eyes for a moment. Whatever else comprised the recital that afternoon is beyond recall. Only the memory of that mesmerizing choreography for solo dancer and spray gun accompaniment has survived.

Within each ensemble of Duncan dancers, beginning with the Isadorables, there have been those dancers singled out for their distinct personality, their physical attractiveness, their artistic excellence. Among the Moscow girls there had been the most gifted, Alexandra (Shura) Aksenova, said to resemble Isadora in spirit and "amplitude of gesture," Tamara Semonova, who lit up the stage with her "lilt and fire," the beautiful Tamara Lobanovskaya, and the admirable technician, Maria (Mussia) Myosovskaya. Now, the Americans could boast of their own special possessions: the lyrical, angelic Hortense (Dolan) Kooluris, Ruth (Kramberg) Fletcher of the high, energetic leaps, the musical and expressive Julia Levien, the energetic Mignon (Halpern) Garland, the breathtaking sheen of Sima Borisovana, and the sturdy, articulate Nadia (Chilkovsky) Nahumck.

The troupe's performance at Carnegie Hall in January 1932 drew an interesting comment from John Martin, dance critic of the *New York Times*, who compared the interpretation and rendition of the Tchaikovsky's Symphony #6 with that of the Russian company's version. " . . . The balance is all in favor of yesterday's performance which appeared to be not only more poised but also less lugubrious and consequently more genuinely tragic." Martin may have sensed that the Russian ensemble more uniformly reflected the strong pedagogical approach of Irma Duncan. The Americans, on the other hand, as a group, were a blend of several Duncan strains, which tempered with a light spiritedness Irma's personal tendency toward the earthy, more solid gesture.

Performing in public in Russia and the United States had become tiresome for Irma. Towards the end of 1932, the travels and the recitals ended. She was thirty-five, and had been, for most of those years, active as a dancer, a teacher, and an artistic director. With her short cropped hair of a blue-black sheen and her light gray-green eyes ("Gay dancing eyes . . . " Edward Steichen had called them) that regarded all intently, she was arresting in appearance. Handwriting analysis (which was a fad of the times) described Irma's personality as dramatic, alert, active, critical, a charm of personality not readily appreciated without extended acquaintanceship. Unsuspected beneath the reserved manner, the tailored chic attire, the firmly handled professional situations was a robust humor, and a spirit of levity that closer relationships savored. On those occasions one could catch a mental glimpse of Irma as a child at Grunewald, and her impish—if not always benign—ways. In her off-guard moments of later years, she could quickly dispel her grandiose "titular head" image with her humor and candor.

Like her famous predecessor, Irma displayed a rare gift for mimicry to which this writer was witness while at the dancer's Hillsdale, New York, home in 1965. A funny moment occurred when, in response to whether she had seen Rudolf Nureyev's recent television debut on the *Ed Sullivan Show*, she screwed up her face, sprang from her chair, and thrusting her pelvis forward, exploded with a full Germanic "Ach! Those ballet dancers and their tights; you can see all their *verks!*"[70]

For the few remaining years before Irma's marriage and subsequent retirement from active involvement with the dance, she continued to teach—both beginner and general classes and the advanced pupils of her concert group. Her students were a mixture of adults and children, those exhilarated and inspired by the Duncan esprit, others who esteemed Irma, and still others lured to the dance environment to bask in the reflected glow of "La Divina" herself, Isadora. Undeniably, Irma was for many, a surrogate Isadora, and in her presence, students stood in awe.

"Each class was a performance and you dressed for it," Sylvia Doner recalled. "You entered her class with seriousness and a concern about your appearance. You saw to it that your costume was attractive and properly worn."[71] (The tunic correctly donned was a happy illusion of a Greek idyll; incorrectly, it was a farcical sight.) Irma would stand close to piano and pianist, trimly dressed in skirt and blouse, her luxuriant hair short and neat. She always looked poised, cool, and serious.

Irma's classes were described as "disciplined—tight. Attention was paid to all details." A member of her dance company would frequently assist with demonstrations. Preparatory barre exercises were de rigueur, followed by Irma's own systematic arrangement of Duncan movement fundamentals. There are memories of classwork favorites: the traditional studies that Isadora based on the delightful sculpture miniatures from ancient Tanagra, for body balance, control, and harmony of attitude proportions; the dreamy, meditative Liszt *Liebestraum* in which the body, in a succession of sustained, *legato* gestures, gradually moved from an upright to a recumbent position on the floor; the energetic and lively polka that took each dancer clear around the studio to Beethoven's *Ruins of Athens*; and the soaring sensation of the high leap, when from a far corner of the room, the body would dart forward, gain momentum and then take off into space—front leg up, somewhat bent at the knee, rear leg back and up, chest high, head back and arms thrust up over head—a charge of the light brigade! Or, as Irma dramatically depicted it—"like Walkyries riding through Valhalla."

In their more intimate relationship with Irma, the members of her advanced group were well aware that the overriding goal of their teacher's life was to propagate Isadora's ideals. No compliment paid her would be equal to that of a favorable comparison with the other Duncan. "Irma's expectations of her own students would be that they justify Isadora Duncan's expectations of her," commented Julia Levien. Scenes of an Irma relaxing after a strenuous rehearsal have lasting memories for Kooluris: Irma sitting by candlelight at the piano, singing Schubert *lieder* in her attractive, resonant voice, or chanting Russian songs to which she had set their dances. "She had such magnetism, humor and drama."

Through her connections, Irma explored and was given some encouragement regarding private financial backing for her center of dance in Manhattan. By 1932, she had leased the handsome brownstone house of the sculptor Elie Nadelman on East 93rd Street. A fine building, it was ideally suited as an official residence for the Isadora Duncan School of the Dance. The large foyer with its sparkling chandelier, the stairway and handsome balustrade, the pedestal upon which stood a small ceramic statuette of Isadora by Stuart Benson (posed for by Irma), the sounds of Schubert and Gluck's music emanating from the dance salon, created an atmosphere redolent, one imagined, of the Grunewald and Bellevue days. But the hoped-for funding never materialized.

The event with which Irma Duncan bid "a glorious and joyful farewell to my dance career," was no modest exit for her. Quite to the contrary, it was a spectacle on a mammoth scale, completely conceived and programmed by the indomitable old man of American music, conductor Walter Damrosch. His lifelong passion for Beethoven's music and the memory of his successful collaboration with Isadora inspired him to counter the rumbling war sounds from Europe with a large-scale music and dance demonstration for peace. He enlisted Irma's participation and she began working on a choreography to accompany the stirring *Ode to Joy* finale of the composer's mighty Symphony #9, the *Chorale*.

At the Art Deco Pan Hellenic Hotel, Irma selected dozens of applicants for the program. Within short order, the great "Pageant for Peace" was staged on January 25, 1933 at Madison Square Garden. No smaller space would do. Damrosch's theatrical scenario called for a symphony orchestra of one hundred musicians, a mixed chorus of one hundred voices, and a group of some fifty dancing figures, men, women, children, to be witnessed by fifteen thousand spectators.

As the *Ode to Joy* motif softly sounded, Irma was introduced on stage. Symbolic of the world anticipating peace, the stirring theme echoed and swelled in volume. The lone figure summoned the others and from different entrances in the hall, people emerged and marched down the aisles with banners and wreaths, the strong rhythms and inspiring "brotherhood of man" music carrying them forward and up on stage where they danced in a joyous intoxication. For Irma, it was an Isadorian vision realized.

The dismantling of Irma's career as she contemplated marriage and professional retirement imposed upon her performing group the need to re-evaluate their own situations. Dissolved as a unit, a few of the pupils desired to maintain the momentum of the past years with Irma and banded together to teach and to perform. They called themselves the "New Duncan Dancers." Irma would have no part of this. She saw the newly formed group as capitalizing on and tampering with her hallowed ground—the institution Isadora Duncan. (*Déjà vu?* The girls were about the same age as the Isadorables when they raised their rebels' voices against Isadora.) The extent of the antagonism toward her former pupils' actions could be read in a *New York American* column on April 21, 1934—"Irma Duncan Sues 'Duncans'!" But the injunction against their appearing under the Duncan name was dropped upon private legal intervention advising Irma to withdraw her suit.

Having come from "the glaring spotlights" of theater stages in the major world capitals, Irma Duncan Rogers now took on the "obscurity of a private existence." She and her husband, Sherman Rogers, settled into an early American country house with a red roof and a long white fence, on an estate with old orchards, a brook, and a fine view of the Catskills in the distance. She became an active painter and a gourmet cook, winning local laurels in both these endeavors. Of more pertinent interest and significance, Irma wrote and published several books on the art and the artist she had served, and contributed her large, unusually valuable collection of documents and personal memorabilia on Isadora to the Dance Collection at Lincoln Center in New York. Her gift marked the thirtieth anniversary of her teacher's death and Irma had this to say: "I want them to be looked at freely by coming generations of dance lovers so that American youth can find new inspiration there and take a national pride in the greatest dance genius known to the world."

In 1966, before Irma relocated to Santa Barbara, California I spent several hours with her. At that time she was anxiously awaiting a response to what she knew would be her final piece of writing about her life with Isadora, her autobiography, *Duncan Dancer*. She stressed the importance of this book for establishing her claim to a professional and artistic identity of her own, which it did. But her tone of voice and serious manner intimated more deeply personal sentiments. She spoke of the long, hard road of dedication to a life in dance stemming from the ideals of her foster mother. With *Duncan Dancer*, Irma wished to finally consider fulfilled her responsibility and private debt to Isadora. The mission was accomplished.

I spoke to Irma about the prolonged absence from the dance scene of a representative Duncan school in the United States. She assured me that plans to revive a school of dance under her directorship had never been completely abandoned, but it was a task that carried great burdens, both physical and financial. She had been too close a witness to Isadora's unsuccessful plights to establish and then to maintain her schools. Irma's own experiences in Moscow and in New York remained an ever present and intimidating specter for her. Financial backing was still essential for the undertaking of a school and a performing company. That very day, as we conversed, Irma alluded, quite vaguely, to a tentative source. At no time was there mention of her former dancemates. Irma seemed to exist as a lone figure on the Duncan horizon.

Irma Duncan's life is inextricable from the history of the dance institution known as Duncanism. As witness, participant, friend, and assistant to the woman whose name she bore, there is no equivalent chronicle to Irma's unique affinity and affiliation with the remarkable Isadora. The keenly coveted recognition for her own standing in dance and among dancers she surely has attained. But the passing of time and events has brought evidence of yet an additional certainty—Irma Duncan left an impressive legacy of her own to world dance.

Today, her published writings are the prize of collectors for their illuminating documentation of one of the seminal chapters in the narrative of our century's culture. *Isadora Duncan's Russian Days and Her Last Years in France,* co-authored with Allan Ross Macdougall and published in 1929, sets down the earliest assembled data on the complex adventure in controversial Russia. *The Technique of Isadora Duncan* (as taught by Irma Duncan) and published c.1937, remains the sole, organized manual on the preparations basic for the study and application of the underlying Duncan technique. Irma's more than autobiographical account, *Duncan Dancer,* demystifies much of the heretofore veiled and little known aspects of life in the Isadora Duncan institutes of the dance. But when Irma shepherded her Russian flock out of Moscow during the 1928–1930 tour abroad and revealed to the outside world her fulfillment of Isadora's noble vision, she also had emerged into safety and world view with the surprising collection of the mature and inspired new dances that marked the "last hurrah" of Duncan's creative energies.

Particularly fortunate and of ongoing consequences for this signal art form was Irma's decision to settle in the United States. Peaking her career with the Russian and American professional dance companies, she had earned world prestige. Her credentials were unrivaled. The years of close collaboration and sharing of Isadora's artistic objectives assured her thorough knowledge and accomplishments in the teaching and performing of the rich, large repertoire. Irma had become the principal player in the supervision and transmission of the inheritance in her possession.

The last decade of Irma's life was spent with her husband greeting friends and devoted former pupils, speaking to the media, and on occasion— health permitting—teaching a private master class in the dance that had constituted her life.

Into 1977, the year that marked the centennial of Isadora's birth, Irma continued to reiterate her regret that no financial opportunities had been made available to enable her to produce the only documentary of Isadora's life in dance with an authenticity she alone could provide. She died later that year, that one remaining dream unfulfilled.

NOTES

1. Minna Lederman, *The Mail*, June 27, 1918.
2. Sigmund Spaeth, *The Mail*, June 17, 1920.
3. *Literary Digest*, May 1, 1915, p. 1019.
4. Minna Lederman, *The Mail*, June 27, 1918.
5. *Literary Digest*, May 1, 1915, p. 1019.
6. Redfern Mason, *San Francisco Examiner*, 1919, quoted in Irma Duncan, *Duncan Dancer*, p. 174.
7. Minna Lederman, *The Mail*, June 27, 1918.
8. Martha Graham in Margaret Lloyd, *Borzoi Book of Modern Dance*, p. 49.
9. Sigmund Spaeth, *The Mail*, June 27, 1920.
10. Letter from Anna Duncan to author, June 5, 1966.
11. Michel Georges-Michel, "Dans la Chapelle d'Isadora Duncan," *Paris-Midi*, November 26, 1920.
12. *Ibid.*
13. *Ibid.*
14. *Ibid.*
15. Louis Payen, "Dans le studio d'Isadora Duncan," unidentified source, November 28, 1920.
16. *Ibid.*
17. Fernand Divoire, "Danse et mimes," unidentified source, November 29, 1920.
18. Michel Georges-Michel, *Paris-Midi*, November 26, 1920.
19. "La Rentrée d'Isadora Duncan et son école de danse," unidentified source, November 18, 1920.
20. "Quelques mots sur les élèves d'Isadora Duncan," unidentified source, November 18, 1920.
21. Louis Handler, "Isadora Duncan at the Champs-Elysées," *La Danse*, January 26, 1921.
22. Emile Mas, "Les premières Champs-Elysées," unidentified source, January 27, 1921.
23. Antoine Banès, "Courrier des Théâtres Champs-Elysées," unidentified source, January 27, 1921.
24. Adolphe Julienne, *Débats*, February 6, 1921.
25. Two years into the war (1916), Paris Singer disaffiliated himself from Isadora's school, according to André Arnyvelde ("Isadora Duncan va rouvrir son école sous le patronage de l'Etat," unidentified source, May 5, 1920). Rather than this act be misconstrued as an about-face on Singer's part, it was speculated that he had suffered financial reverses brought on by the war.
26. Arsene Alexandre, "L'Art, les luttes, et les projets d'Isadora Duncan," unidentified source, May 5, 1920.
27. Lisa Duncan in Fernand Divoire, *Les Spectacles à travers les âges*, p. 23.
28. *Ibid.*
29. Odile Pyros interview by author, 1984.
30. Fernand Divoire, *Pour la Danse*, p. 64.
31. Letter from Lytton to author, 1986.
32. Fernand Divoire, *Pour la Danse*, p. 64.
33. "Lisa Duncan," *Journal of the Sorbonne*, July 1983, p. 4.
34. Fernand Divoire, *Pour la Danse*, p. 64.
35. Lady Madeleine Lytton, "Isadora Duncan," *National Review*, July 1948.
36. Jean Laurent, "La Danse Isadorisme," *Les Nouveaux Temps*, July 27, 1941.
37. Anita Zahn interview by author, 1985.
38. Anita Zahn interview by author, 1984.
39. Letter in Louise Craig Gerber collection.
40. Anna Duncan, "Does Classical Dancing Pay," *Dance Magazine*, July 1929.
41. W. A. Roberts, *Dance Magazine*, May 1928.

42. Madeleine Babian, *Dance Magazine*, November 1929.
43. C. D. Isaacson, *Dance Magazine*, December 1930.
44. Sylvia Garson Doner interview by author, 1983.
45. Julia Levien interview by author, 1984.
46. Hortense Kooluris interview by author, 1983.
47. *Dance Magazine*, January 1926.
48. Mary Watkins, *Dance Magazine*, May 1929.
49. *Ibid.*
50. Edwin Denby, *Looking at the Dance*, pp. 337, 339.
51. Letter from Theresa Duncan to author, January 16, 1967.
52. Letter from Irma Duncan to Louise Craig Gerber, 1977.
53. M. Onchurova, Introduction from *My Life* (printed in Russian in the Soviet Union in 1989), p. 10.
54. Irma Duncan and A. R. Macdougall, *Isadora Duncan's Russian Days*, p. 12.
55. Natalia Roslavleva, "Prechistenka 20: The Isadora Duncan School in Moscow," *Dance Perspectives* #64, Winter 1975, p. 45.
56. *Ibid.*
57. *Dance Magazine*, June 1954, pp. 33–34.
58. Irma Duncan and A. R. Macdougall, *Isadora Duncan's Russian Days*, p. 275.
59. Natalia Roslavleva, "Prechistenka 20: The Isadora Duncan School in Moscow," *Dance Perspectives* #64, Winter 1975, p. 45.
60. Irma Duncan, *Duncan Dancer*, p. 275.
61. *Ibid.*
62. Sol Hurok, *Impresario*, p. 124.
63. Irma Duncan and A. R. Macdougall, *Isadora Duncan's Russian Days*, pp. 276–277.
64. *Dance Magazine*, April 1929; July 1929.
65. Irma Duncan, *Duncan Dancer*, p. 331.
66. Fernand Divoire, *Pour la Danse*, pp. 72–73.
67. Natalia Roslavleva, "Prechistenka 20: The Isadora Duncan School in Moscow," *Dance Perspectives* #64, Winter 1975, pp. 43–45.
68. *Ibid.*, pp. 43–44.
69. Irma Duncan, *Duncan Dancer*, p. 334.
70. Irma Duncan interview by author, 1965.
71. Sylvia Garson Doner interview by author, 1983.

PART III

The Legend
and Legacy

CHAPTER SIX

La Presse

"What a miracle that such a tender blade should
Have grown on such a stony soil as America; like
a voluptuous blossom in a garden of snow, heat born
of ice, harmony born of chaos."

YVETTE GUILBERT,
Song of My Life

"Duncan was the single flaming spirit which our generation had contributed to
the international world of art."

OLIVER SAYLOR

THE IMPORTANCE OF FRANCE in the formulation of Isadora Duncan's
artistic image was emphasized to me by artist Abraham Walkowitz during a
conversation at his Brooklyn home. He spoke of France's esteem and respect
for creative people; how "without France, Isadora would not be Isadora . . . the
French created her and the French got the best out of her." No other country
had the opportunity to accumulate the quantity and variety of documentation

concerning Isadora, who established the longest residency of her quasi-nomadic existence in Paris.

Writer George Delaquys reminisced how Isadora seemed to have dropped in on Paris in 1900, from out of nowhere, so to speak.[1] She was not French; she was a foreigner. He pondered if she was even necessary. Parisian culture lacked for nothing; there were operas, café-concerts, and ballerinas galore. The suddenness of Isadora's appearance caught Parisians off guard, and after a brief display of her dancing before private gatherings, she took off as mysteriously as she had come.

Isadora's first public appearance in Paris took place at the Théâtre Sarah Bernhardt during May and June 1903. "She was not successful," Delaquys noted. Objecting to "payoffs," Isadora earned herself a press who were "indifferent or hostile . . . the critics who lived on their reputation for making discoveries of persons of genius discovered nothing that year . . . not Isadora Duncan." Nevertheless, curiosity about this mysterious young woman and her mysterious dance had begun. Rumors circulated "like the flying winds," but the dancer eluded reporters who pursued her. "The truth is," said Delaquys, "Miss Duncan doesn't give a damn."

Isadora pulled off some adroit capers to safeguard her privacy. Wherever she was sought she proved to be elsewhere, but the shadows of stalking journalists were to hover permanently over her extraordinary life's events. With the increase of her concert activities, her fame flowered. She came under the scrutiny and judgment of the many writers and critics who penned the staggering quantity of printed material available to early twentieth-century Parisians.

On the subject of Isadora Duncan, these writers swung a wide critical pendulum, from full-blown emotionalism and adoration to fierce cynicism and rejection; few were middle of the road. One might parody, extol, or lampoon her efforts, but one rarely, if ever, was dispassionate. Journalists, on occasion, were known to make use of their newspaper column to take a serious "poke" at an irksome colleague for either his overenthusiasm or underappreciation of the dancer. Isadora herself became a "journalist" at crucial times. Responding to unflattering remarks, she was always ready to offer her "corrections" in a letter to the press.

It took Isadora one year to convert the 1903 setback at the Théâtre Sarah Bernhardt into a 1904 conquest at the Trocadéro Palace. No less than the titan of music, Beethoven, now graced her expanded repertory. For her *Soirée Beethoven* she included two piano sonatas (the *Pathétique*, Opus 13 in C minor and the *Moonlight* (*Quasi una Fantasia*) Opus 27 no. 2 in C-sharp minor), some minuets (arranged by Hans von Bülow), and two movements from the Seventh Symphony (Opus 92 in A major)—her first attempt at symphonic choreography. She was assisted by the famous Colonne Orchestra and its venerable conductor, Edouard Colonne.

A cavernous theater, the Trocadéro was filled to overflowing. The musicians in the audience were especially wary of choreographed Beethoven. Afterward, composer Gustave Charpentier commented that "she has understood that the most elusive, complex, and evanescent movements of the human spirit can be mirrored through the contours and lines of the dancer's body. With her, dance encompasses everything . . . the drama, the symphony. . . . With all the refinement of her own person, her leaps, her languors, the tremblings of the nakedness beneath the veils, she has created a new vocabulary, an ensemble of metaphors capable of speaking in the most immediate and musical of languages."[2]

Musicologist and critic Louis Laloy indicated that he was usually reluctant to apply a term like "genius" to the dance, in view of the deteriorated state of the ballet of his time, but found Isadora's dance altogether a different matter.[3] He had come to her concert fully expecting to find the manner of her dance "poor and puerile compared to the sumptuous music she wished to interpret. It was nothing like that."

Like other arts that reveal the most beautiful secrets of life, Laloy referred to Isadora's new dance as "mute music and moving sculpture." He was impressed that the presence of a full orchestra was not able to eclipse the dancer; she sustained full interest in her dance. Furthermore, in the more subtle, underlying themes of the "Adagio" of the sonata *Pathétique* and the "Adagio Sostenuto" of the *Moonlight*, her gestures transmitted the more profound human emotions that existed in the music.

For Laloy, the interest and beauty of Isadora's performance lay in the personal nature of her expressiveness through movements that were "nowhere to be found in any prior or existing textbook on dance. . . . Here a spirit is sensed and materialized before us." Laloy assured his readers that Isadora Duncan was a priestess "worthy of her God . . . she has piety, purity, and nobility of thought."

The swift-moving dances in close rapport with the music roused the critic's enthusiasm: "Melody and movement are here as twin flowers of the supporting rhythm. One does not know which of these flowers has the most grace and perfume." The minuets, he said, revealed a virginal face; Isadora's turnings were delicate, somewhat demure, and reminiscent of the maidens of the Parthenon. Finally, Laloy commented on the Beethoven symphony, after first subduing those who protested Isadora's use of the composer's music. The symphony, Laloy conceded, was in itself a complete work that required no supplemental clarification from another medium, such as dance, but the dance of Isadora Duncan was also to be regarded as "a work of art."

Beginning with the second movement (the first was an orchestral prelude), Laloy remarked on "the mystic weeping, which invokes in her alone a whole procession of moods, alternately sad and weary, or bathed in elysian light." In the rondo, "one imagines seeing nymphs reaching for one another's hand." Finally, there was the "seraphic bacchanale" of the last movement, in which Isadora's brisk movements and the accentuated bounce of her body on the final note of the main phrase infused the music with "fine images of nymphs dancing at the festivals of Dionysus."

Other European performances, motherhood, and her first tour of her native United States in 1908 consumed the almost five years until Isadora once again appeared in concert in the French capital from late January into February 1909, at the Théâtre-Lyrique Municipal de la Gaîté. Two distinctive premières took place on that occasion: Gluck's *Iphigénie* (which had first been presented in Germany in late 1904) and the Paris debut of the children from her first school of dance in Grunewald (the children had already been widely seen in Germany and throughout Europe).

Gluck's two operas—*Iphigénie en Aulide* (1774) and *Iphigénie en Tauride* (1779)—were revered by the dancer and were long a choreographic preoccupation of hers. From them, she fashioned a single concert-length production. Into the second section ("Tauride") she interpolated an orchestral arrangement by Felix Mottl from yet another Gluck opera, *Armide*, which furnished the accelerating mood of celebration in the closing portion with dances of an added joyous character. With *Iphigénie*, another block of Isadora's broadening exploration into music for her dance was set in place. It was possibly her *chef-d'oeuvre*, the apex of her lyric-dramatic style, and remained an actively integral part of her repertory.[4]

At the Gaîté-Lyrique Isadora was assisted in her series of performances by the Concerts Lamoureux Orchestra, conducted by Camille Chevillard, under the artistic management of Lugné-Poë. A second engagement at this theater, with a seating capacity of approximately 2,200, took place in May and June 1909, when she was accompanied by the Colonne Orchestra and by her pupils as well, who charmed audiences with their innocence and grace in a group of incidental dances.[5]

Reviewing for *Comoedia Illustré* in February 1909, André Marty described the scene at the Gaîté-Lyrique:

> Let's imagine a stage, completely hung with gray-blue draperies, a carpet of the same color; a soft light facing toward the back of

the stage. The curtain parts, and with the first measures of a Gluck air we see emerging from the shadows the strangest, most exquisite of apparitions. Have we seen her on one of those immortal paintings that adorned Greek vases; does she step live from the land of Tanagra; is she the serene muse on Parnassus out of a Mantegna, the most perfect of Clodion's statuettes? She is none of these, she is all of them; even more, one makes a mistake to compare her with anything else. Her dance is not imitative of other plastic arts, nor an appealing accompaniment for music; it is an art in itself, she attains the beautiful by means all her own.[6]

Marty observed that Isadora, in her expression of feelings and in her representation of human actions, created something simpler and more forceful than reality. He referred to this as a "superior synthesis," a stylization seen in the games she played in the "Aulide" segment—ball and knucklebones. Not literal images, they were devoid of relation to a specific time, place, or period. And when in the "Bacchanale" "she might seem an intoxicated bacchante incited by some god to irrational behavior, we are actually seeing the symbol of divine folly itself."

Pierre Mille started his account of Isadora's concert in the February 1909 issue of *Le Théâtre* by quoting his colleague, Fernand Nozière: " 'One wants to get down on the knees and pray, even to cry' . . . It seems insane that a dance, only a dance—two feet, fast or slow, the arms open or folded, and the supple body of a woman could inspire you to pray or cry. Yet this is the truth! Nozière is right. There is a great mystery here." To his own rhetorical questions he provided answers: "What is it that she does, this large woman with long legs, an undulating torso, and muscled like the statues of virgins sculpted by Polycletus?" Whatever it was that she did, Mille was certain of one thing: "She dances and no one has ever danced as she."

To describe her attire, Mille referred to the virgins of the Parthenon frieze, the priestesses in flowing robes standing before the temple of Athena, the winged victory, the seductive folds that cover without concealing, the forms of Botticelli's nymphs. "And then, what is it that she does? Certainly others have danced better, if it were solely a question of . . . beat and step. But what she does is so very open, so very unsophisticated—a simple manner and that is all that is necessary." Utterly convinced that Isadora knew at all times what she wished to achieve, Mille went on to describe the heroine Iphigenia as she played along the shoreline with knucklebones: "They are like flowers in her hands. She tosses them in the air; they fall back downward. She seizes them. So convincing are all her actions that spectators do not question that she truly sees the sea before her and that her eyes are filled with the shape of the waves." With certainty and pride she runs to welcome the victorious Greek fleet, arriving to the reverberations of trumpets, "her bosom heaving, her figure seeming to grow taller."

Still later Isadora returned as a young warrior, dressed in a short red tunic, her arms bare. Then, during the clash of weapons (the "Dance of the Scythians" from *Tauride*), she brought an exaltation to the combat: "How vivid are the simulations of battle, the fist that strikes, the feigned flight, the bold young head warding off the blows, eyes brilliant in valor; and when the final assault fells the foe, her arm is raised in triumph. No longer does she battle, she remains still—a monument to glory."

For the *Finale* Isadora appeared as a bacchante, clumps of ivy and flowers in her hands. "First she tosses the flowers, then brandishes the vines, all the while continuously dancing and ever faster." If the role of the poet and artist was to awaken and to reveal, then "she is indeed artist and poet, this Isadora."

The American dancer and her revolutionary approach to her art created a furor, reported the *New York Times* on May 23, 1909. Her pursuit of acceptance by the French had been a resounding success. "Of all the cities where I have danced, Paris is the one from whom I most wanted admiration. . . . "[7] The extraordinary success of the two Gaîté-Lyrique engagements placed Isadora firmly in the French consciousness. Increasing attention was paid to all aspects of her personal and professional life. Journalists wrote of her individual craft and style, music critics of the aptness of her choice of music, dance experts of balletic tradition vis-à-vis Isadora's more radical concepts. Feature articles spotlighted her choreography, her school of dance, and her young pupils.

One of the few professional women to write on Isadora during this time was Jeanne Gazeau, whose lengthy essay in *Les Entretiens Idéalistes* on December 25, 1909, presented a discriminating and favorable assessment of the philosophical and esthetic underpinnings of the new dance and its theorist. Reacting to the choreographies, Gazeau described moments of wonder and excitement: Isadora's run in the "Scythian Dance" was "steady and fiery as an ephebe"; in the "Bacchanale," "she is possessed"; in her "glide into a Chopin waltz" she effected an easy transformation of mood and form.[8]

Of the Chopin numbers on the dancer's programs, Gazeau considered that Isadora reached the peak of tragic emotion in *The Maiden and Death* to the Mazurka in B minor (opus 33, no. 4). "I know nothing more beautiful than the sudden transformation of this young being dancing with the exuberance of life, who now feels gripped by Death; there is a shudder, then an effort to shake off the icy embrace, finally a desperate stiffening of the entire body, a supreme convulsion, where she seems to raise herself erect like a fragile flower that shoots up from a blow, then falls lifeless. It is the eternal mystery of death in all its simple anguish. . . . "

One of the lengthiest and most detailed examinations of "The Dances of Isadora Duncan" appeared in the March 1910 issue of *Mercure de France*.[9] In analyzing *Iphigénie* the author Ovion was intrigued by its archaeological character and the two distinct classifications of movements at work in this dance: movements of action, descriptive and evocative of the style of Greek art, and gestures expressing human emotion. Ovion did not find these derivative of earlier influences, but personal in nature and decidedly more interesting and original.

The best example of the action motions and the set figurative patterns of Greek origin, were the youthful scenes from *Iphigénie en Aulide*: the Tanagra figurine half-kneeling, counting the score points from the imaginary knucklebones caught on the back of the hand, the recumbent pose in the classic position of the Greeks—underleg bent, upper leg extended—or in the symbolic lamentations of Iphigenia, who, believing Orestes dead, makes her final tribute, articulating maddening grief by simulating the tearing of her hair.

Unmistakably derived from ancient artifacts, Ovion believed, were the physical gestures employed in the warrior's conflict: "One can point out by the hundreds the designs on vases where the poses of Isadora Duncan in this dance . . . can be traced." Ovion drew close parallels between the gestures in this dance, in which Isadora was both the attacker and the attacked, and Plato's description of the Pyrrhic dance in which he had written of those natural bodily modulations employed in battle: " . . . the posture of a man letting fly an arrow or hurling a javelin." Gestures characteristic of the one being attacked were associated with the body's mechanisms for self-defense, "be it flinging oneself to the side, drawing back, leaping, or bending."

But the dances of joy, as in the *air gai*, the delirious climax of the "Bacchanale," even the undulating motions of Isadora's arms in the "Entrance of the Priestesses" in *Tauride*, had the individuality of personal, interpreted gestures. Here one encountered the emotional, expressive movements that Ovion properly credited to Isadora—creative movements of "unusual novelty, a return to symmetrical form, architecture in dance, movements regular and broadly structured, well-proportioned, and evincing a sureness of balance and deliberate control of the emotional dynamics." In the music of Gluck, Isadora seemed to perfect her unusual art, the writer concluded: "She is the remarkable interpreter . . . a gesture from her radiant purity of style remains imprinted on the retina, a joy forever."

French deputy Paul Boncour eulogized "The Art of the Sublime Dancer" in his article for *Le Figaro* on May 22, 1909. When he called for the creation of a society to perpetuate Isadora's work in dance, he caused quite a stir. When his report on the fiscal state of the arts was carried by the newspaper *Excelsior* on November 30, 1910, it raised eyebrows in "parliamentary circles" and upset the "small, charming world of danseuses."

Boncour had provocatively made known his opinion that all ballet had had its day. He cited Isadora as a most important figure among new artists of the dance, suggesting in fact, that her fresh perceptions and innovative ideas had far more contemporary relevance than did ballet and should be considered for a needed renovation of the old system. *Excelsior* also aired the results of a survey it had conducted on the controversial subject: "Tutu vs. Peplum—Will Isadora Duncan Reform Our Corps de Ballet?—Freedom of Art vs. Tradition—What Are the Big Stars Saying?"

The first "big star," Mme. Rosita Mauri, who was then in charge of dance training at the Opéra, spoke well of Isadora, but defended traditionalism. A dancer could no more divorce herself from the established disciplines of the profession than a writer could violate grammatical rules. Opening the doors to innovation, as Boncour suggested, could not work. "Classic dances [ballet] cannot be changed and the tutu remains the only costume appropriate for the dancer." Of course she had seen Isadora and her pupils who were so wonderfully graceful, but never could one of the children accomplish what the children of her own studio did. "Look at her!" She indicated to the *Excelsior* interviewers a thirteen-year-old child in tights and a pink and white tutu, with a strong, supple, arched back, momentarily wobbling to balance herself on left pointe.

The ballet mistress at the Opéra-Comique, Mme. Marquita, was cautious about giving an opinion, not having seen Isadora in concert. "I did not know that she had already become a school."

The reporters next caught up with the famous Mme. Carlotta Zambelli, who was rehearsing on stage at the Opéra. A champion of ballet, she was reluctant to talk, but told them straight away: "What Isadora Duncan does is not very difficult; one has only to move the legs freely. We could perform her work easily, but the reverse is not true." One reporter tenaciously pressed the point further. Isadora Duncan, he advised, had been through a thorough physical training in preparation for her dance and had as strong a technique as she. Zambelli's reply: "You think so? It would show." She terminated the interview with that, and proceeded to transform herself into a Snow Fairy.

"Aflutter, pretty, amiable, and in a feathered hat," Mme. Regina Badet limited her interview to five minutes; she was late for her rehearsal at

Gemier's. The subject of Isadora Duncan merited some sympathy from this ballet mistress. Isadora's was an art that offered much of interest, but was unlikely to realize any permanent success because, Mme. Badet explained, "the Opéra is so solidly entrenched an organization that to penetrate it will be most difficult." However, she could recognize the benefits of new ideas on the old traditions. "We are martyrized, you know, in childhood . . . they deform and dislocate us. Very fortunate are Isadora's young girls who are let free to dance and follow their own instincts."

The central figure in the controversy had the final say. Isadora Duncan's studio, where the interview took place, was located in the Hôtel Biron on rue Varennes (the current Rodin Museum). There, she told her visitors, she spent hours daily working on her technique and compositions, "proving well that what she does is not all that easy." (The composition in preparation on that occasion was her new version of *Orphée et Eurydice*.) She professed to not being entirely familiar with Paul Boncour's report on the state of the arts or aware of any investigation into her dance, but, in general, she was of the opinion that most people were mistaken about what she believed.

In the nine years since her arrival in Paris, Isadora claimed to have become much wiser, talking less and doing more. She accepted the fact that her art had no chance of supplanting the classical dance because it was not an art of the theater. Hers was a self-sufficient art expression, and her true ambition was to focus on founding a school of fine arts in a milieu of painters and sculptors, where the plastic arts would become an official study and where she could expound and reveal the principles of her work in dance and train future exponents of her ideas. She expressed distress over "the wretched imitations they do of me," and desired only to be left alone to live quietly, read, and listen to music. "I have nothing more to say now. I have already talked too much."

Isadora's fuller version of Gluck's long-surviving opera, *Orphée et Eurydice* (a short suite of pieces from this opera dated from her early programs, c. 1900), was completed by the close of 1910 and presented at the Châtelet Theater on January 18, 1911, with the participation of singers, a chorus, and the Colonne Orchestra. The *Orphée* was the second Gluck adaptation to reinforce the public's recognition of the dancer as an artist. She was not solely a captivating charmer and invigorating spirit in the music of Strauss, Schubert, Brahms, and Chopin but an earnest interpreter of simple and powerfully beautiful musical scores, capable of integrating great music with human gestures of dramatic truth and eloquence. Whenever it appeared in Paris, Isadora's *Orphée* was announced in the press as a cultural event of commanding magnitude; all were summoned to the theater.

Walter Rummel, Isadora's musical advisor and accompanist, some years later, wrote on the dancer's interpretive approach to Orpheus.[10] Her role was neither representative of the word nor illustrative of the dramatic action. She placed herself within the panorama of the narrative as did the Greek chorus in the performance of ancient tragedies, rendering "the primordial and imper-sonal emotion that rises from the innermost depths" of the character in the drama. Such emotion, Rummel stressed, could not manifest itself other than through music, and only the dance could make it visible. Thus the chorus (Isadora's role) was not a depiction of the story development; it assumed the silent and concentrated focus of the drama's emotion, "the distillation of its passionate essences."

André Nède's January 18, 1911, article, "Isadora Duncan at the Châtelet," provided a preview of the major scenes of her *Orphée*, a run-through as helpful to his fellow Frenchmen as to today's readers:

> The orchestra will play the overture, the curtain will rise, and
> the chorus will be heard; Orpheus's companions lament the
> death of Eurydice and Miss Duncan will dance these
> lamentations. At Eurydice's tomb she becomes Orpheus, who can
> be recognized by the grief that marks her pantomime. She is
> alone on stage.

For the performance, there were usually two voices—Orpheus (con-tralto) and Eurydice (soprano)—and a small chorus, all seated among the orchestra players. On stage, Isadora constituted the entire spectacle.

> The orchestra plays the dance of the lost souls and we are now in
> Hell. A harp is heard, Orpheus's arrival is announced, and the
> chorus begins the melody of the lost spirits. Miss Duncan dances
> the dance of these wretched souls. . . . The following scene
> transfers to the Elysian Fields, where Miss Duncan, in her dance,
> reveals the now happy shades leading Orpheus toward
> Eurydice. . . . The end of the poem is the triumph of love, and
> Miss Duncan dances the processions, the sacrifices, and the
> placing of flowers on love's altar.

There was no unanimity among the critics. Paul Souday's response to the Châtelet *Orphée* found Isadora's choice of music faulty. "Even a dancer such as Isadora Duncan cannot alone adequately synthesize a complete lyric drama."[11] He thought her meanings were obscure as she shifted her portrayal from that of Orpheus to that of the Shades who obstruct her entrance into Hades. Strange and disconcerting though, "it was not at all unbecoming or tiresome." As for the rest of Isadora's program, Souday commented that "Miss Duncan merited the most glowing of compliments."

A personal apprehension was disclosed by André Marty in his February 1911 *Comoedia Illustré* article, "Isadora Duncan at the Châtelet." Might she not in her latest undertaking perhaps destroy the sublime memory of her earlier perfection, "treasured in us like a jewel?" His fear that the "new" that might shatter the spell of the "old" dissolved upon seeing "the priestess" once again. Sometimes the same, sometimes different, Isadora was always beautiful to Marty.

Isadora's handling of the beginning of *Orphée*'s second act demonstrated to the reviewer how deep intuition and artistic intelligence could inject art with an exceptional character. While the off-stage voice of the hero was pleading for the return of his Eurydice, the dancer began moving to the haunting theme of the lost souls—she had become one of those pitiful, infernal creatures, wandering along the banks of the Styx. "At no moment in this dance could one say her gestures recreated figures from the Sistine Chapel . . . still, Michaelangelo's name was on everyone's lips. She does not imitate the great creator, but by her energy and superhuman effort she rises to the height of his genius."

Pierre Lalo, the brilliant son of composer Edouard Lalo, was music critic for *Courier Musical*, *Comoedia*, and *Le Temps*. He was an arch conservative, known for his astuteness and caustic wit. With Isadora he made little progress, despite his undiminished antagonism. His lengthy critique ignored direct reference to the *Orphée* première, tackling instead her ideas and doctrines and their fallacies.[12] Altogether peculiar in view of its past disdain was Paris's unwholesome infatuation with her dances and her bare feet. "There is not in what she does today any less pretension or less mediocrity than at another time."[9] But it was Isadora's remark in *Excelsior*, to the effect that a collection of more or less arbitrary steps does not constitute an art, that incited Lalo to the virulence of his critique.

The classical dance to which the dancer had referred *was* an art, Lalo asserted, because it defined its gestures and attitudes with precision and eliminated "useless, obscure motions." Ballet cultivated, developed, and perfected a style by "logically studied methods based on a body of rules." Citing Gautier and Mallarmé, who were fervent admirers of the ballet, and pointing to Degas, the greatest painter of the day, who esteemed ballet sufficiently to devote a significant portion of his work to studies of it and its practitioners, Lalo challenged Isadora to make such a claim for herself. "Merely fluttering about and trying to express her soul, this presumptuous American, without any understanding of the medium, not even a shadow of technical competence, thinks she is creating a revolution. . . . She seems entirely devoid of a musical sense . . . like one of those Anglo-Saxons of whom Nietzsche said, 'they possess no music in them.' "

Under attack were Isadora's "false simplicity and affected naiveté." Lalo, with his well-known anti-German prejudice, called the children from her school "heavy little girls from beyond the Rhine, whose ankles were as thick as their thighs . . . their naked legs skipping around monotonously while following Miss Duncan in a row." The public, who aided and abetted her successes, were not spared his attack. "They are the dupes of a Parisian pro-Duncan coalition composed of snobs: ringleaders, agitators preying on the bovine throng, who blindly follow the caprices of fashion." He found incomprehensible "their stupid tendency to confuse the amateurish, underdeveloped efforts of the foreigner with those of a genius." Denying any prejudice on his part, he pointed to his acceptance of the foreigner "who is a Wagner, Tolstoi, or an Ibsen—not a Puccini, Caruso, or an Isadora Duncan."

Composer Reynaldo Hahn's music review of an *Orphée* performance given by Isadora in March 1913 at the Trocadéro was critical of her treatment of the Gluck score. "Regretfully, I must confess that this Orpheus is not an example of her notable art I prefer."[13] He faulted her disregard for the composer's tempo markings, the vagueness of her interpretation of Eurydice, of Orpheus, and the Blessed Spirits, which ultimately undermined her artistic intentions. Furthermore, the Gluck music bore characteristics of eighteenth-century operatic style quite incompatible with the dancer's attempt to apply it to movements of the Chorus in Greek tragedy.[14] In Act Three, "The Elysian Fields," mention is made of seven of the pupils led by Isadora, who became the "living realization of all sylvan myths. . . . " The renowned dramatic actor Mounet-Sully recited the prose uniting the narrative extracts, while the distinguished singer Rudolf Plamondon sang the role of Orpheus.

When Hahn turned to the Schubert numbers on the program, his review lightened. There was, in Isadora's ease of rhythms, in her serenity and tranquility of repose, that which excited in the spectator "a penetrating sense of well-being, to be alive and to feel the world so acutely."[15] What irresistible magic in her forms and exhilarations in her vigor, the critic marvelled. He would not find the term "genius" excessive in one who could realize the summit of beauty and emotion attainable by a human being. "In those moments where beauty and emotion fuse and climax, something of the immortal floats about the dancer; she wanders in a divine ray, in a mist where all works of art circle in unison with her . . . As Goethe once said: 'Hold this moment, do not flee, you are so beautiful!' "[16]

One of a favored circle of journalists whose supportive reviews were appreciated by Isadora, Michel Georges-Michel attended her performances in late November 1911 at the Châtelet. In his "Les Ennuis et les Rêves d'Isadora Duncan" ("Isadora Duncan's Anxieties and Dreams") that appeared on December 3 in *Gil Blas*, Georges-Michel made note of the seven young pupils, "the little dancing roses," who entered the stage and stood within the blue shadow of the heavy curtains. At that point Isadora approached the footlights, crossed her arms, and addressed the rather surprised audience: "Look at these children. They are healthy and robust; eyes are clear and no one is tired or weakened. To the contrary, listen as they breathe freely. Do you think it is wrong for them to dance?"

What prompted the brief and unexpected speech became apparent to Georges-Michel when, in her dressing room, Isadora told him: "I am pampering a big dream—my school of dance. I want not 50, not 500, but 5,000 pupils. The dance is play, it is art, health, joy and poetry. I would wish for the whole world to dance with me! And the whole world, even with its idiosyncracies, delusions, pathos and passions and would come to realize a more pleasurable existence."[17] How should she not be irritated, Georges-Michel wrote, when that very day, she had been informed by a reputable critic that her pupils were to be the subject of an investigation? A prominent society member found objectionable the commercial exploitation in Parisian theaters of young children, parading around in skimpy outfits and baring their naked legs. Moreover, Georges-Michel added, Mme. Duncan was apprised by her informant that all young children dancers in Europe usually wound up as prostitutes—lost by the time they reached the age of fifteen!

There was more to come. Isadora herself was threatened with cancellation of her concerts if she dared to appear in her transparent veils for what was described as her "sensuous" "Bacchanale" from *Tannhäuser*. The daily papers made it known that a police deputy was to be on hand in the theater to enforce the restraining order on her attire (waiting to close the curtain at the first drop of her modesty). The harried dancer tried to put the matter into some rational perspective with a letter to the newspapers. She was hoping to diffuse the situation by clarifying her personal concept of Wagner's score and her choreography. Those familiar with Isadora's interpretation of this music were equally cognizant of her belief that the spirit of the dance must transcend the corporeal, so that in the treatment of the love and carnal themes suggested in the music, only the imagination was titillated, not the flesh. To Georges-Michel she vented her frustrations: "If they annoy me about this, I will dance in a forest naked, naked, naked . . . with the song of birds and elemental noises for an orchestra."[18]

To unruffle feathers, Isadora wore for this performance (according to one source) a double layer of light scarves. Inevitably, with all this commotion, public anticipation was high for the "Bacchanale" and the audience, not disappointed in the overall presentation, had actually awaited a less restrained interpretation. All in all, things proceeded without incident. Isadora was seen leaving the theater wrapped in ermine from head to foot, utterly fatigued and utterly delighted.

The death of Isadora's children in 1913, followed by the four-year war that engulfed first Europe and subsequently the United States, brought years of disruption and turmoil to Isadora's life. She restlessly kept moving with more and more concerts in the United States, as well as South America; in between she returned to France, where she presented in Paris, in April 1916, two benefit performances to aid French war relief and did a short tour of the provinces in recital with a piano accompanist. The French press kept track of it all.

Isadora's first major reappearance in Paris after the war took the form of a year-long Festival of Music and Dance throughout 1920. This year celebrated two decades since the dancer's arrival in Paris in 1900. Art critic Waldemar George, in an article on the new dance, addressed part of his essay on the now familiar and reputable artist and the implications of her dance.[19] A broad and rhetorical question framed the purport of his assessment. Could the dance have the potential for becoming a viable art, one no longer peripheral, but within the scheme of the modern esthetic? He believed it could and found in Isadora the initiator and the reactivator, evidence of the renewal of this medium and the new spirit infecting the plastic arts. She had, in the twenty years of her opposition to the balletic tradition, brought credibility to a technique at first thought to be based solely on intuition. Surprisingly and more precisely, George viewed this technique as stemming from a perfect knowledge of the rules of rhythmic structure. This is an art, he reasoned, that could be learned and taught with authenticity.

The press had been informed by Isadora that her dance now had a new character. The horrendous events affecting the world had deeply touched her and she desired to express through her dance ideas and emotions more relevant to those experiences shared in common by all people. It was her earnest wish to offer some consolation to the sorrowing and to the afflicted.

Afflicted but not consoled by Isadora's words was Paul Abrams who, in an article in March 1920, vented a wary response.[20] He addressed himself to the men of his generation who were witness, as was he, to two events in the art of choreography—both indelible, "never to be stricken from memory." The first came with the entrance of the Ballets Russes, the decors of Bakst, the performances of Nijinsky, Karsavina, and Rubenstein, and the sumptuousness of the Orient. The second landmark event, less ostentatious but more profound and memorable in its appreciation and alliance with the values of beauty in the classical sense, was the appearance of Isadora Duncan. Then Abrams got to the heart of his displeasure. He and several of his colleagues had received letters from the dancer in which she promised a departure from the earlier character of her dance. He was apprehensive. For Isadora to complicate or even to become pretentious just to produce other effects "which she little needs" worried him. It would be, he commented, "like having grains of pepper thrown into a glass gilden by the Hellenic sun and filled with wine from Samos."

Newspapers carried the announcement of Isadora's concert dates and program schedules with a jubilation befitting the return of Ulysses to Ithaca: "A date in the History of Beauty," "She will reclaim her Apostolic Esthetic." As the momentum gathered, her appearances took on the dimension of immense cultural happenings—masterpieces from the greatest composers and the most acclaimed dancer of her epoch together in the prominent theaters of Paris. Isadora began her concert series at the Trocadéro in March and April, continuing at the Théâtre des Champs-Elysées in May and June, again performing at the Trocadéro in November and December, this time with the Isadorables, finishing at the Champs-Elysées, again with the Isadorables, in January 1921.

Paris resounded with the "big guns" of Isadora's creative achievements, the mainstays of her career and her artistic signature, *Iphigénie* and *Orphée*, the sensitively probed works of her maturity, Tchaikovsky's Symphony No. 6 in B minor (1916), César Franck's *Redemption* (1916), Liszt's *Les Funérailles* (1918–1919) and his *Bénédiction de Dieu dans la Solitude* (1918–1919), her revised and enlarged excerpts from Wagner's *Parsifal*, and her gestural dramatization of the French anthem *La Marseillaise* (1915–1916). For her numerous "loyalists" Isadora tossed floral bouquets in the form of the beloved Schubert, Brahms, and Chopin waltzes, which rekindled treasured remembrances of the vivacious and nimble Isadora of her younger days.

The cavernous, antiquated, and acoustically faulty Trocadéro did not impede the tumultuous reception accorded Isadora. Across its enormous stage had passed France's great orators, beribboned men of state, and members of L'Académie Française. Isadora now stood there in her light peplum and bare feet, first expressing her gratitude to the full house for so grand a welcome and then announcing her plan to endow Paris with a school of the dance. She called on her faithful followers to aid her in her task. "I have but opened a door. This door must never be allowed to close." On hand and in good number were the members of the press, many familiar figures reconvening for such an auspicious occasion. Seen with some frequency during the gala season were the notables among artists and intellectuals in Paris, several of whom would continue to cast their shadows over cultural events for some time to come: Gabriel Astruc, Henri Bidou, René Blum, Colette, Kees van Dongen, Lanvin, Louis Jouvet, Steinlen, Picasso.

As in the past, eulogistic terms—"Priestess," "Goddess," "Statue"— headlined article after article. Charles Mère described Isadora's effect on the crowds as a "magnetism of intelligence and benevolence." Fontrailles exclaimed: "She's a prodigious thing!" As Isadora danced the *Marche Slav*, Nozière, drama critic for *Gil Blas* and *Au Matin*, was seen standing in his loge, writing and uttering "She is an entire temple, this woman!" The crusty critic of *L'Oeuvre*, known to his colleagues as La Fouchardière, grumbled aloud: "To dance to Wagner with this corpulence . . . this Isadora! I must do an article, but . . . cannot handle it with this woman. She's a national glory!"

Following are some of the collected impressions of the Schubert *Funeral March* (*Marche Héroïque*) composed by Isadora in 1914 as a memorial to her children.

> The Goddess appears; first, a pale shadow moving against the tall, dark backdrop. . . . The years, heavy with grief and anguishes, have weighed oppressively on the shoulders of the divine Iphigenia who not long ago danced on the shores of Aulis.[21]

> Still and white in long vertical folds and staring with an inexpressible sadness . . . the poses, the walk of the great artist suffice to cause spectators to tremble.[22]

> The sadness and gravity of the Funeral March, a dance? No—it is a mute tragedy.[23]

For Isadora's fans, her return to the Trocadero with her *Orphée* was a time for elation. Her performances of December 11 and 16, 1920, featured singers M. Francell of the Opéra Comique, Rudolphe Plamondon of the Opéra, Mme. Marcelle Doria and an ensemble of Singers from Saint Gervais, and eighty musicians from the Concerts Colonne Orchestra with the much admired conductor Georges Rabani.

Sublime and "hieratic," Isadora took charge, reported critic Guillot de Saix. On this occasion her Orpheus took on a particular dignity. While interpreting the Gluck score, yellow, violet, and red lights created a phantasmagoric atmosphere. Guillot de Saix noted how the composer Gluck had transcended his epoch, but how the dancer in her turn had surpassed the composer. He called attention to how she had rejoined the statuary of antiquity, of how she brought animation to the paintings of da Vinci. She now led her audience as she dreamily wandered from the tomb of Eurydice to the infernal caverns where monsters and furies became tamed by the strumming of Orpheus' divine lyre, and when she guided them into the Elysian Fields studded with flowering narcissus, artists in the hall watched this scene with ecstatic eyes, believing they were seeing live before them, their own dreams.

During Easter week in April 1920, Isadora offered a "Spiritual Concert" that featured the *Childhood of Christ* of Berlioz, the *Redemption* of César Franck, and the *Holy Grail* music from *Parsifal* of Wagner. Leading into his review of the concert, Pierre Scize asked a question: "Who, then, said this woman was a dancer? The most agreeable of mimes, a tragedian, perhaps, a sculptor, as well. A dancer? Truly no!"[24] Appraising Isadora, Scize regarded her as a sculpture of flesh with movements ecstatic and of prayerful supplication; he beheld in her the collision of two worlds—ancient and modern, Dionysus in full sunlight and Jesus in Christian austerity: the reign of humiliation and sacrifice. "And when the splendid statue of flesh finally lies outstretched under its shroud as the bells and fanfares of the Grail ring out a new Assumption, we realize that something august came to pass here—a kind of Mass for paganism crucified. But who, then, who said this woman was a dancer?"[25]

Well regarded and of established reputation within the community of writers was Fernand Nozière, alias Guy Launay. Under either name he was a staunch partisan of Isadora, strongly receptive to her form of dramatic expression and humbled by the physical beauty of her movements. Throughout the year-long extravaganza his reviews recorded some of the details and on-stage actions in the lesser known choreographies. In his sensitivity to his subject, Nozière was able to depict clearly the physical woman as well as her creative spirit, and her intellectual and psychological influence on the spectator.[26]

Observing her during the Easter week concert, Nozière profiled Isadora noting that she had the decorative beauty of the angels imagined by the artists of the Renaissance. Her arms extended were caressing, "heavenly nourishment"; the slope of her neck, the clearness of the gaze, and the smile on her lips were "evocative of those Botticelli compositions . . . of a religious serenity." (César Franck's oratorio in three parts, *Redemption*, was based on a poetic text that set forth and acclaimed the spiritual reformation. Isadora danced only the second part, the "Symphonic Interlude," in which she conveyed the regenerative transformation of mankind's depravity into the age of enlightenment. It was first performed on April 9, 1916, at the Trocadéro for a war charity matinee.) Nozière began by describing Isadora as having risen from the dust. First sitting, then kneeling, she executed a sequence of positions that were forceful and tremendously stirring, "calling to mind Bourdelle's sculptural studies of the torso." With deliberate resolve she steadily pulled herself upward, "as the seed raises itself to the sun. Standing erect, her hand signals the canopy of heaven and the revelation of divinity. It is simple and it is great."

For her picturesque movement images to Berlioz's *L'Enfance du Christ*, Isadora brought a quality of light and the sparkle of joy. Through Nozière's eyes, a woman lingered maternally before the divine child, lovingly regarding his slumber. She smiled to him, rocked him, and suddenly, "accompanied by flutes and harp, she goes off seeking wondrous gifts for him: brilliant, full flowers, fruits of luscious shape and color, rich fragrances." All the while, the critic observed, the dancer scarcely touched the floor, gliding with an ethereal grace that enveloped onlookers, including Nozière, in an atmosphere of awe.

Of Tchaikovsky's Sixth Symphony Nozière reported the following:

> The orchestra plays the Adagio [first movement]. The Scherzo [second movement] inspires Isadora. She is the Isadora Duncan we have known, the one who runs blithely across the green and gathers a flower, who dances in sunlight, and who abandons herself to her youthfulness. It is the Isadora of yesterday—the one numerous ballerinas have imitated; she now appears to be imitating herself. But the Allegro Vivace [third movement] reveals the new Isadora Duncan . . . She has become the very symbol of battle—of its intoxication, its sadness, its glory. With her index finger she seems to have traced on the pediment of the temple a sign of heroic duty. When her forces diminish, when she seems to waver, she returns to this sacred and radiant inscription where she renews her courage and vigor . . . It is no longer a woman who dances—it is a divinity rousing the crowd. Behind her she urges a whole people toward a superhuman task—toward challenges, toward triumph. Alone on stage, nevertheless, a feverish procession follows, walks, and dances with her toward invisible arcs on which are inscribed the superb criteria of heroism, dedication, goodness.

It is in the fourth movement, the Adagio Lamentoso, that Nozière gave testimony to Isadora's intense imagination and emotive depths. With forceful symbolism she is earth-mother in a dolorous plaint for the slain in battle. A striking metaphor for maternal grief, she kneels and weeps for the dead children of man, and with an immense, surging movement of torso and arms, she wrests them from the void, pressing them against her body, to shelter within her womb. The critic wrote: "Such feelings demand symphonic scope. Beyond words is the sublimity of these movements; the most moving, most profound and human homage that could have been rendered the dead."

No longer suggestive of Greek sculpture or Botticelli paintings, Isadora's arrangement of the march toward the Holy Grail from Wagner's *Parsifal* transformed her into a Wagnerian hero, "posing the eternal polemic of Dionysus and Christ, earth and heaven, darkness and light, the weight of lust, and liberation through renunciation." There was authority, subtlety, and nobility in her characterization of Kundry: "How she makes us feel the torment of doubt, the invigoration of faith, the hesitancy of anguish, the ascent toward the light." As for her *Death of Isolde* (dramatized on about four square feet of space), Nozière had reached a verbal impasse: "I give up explaining it; I bow before this marvel of intelligence . . . of the sublime artist and the creator [Wagner]."

Neither nymph nor bacchante, Isadora's art had become prouder. She was seen as a powerful sculpture, her gestures more solemn, her stances solid and her expressions intense. Criticized elsewhere for her unsatisfactory conception of the frail Isolde, Nozière questioned whether it was ever Isadora's intention to interpret the legendary princess. "It is not the heroine," Nozière conjectured, "but the very inspiration of the composer that she strives to manifest in the music. There are formidable forces of love and death in evidence here."

Music critic Louis Laloy, however, who justifiably took credit as one of the first critical voices to herald the arrival of Isadora's unusual and earnest talent, now persisted in objecting to her free adaptations from Wagner, whose music was least representational for dance purposes. Meritorious though they may be, her energetic evocations of the *Ride of the Walkyries*, the "Bacchanale" from *Tannhäuser*, or Isolde's *Love-Death*, were not works, Laloy cautioned, to become models for other artists of the dance, or replacements for classical ballets. "Isadora Duncan's dance is not, and cannot be, the whole dance."

Just as Isadora's *Blue Danube* waltz years earlier had brought ecstatic audiences to their feet, her *La Marseillaise,* since its first performance in wartime Paris in 1916 had ignited the public's fervor. Unsurpassed for its sheer theatrical power, this semi-mimed interpretation of man's eternal quest for freedom produced the *tour de force* of her career. It remained a crowd favorite whether performed in Europe, South America or the United States. Audiences wept and went wild.

Allan Ross Macdougall, friend, secretary, and biographer of Isadora, described the emotional outburst that rang through the Trocadéro in 1916 when the dancer, robed in a blood-red tunic and red shawl, mimed with "incredible intensity" the four stanzas of the French anthem: "She stood filled with patriotic fury, her left breast bare as in the Rude statue in the Arc de Triomphe which had been her inspiration . . . "

François Rude's 1836 sculpture relief in stone on the lower right quadrant of the Arc de Triomphe in Paris overwhelms in its personification of Liberty. The central figure of the *Marseillaise* herself "raises high her left arm to rally all the brave to her side. With the other hand she points her sword toward the enemy. Her legs are wide apart. Her mouth of stone shrieks as though to deafen one." An examination of the sculpture and then a closer study of the art and photographic reproductions of Isadora reveal an almost literal transfer from the physical force of the stone's gesture and its embodiment of patriotic ardor to the dancer's bodily stances and expressive demeanor.

For anti-war intellectuals and those on the political left in the United States, the dancer's overpowering effect and success in her *Marseillaise* were a severe disillusionment. Up to now she had been a symbol to them of "life lived frank and free"; they now rebuked their lady of liberty for accelerating American pro-war sentiments.

For quite different reasons, sounds of disapproval came from a small critical enclave in Paris. Isadora's dance translation of the French anthem during her 1920–21 festival once again raised the familiar dichotomous issue: the appropriateness of dancing to certain kinds of music, specifically a literary piece and none other than the supreme pride of France—the national anthem. It was an affront to the public! Tampering with the Rouget de Lisle poem to indulge choreographic whims was an impiety! One did not desecrate a glorious poem by dancing it. "Botch the works of foreign composers," [27] she was told, but leave their compatriot alone.

Also biased in favor of the French "soul" as alone capable of appreciating and conveying the *Marseillaise*, was Emile Mas.[28] Generally supportive of her other undertakings, he rejected Isadora's dramatization. Her fierce stances, the unattractive facial grimaces, then her unbecomingly lively change were seen as a grievous error. She understood nothing of his anthem! Less mocking than disappointed, he described how at one point in the dance when she had not stirred, one hand was finally raised up and cupped around her ear, leaving the impression that she wanted to telephone. This *Marseillaise* was not theirs!

The excerpt that follows appeared in print after a 1920 performance of the *Marseillaise*.[29] Incomplete, it nevertheless comes closest to being a choreographed text and provides vivid clues to the dancer's movement phrase in correlation with word and music. This choreographic description ends at the point of the galvanizing refrain, "Aux Armes, Citoyens" (To Arms, Citizens), when the entire hall breaks loose into feet stamping, hand clapping, and general commotion climaxing the dance.

LA MARSEILLAISE

ALLONS ENFANTS DE LA PATRIE

The dancer places her right foot in front and raises the right arm. Hand is wide open, fingers separated, palm facing the audience, her fixed glance is in the direction of the first balcony.

LE JOUR DE GLOIRE EST ARRIVÉ

The torso is brought forward, plexus trained on the first balcony, the mouth in the direction of the second balcony and the eyes on the rim of the theater; both arms are flung backwards, lightly raised from the body and forming an angle with it of approximately twenty-two degrees. The right foot rejoins the left foot which has not moved.

CONTRE NOUS DE LA TYRANNIE

Here the dance begins. The dancer steps off with the left foot and executes a half turn of the stage while moving to the right and seeming to hold some invisible cord: it is this "pulling" that designates the "tyranny" of which the poet de Lisle speaks.

L'ÉTENDARD SANGLANT EST LEVÉ

The dancer stops point blank in the rear center stage. She raises both arms high above her head which has been thrown backward. At this moment the spot lights hit her robe with a flaming red color.

ENTENDEZ-VOUS DANS LES CAMPAGNES

The ear is thrust toward the east and the gaze becomes strangely pained; the arm at that side is stretched out to this central point; the foot of that side readies to move.

MUGIR CES FEROCES SOLDATS

The dance begins again here and the dancer does the second half turn on stage while pushing with feet and hands against the on-rushing forces. The forcefulness of the feet is obtained by first causing the thighs, then the calves, to quiver. As for the hands, the powerful vibrations from the upper arm muscles tremble down through the entire arm, through the palms.

ILS VIENNENT JUSQUE DANS NOS BRAS

The dancer has returned to center stage. Starting first with the left arm, she slaps herself across the right arm, then, simultaneously on both arms, each with only four fingers of the opposite hand.

ARRACHER NOS FILS, NOS COMPAGNES

There are gestures of wresting, battle, struggle, resurge, and at the end, despair. The wresting on "arra," the battle on "cher nos," struggle on "fils nos," the resurge on "comp," despair on "gnes." These movements must be synchronized to produce their full effect.

Looming large on the Duncan landscape was Fernand Divoire, editor-in-chief of *L'Intransigeant*, dance critic, and author of works on theater and dance. One of the most consistent and interested of witnesses to the growth of Isadora's influence on twentieth-century theater, Divoire was devoted to "Isadorism." His published writings contain major segments on her dominant choreographies and her individual artistry, on Duncanism as an art ideology, and on the Isadorables as the fruition of an ideal vision. Commenting on Isadora's 1920–1921 Paris appearances, Divoire discerned an ever-evolving artist, surprisingly more supple and diverse, "richer of fine and fluid ease, more replenished. And the curve of her gesture each time seemed larger and bolder." Divoire next saw her in 1923. He sensed, as did others, her bodily fatigue, her spiritual frailty. He made mention of the lost happiness, the many sadnesses, and the greatness: "Have they not withered and wearied her spirit?" Through Divoire's compassionate, humane words could be heard genuine empathy from one long attracted to Isadora as a person and as an artist. The body on stage that had so captivatingly articulated beauty, grace, and strength, now registered the cumulative effect of life's multiple tragedies and thwarted dreams. (Coinciding with Isadora's appearance at the Trocadéro in May 1923 was her realization that her chaotic relationship and marriage to the Russian poet Essenin would have to be dissolved.)

Erudite, aristocratic André Levinson critiqued Isadora's concert of May 27, 1923, explaining first how repugnant it was for him to speak about the physical decay of an artist and the inevitable ravages of time, but then proceeding to do so.[30] From the entire performance a single memory remained with him. "I see again the dancer, arms crossed as on an imaginary crucifix, torso slumped, knees bent, limbs . . . brutally apart. Then the head falls, the torso following it and the short hair brushes the floor. These two positions, while close to the grotesque, attain a painful grandeur." He referred to the Tchaikovsky and Scriabin that Isadora interpreted, as "music of the defeated and frenzied Russians. But it is the music that is necessary for Mme. Duncan; it is the score that provides the emotive shock, the psychological stimulant."

Levinson possessed a refinement and specialized knowledge of the theatrical arts that made his critical essays of the heretic Isadora stand in a class by themselves. On record in *Comoedia*, *Les Nouvelles Littéraires*, and in many published volumes are his contributions distinguished for their precise detailing of Isadora's gesture in its physical character and subtleties of expression, in its mimetic clarity and persuasive manner of projection. But his nineteenth-century elitist sensibility found much to challenge in "the intrinsic value of her reform." He seriously questioned her claim that through the unrestricted movements of the body lay endless paths to one's identity and individuality. With his rational criticism, the sophisticated Levinson intellectualized deeper resentments toward her: her dance vocabulary was too simple, she subjugated the dance to music, she lacked formal elements in her dance, and— the source of blatant irritation to him—she dared to reject the time-honored classic traditions and scorn a distinguished esthetic order, a most venerable discipline. Ultimately, he was certain that Isadora's "negation of all doctrine" would doom her role as evangelist. All the more was his wonderment over the "psychic contagion" by which the barefoot dancer was able to win the "enthusiasm of an immense public."

There was obvious chagrin when Levinson charged Isadora with wrenching theatrical dance out of the gentle and caring hands of the privileged few, democratizing it through her open, revolutionary channels. Her dance, he contended, would release the floodgates of dilettantism and imitation. Levinson could not conceal his private dismay and frustration that the brilliant and royal art of ballet that he loved, his sacred and "golden art," his personal fantasyland, had been invaded, injured, and changed by the woman who, for the integrity of her ideals, "braved all, risked all," and who, "by a miracle of will and faith . . . had imprinted her seal on a whole epoch." How to explain the complacency, the impotence of ballet officialdom in not launching a counteroffensive to Isadora's esthetic onslaught? Almost sheepishly, André Levinson surmised that they, too, had been "captivated by the glowing candor of the intrepid amazon."

Levison did not acknowledge Isadora's dance as a viable art form. His analyses were thoughtful, forthright, penetrating, and beautifully written. In essence, he appreciated her negatively, but for her convictions, her sovereign presence, and her effect on the world's perception of dance, his admiration was boundless.

These men of letters, composers, dramatists, opera and theater critics, poets, and journalists were prominent chroniclers of their time. Out of their own diversities of temperament and esthetic proclivities they presented the many facets of Isadora Duncan, all somehow valid and appropriate for the complex, larger-than-life persona and her individual imprint on a culture in transition. Their words alone, in this instance, have become the conservators of one unique being's creative existence. Collectively, their writings constitute the principal archive of Isadora's twenty-five-year effort to convert the consciousness of the world to the dance as art.

NOTES

1. George Delaquys, "Isadora Duncan," *Mercure de France*, December 15, 1906, pp. 539, 542.
2. *Ibid.*, p. 544.
3. Louis Laloy, "Isadora Duncan et la danse nouvelle," *La Revue Musicale*, 1904.
4. Louis Untermeyer, "Isadora Duncan Dancing (Iphigenia in Aulis)," in E. Dickson, *Poems of the Dance*, p. 243.

I

Fling the stones and let them all lie;
Take a breath and toss the ball high. . . .
And before it strikes the floor
Of the hoar and ancient shore,
Sweep them up, though there should be
Even more than two or three.
Add a pebble, then once more
Fling the stones and let them all lie;
Take a breath, and toss the ball high. . . .

II

Rises now the sound of ancient chants
And the circling figure treads more slowly,
Thus the risen gods themselves must dance
While the world grows rapturous and holy,
Thus the gods might dream a new Romance
Moving to the sound of flute and psalter;
Till the last of all the many chants,
And the priestess sinks before the altar.

III

Cease, oh cease the murmured singing;
    Hush the numbers brave or blythe;
For she enters, gravely swinging;
    Lowering and lithe—
Dark and vengeful as the ringing
    Scythe meets scythe.

While the flame is fiercely sweeping,
    All her virgin airs depart;

She is without smiles and weeping,
Or a maiden's art,
Stern and savage as the leaping
Heart meets heart.

IV
Now the tune grows frantic,
Now the torches flare—
Wild and corybantic
Echoes fill the air.
With a sudden sally,
All the voices shout;
And the bacchic rally
Turns into a rout.

Here is life that surges
Through each burning vein;
Here is joy that purges
Every creeping pain.
Even sober sadness
Casts aside her pall,
Till with buoyant madness
She must swoon and fall.

5. Clearly evident from the numerous and differing programs featuring the *Iphigénie* was the variability of its format. The orchestral score was supplemented at times with principal voices (Clytemnestra and Iphigenia), or a small singing chorus seated in the orchestra, or a speaking chorus, or poetic readings from a text interspersed. Initially conceived as a solo vehicle, Isadora gradually allowed her maturing disciples to dance certain segments.
6. André Marty, *Comoedia Illustré*, February 1909, p. 122.
7. Isadora Duncan, *My Life*, pp. 122–123.
8. Jeanne Gazeau, "Isadora Duncan," *Les Entretiens Idéalistes*, December 25, 1909, pp. 299–305.
9. Ovion, "Les danses d'Isadora Duncan," *Mercure de France*, March 1910, pp. 69–82.
10. Walter Rummel, "Isadora et ses élèves," Program notes for Trocadero performances, December 11 and 16, 1920.
11. Paul Souday, "Representations de Mlle. Isadora Duncan," *Excelsior*, January 1911.
12. Pierre Lalo, *Le Temps*, January 24, 1911.
13. Reynaldo Hahn, "La Musique," unidentified source, March 29, 1913.
14. Gluck believed that neither time nor fashion were relevant for the survival of certain of his scores and that equal pleasure could be reaped two centuries hence. Isadora as well perceived the style and form of her dance as resistant to temporal influences.
15. Reynaldo Hahn, "La Musique," unidentified source, March 29, 1913.
16. *Ibid.*
17. Michel Georges-Michel, "La Danseuse Nue," *Gil Blas*, December 7, 1911.
18. *Ibid.*
19. Waldemar George, "La danse et l'esprit moderne," unidentified source, July 26, 1920.
20. Paul Abrams, "Propos de Théâtre," unidentified sources, March 8, 1920, and April 5, 1920.

21. P. Fontrailles, "Isadora Duncan au Trocadéro," unidentified source, March 8, 1920.
22. *Ibid.*
23. Fernand Noziere, "Isadora Duncan," unidentified source, March 8, 1920.
24. Pierre Scize, "Isadora danse," unidentified source, April 4, 1920.
25. *Ibid.*
26. Fernand Nozière, "Un Festival de danse et de musique," unidentified source, November 29, 1920.
27. Antoine Banès, review of Isadora Duncan in performance at Théâtre des Champs-Elysées, unidentified source, January 27, 1921.
28. Emile Mas, "Les Prèmieres, Théâtre des Champs-Elysées," unidentified source, January 27, 1921.
29. Jean Bastia, "Au Champs-Elysées," unidentified source, January 27, 1921.
30. André Levinson, "Mme. Isadora Duncan au Trocadéro," *Comoedia-Illustré*, May 29, 1923.

CHAPTER SEVEN

Artists and Confrères

Abraham Walkowitz

"His work is his personality. . . . absence of pretension and strife . . . affection for humanity . . . a living antithesis of the academic . . . composed of lineaments, formations, tonalities that precisely correspond to the feeling engendered by nature . . . rhythmical feeling . . . impelled by the inner necessity."

OSCAR BLUEMNER

THESE WORDS INTRODUCE THE painter Abraham Walkowitz—the kindly, loquacious, pink-cheeked little man considered in his time one of America's avant-garde artists. Born in western Siberia, most of his life was spent in the United States. He studied art at Cooper Union and the National Academy of Design, continuing his studies at the renowned Académie Julien in Paris, where he came under the influence of Matisse and Rodin. Throughout his life Walkowitz would retain the impression made upon him by the memorial exhibition of Cézanne's paintings in 1907 in Paris. By 1912, Walkowitz's paintings were included in 291, the gallery run by Alfred

Stieglitz. The following year found him represented in the historic 1913 Armory Show that spurred the modern art movement in the United States. The Zabriskie Gallery in 1976 featured both Stieglitz and Walkowitz in an exhibit, *The "291" Years: 1912–1917*, one of the latest exhibitions to present Walkowitz as an artist representative of the formative years of a modern style in American art.

The gentleness of the man and the quality of his painting are immediately apparent upon contact with his subtle and delicate palette. His subjects center around people: where they live, at play and rest in parks, bathing in clear ponds, mothers and children, fishermen working their nets, bearded Jewish scholars of the Lower East Side in traditional garb. His is a "lyrical tenderness, naive but with grace." A retrospective of his work in October 1964 drew a critic's comment: "These paintings are the fresh, direct and felt impressions of an artist who communicated his feelings with youthful daring without abandoning his inherent simplicity and warmth."[1]

Walkowitz first saw Isadora Duncan dance in 1908, the year she returned from Europe as a celebrated performer. She revealed for him "an artistic fervor of great dignity he had not known before."

> In all his figures there is the poetry of subtle, mystical insight,
> especially in the figure of Isadora Duncan. How tender and
> caressing they are; how filled with psychological insight. He
> creates in a kind of intangible musicality of mood.[2]

It is reported that the dancer had encouraged the painter to work in her studio where he could sketch the structural workings of the human body, a subject that made him turn again and again to her moving figure. She became the turning point in his life. That Isadora Duncan was important to Abraham Walkowitz in more than the sphere of artistic influence was disclosed by art critic Alfred Werner. Walkowitz had loved her and her death "robbed [him] of all desire to live and work."[3] The paintings he would produce in later years were "without consequence and incentive."

The infinite variations of her moving body that constitute his record of impressions are an invaluable source for documenting the past as for indicating future perspectives of Isadora Duncan. In his myriad and swirling forms are visions of the dancer's art, "in every mood, in every posture, through the entire range of human emotion." By recreating her movement in his line drawings Walkowitz, in Carl Van Vechten's appraisal, captures "the precise feeling of her rhythm, the precision and intensity of her line, her flowing grace, and the massive proportions which served her to design nobility."[4] In this regard, Walkowitz may have come closest to "completely analyzing and describing and reviewing the work of another artist in another medium." For photographer Arnold Genthe, the lack of filmed record of the dancer "is a calamity." He sees the work of Walkowitz assuming a "special significance for posterity's perception of Duncan's dance art."[5]

Evidence of his fascination and preoccupation with Isadora is the staggering quantity of drawings, estimated to be more than three thousand. Using pencil or pen-and-ink enriched by watercolor, most of the sketches, Walkowitz told this writer, were done from memory—the memory of a love and inspiration that guided the artist's hand to create repeatedly in her image. So complete a record of her every posture and rhythmic design are his impressions that they become testimony before the residue of false interpretations of her as dancer of sentimentality and naiveté. They establish the more accurate conception of the woman who explored the broadest range of emotional experience. Walkowitz's Isadora was

> a woman who was ponderable; a body incomparably alive,
> mobile, graceful, expressive, but a body that had weight; feet that
> could stamp; legs that could brace to the earth as firmly as a
> peasant's. . . . No delicate creature, but a woman of flesh and
> bone and passion. . . . Only such a woman could have made the
> dance . . . so intense, so overmastering an art.[6]

Today, Walkowitz is best remembered for the Isadora Duncan drawings and is rarely disassociated from her. "The vibrant Californian Isadora found her most devoted celebrant in the gnomic Siberian Walkowitz," was Shaemas O'Sheel's droll observation.

"This exhibition is the presentation of an experiment," Walkowitz wrote in his foreword to the museum catalog for the large, colorful, and thought-provoking exhibition "One Hundred Artists and Walkowitz," which took place at the Brooklyn Museum of Art in 1944. Walkowitz had proposed a challenge to his artist friends: explore the relationship between artist and the object to be portrayed, a dynamic "complicated and little understood." The medium, form, and interpretation would be each artist's choice; the object was to be Abraham Walkowitz. The results would be based on his premise that no two people see the same subject in the same way; furthermore, that artists reveal themselves more than the object they portray. His premises were borne out. The unique project brought together one hundred creative pieces covering a wide range of media, including oil, pastel, watercolor paintings; sculptures in stone, wood, plaster; and photographs. Among the participants in the experimental event were painters Reginald Marsh,

Guy Pene du Bois, Raphael Soyer, Gifford Beal, Alexander Brook, Milton Avery, Yasuo Kuniyoshi, Moise Kisling, Isabel Bishop; sculptors Chaim Gross, William Zorach, Max Weber; photographers Alfred Stieglitz, Arnold Genthe, and Carl van Vechten. The dancing figure of Isadora Duncan—as a decorative motif around the subject Walkowitz—was a repeated theme.

Through his generosity and foresight much of his prolific output can be found in major art institutions throughout the country. Among the museums are the Whitney, Metropolitan, Brooklyn, Newark, Philadelphia, Boston and Washington. The Dance Collection of the New York Public Library at Lincoln Center received a large collection from him in 1952. Those drawings sampled in the archives of print departments of museums and in private collections demonstrate the extraordinary evolution in Walkowitz's rendering of the dancing figure. The closer the distance between artist and model (the early years when he drew from immediate impressions), the more realistically delineated is the treatment of the anatomy. Between the drawn lines the able draftsman suggests volume of space and weight of gesture.

Two fine pencil studies dated 1910 are of this early period and style. One of her standing form is in a dance attitude from the series of movement studies inspired by the figurines from Tanagra, which Duncan taught to her pupils. The quiet grace and repose of this solidly drawn figure contrasts with the second study. Here the dancer's form, sturdy and full, displays a concentration of force in the torso that seems to propel the arms overhead. Quite characteristic of Walkowitz's early work is his use of a great surface area and large figures, as well as his introduction of watercolors. The dancer's costumes are in strong reds, yellows, blues and oranges; backgrounds are washed in color with rhythmic brush strokes activating her soaring motions.

Later, the surface area was reduced, the body configuration less defined, the wash was paler in hue, and the backgrounds less intrusive. Still later, the sketches were no larger than two by seven inches. Though the pen-and-ink lines are astonishingly facile, the image—the moving body—is all but dematerialized; its essence embodied in the design of linear abstraction, graceful, curving strokes, charged with energy.

Waning interest in his work and the deterioration of his eyesight that eventually led to his blindness separated him from the community of art and discouraged his creative activity. American artist Raphael Soyer speaks in his memoirs of his white-haired, rosy-faced colleague who for years was seen on 57th Street in museums, at concerts and dance recitals, and then, "dropped out of the artistic scene of New York."[7] However, Walkowitz was honored before his death by an award from the American Institute of Arts and Letters and a standing ovation from the audience.

Isadora in Iphigénia, pen and watercolor by José Clará. (Collection of the author)

Marche Slav, pen and watercolor by José Clará. (Collection of the Museo Clará, Barcelona)

Love Death of Isolde, watercolor by Joseph Paget-Fredericks. Based on Isadora's last concert at Mogador Theater, Paris, 1927. (Collection of the Fine Arts Museum of San Francisco)

La Marseillaise, *bas relief on Arc de Triomphe by Francine Rude. (Roger Viollet Collection)*

Isadora in La Marseillaise. Drawing by José Clará. 1916.

*Pencil studies by Abraham
Walkowitz, 1910.
(Collection of the author)*

Poster attributed to Kees van Dongen, but possibly by Antoine Bourdelle.
(Roger Viollet Collection)

Isadora, ink and watercolor by Antoine Bourdelle. (Collection of the author)

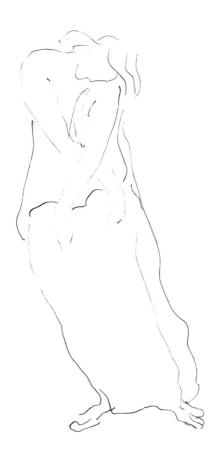

Tristesse, *pen and ink by Antoine Bourdelle. (Courtesy of Rhodia Dufet and the Musée Bourdelle)*

Gravitation, *pen and ink by Antoine Bourdelle. (Courtesy of Rhodia Dufet and the Musée Bourdelle)*

Danse des Scythes, *first study.*
Pen and ink by Antoine Bourdelle.
(Courtesy of Rhodia Dufet and
the Musée Bourdelle)

Danse des Scythes,
second study. Pen and ink
by Antoine Bourdelle.
(Courtesy of Rhodia Dufet
and the Musée Bourdelle)

Isadora, print by Maxwell Stewart Simpson. (Collection of the author)

Isadora surrounded by (left to right) *André Arnyveld, Edward Steichen, Henri Gervex, Kees van Dongen* (holding the dancer's left hand), *Antoine Bourdelle* (holding her right hand), *and an unidentified man* (behind Bourdelle).
(Roger Viollet Collection)

(left to right) *Elizabeth, Augustin, and Raymond Duncan.*
(Roger Viollet Collection)

Raymond Duncan and his partner, Aia Bertrand, on a quay along the Seine, Paris, October 1963. (Roger Viollet Collection)

(overleaf) *Isadora, Paris, 1913, photographer unknown. (Collection of the author)*

* * *

Toward the beginning of 1965, I interviewed the blind and ailing Walkowitz—only weeks before his death.[8] On that day he was alert, receptive, and most patient with questions. His voice was steady and his thoughts were clear and came easily to him. What he had to say rang with the confidence and conviction that longevity can bestow.

With eyesight he might have realized that we had met twenty-five years earlier at dance recitals or in the hospitable Horn and Hardart cafeteria down the street from Carnegie Hall. There, with a handful of nickels for endless cups of coffee and a few young dancers eager to listen, he held forth on Art, Dance, and Isadora Duncan. The occasion of this later meeting provided a long-desired opportunity to express gratitude for his Duncan line drawings in that they made vivid the splendid clarity of line and fluidity of motion that were marvelously unique to this woman.

He spoke of his awareness of dance as beginning with Isadora. She was not to be explained, he kept reiterating. "You had to feel the movement she made. . . . She was a creator and creation is never imitation. You must break all laws and rules of art. She broke laws and rules to create her art. . . . But she was never the same in her dances. Always changing. In the same dance the interpretation would be different."

The subject of his youth in Paris evoked a warmth and sincerity of response. "France allowed the artist freedom for creation. That country valued and respected creative people. Without France, Isadora wouldn't be Isadora. And there is only one Isadora. The French created her and the French got the best of her." He felt strongly that Paris was where the dance was born to Isadora and where many artists, as himself, had been inspirationally enriched by their encounter with the art of the American dancer. "In order to complete Isadora, to really know her, you must go to Paris. I tell you, you must go to France to find Isadora."

Antoine Bourdelle

"A sculptor is inevitably attracted to a dancer. Theirs are complementary arts. Dance is the movement forever tending toward a pose; sculpture is the pose suggesting movement. The body evokes the marble; the marble dreams of flesh."

FRISCH/SHIPLEY

Rue Antoine Bourdelle, within the shadow of the old Gare Montparnasse, bears the name of this gentle and esteemed sculptor from Languedoc. Down this obscure and unimpressive little street one comes upon a wall and a gate behind which is housed, unexpectedly the loveliest, museum in Paris—the Musée Bourdelle.

Entering through the tall wrought-iron gate was like following Alice though her looking glass into the unexpected—a sanctuary of green shrubberies, slender young trees, and Bourdelle's sculptures, none more imposing than the larger-than-life-size *Penelope*, at the rear of the garden. Huge and majestic, she stands somewhat wistful, the columnar folds of her sculpted gown giving a gentle sway to the full, womanly form. Directly behind her lies the entrance to the museum, a large, new structure connected to the original quarters and studio of Bourdelle, and before him, the atelier of the symbolist painter, Eugène Carrière.

Antoine Bourdelle came to my attention by way of his drawings of Isadora, that illustrated a handful of books available in the United States in the 1960s. In his early recognition of Isadora's unique dance art, Bourdelle was not alone among sculptors. The French Rodin, the Spanish Clara, and later in America, Lorado Taft, Gutzon Borglum, and George Gray Barnard—all found a magic in the sculptural form of her movements and in the eloquence of her mobile body. But Bourdelle, who in his writings acknowledged the profound way in which her dance influenced his creative life, was the one to visibly embody the rhythmic design and dramatic character of her gesture into his stone and clay forms.

The collection of drawings of the dancer preserved in the archives of the Musée Bourdelle sparked my curiosity. I envisioned scores of dance action impressions revealing more specifically the nature of her gesture; I anticipated uncovering references to choreographies that vanished with Isadora's death. I viewed this as an archaeological expedition.

I made the necessary arrangements to spend time at Musée Bourdelle and was cordially received by the sculptor's daughter, Rhodia Dufet and her husband, Michel Dufet—the present curators of the museum—and the sculptor's widow, Mme. Cléopâtre Bourdelle.

My orientation to the museum began with a tour of the galleries. The multilingual Mme. Bourdelle assumed her able role as personal docent, thus eliminating any communication barriers. Starting in the old studio we entered one room of overwhelming impact. The entire area was dedicated to that musical genius, Beethoven. Cléo Bourdelle told me of her husband's long affinity and reverence for the composer. A photograph of the sculptor when young bears a strong likeness to the young Beethoven. It was said of Bourdelle that the shepherds of his childhood played the flutes of Pan but it was Beethoven's music that sang through the pipes. Beginning in 1880 and continuing until the final year of his life, he returned repeatedly to the Beethoven theme, producing dozens of studies—heads, torsos, the hand, the draped full-length figure, Beethoven with long hair, a mask—in various media—gouache, chalk, bronze, stone, and plaster. There was Beethoven, contemplative, scowling, anguished, melancholy, but always monumental.

In this room I understood Rodin's statement in which he observed "a fire . . . a poet and a sculptor . . . deliciously strong" in Bourdelle.[9] Here, where Beethoven dominated, the intellectual and artistic bond between Isadora Duncan and Antoine Bourdelle became apparent; the composer and his music served both artists as a major source and focus for their creative ventures.

That the dancer and the sculptor shared an ideological ancestry was readily manifested in the exhibits that followed. In common they espoused a concept of the human ideal by incorporating in their work sentiments of character nobility and grandeur of spirit as revealed to them in their study of the ancient arts. For Bourdelle, the heroic proportions and craftsmanship of the Grecian archaic sculpture and architecture had lasting influence. For Isadora, the idealized movements of figures adorning urns, friezes, and temples of antiquity, in their varied states of naturalness and simplicity of manner, formed the shape and philosophic root of her dance.

The sculptor and his muse, Isadora, did not dwell nostalgically in these past regions nor did they revert to emulating or reviving the old images. Quite the contrary. Each took from the past to endow the future. Each, a modern artist, forged in an individual medium of art a vigorous originality. However, in their assertion of the primacy of the human spirit and in the lyrical vein that flowed through their work, one cannot deny that the products of both their oeuvres glowed with the expressive beauty and intellectual energy of the earlier civilizations. Both, declared Mme. Bourdelle, shared the grand monumental character of the "époque" in their art.

My knowledgeable guide next led me into the Salle des Monuments, the new wing built to accommodate the unusual height of many of the sculptures, some, more than three times life-size. Her husband's favorite model, Mme. Bourdelle's features were recognizable in the marbles and the bronzes. Nowhere was there a work on display of Isadora herself, as the woman or as the performer. Yet, her presence emerges throughout the large gallery, in the *Fragment of the Monument to the Falcon* (1911), in the *Study for the Soca Memorial in Montevideo* (1927). From the sculptured folds of the figure's tunic, to the form discernible beneath the woman's garment and in the heroic stance and gaze—there is Isadora. Despite the fact that she resisted posing for Bourdelle and did so on only one or two occasions (she disliked posing, in general), "she was la grande inspiratrice," Mme. Bourdelle remarked frequently.

Bourdelle had been given the prestigious but challenging commission to create daring art works for Paris' most modern Théâtre des Champs-Elysées, the newest home for the arts of music, dance, and theater. Impresario Gabriel Astruc, always motivated by a taste for novelty and pomp, envisioned this new structure as the center of luxury and opulence. At the time of its inauguration in 1913, the theater stood as the most interesting architectural structure in Paris, but its Art Deco design polarized its critics, although not for long. The building went on to make theatrical history.

Bourdelle's eight bas-reliefs, powerful and original, ornamented the marble facade of the theater. In the gallery of the museum, along the length of the walls, were numerous large plaster studies in high relief, executed in preparation for this assignment. The arresting, three-panelled frieze that comprises the *Meditation of Apollo* and decorates the pediment of the theater was created as a direct consequence of Isadora's influence, Michel Dufet has indicated in his writings on Bourdelle. It is an excellent example of the sculptor's ingenuity in portraying the nine muses as they move toward and surround the central figure of the God and his lyre; how he was able to contrast the postures of their moving forms and subtly alter their essential sameness, for as Mme. Bourdelle pointed out, they all were Isadora? "She was his principal source." Not only did the figures carry the imprint of her élan, but also her physical characteristics—a facial feature, the shape of her thigh, the positioning of the head and neck, and the Duncanesque arm gestures.

Models in terra cotta and in plaster for the theater's frescoes, pillars and panels, could be examined at close range. Today they still enrich the Théâtre des Champs-Elysées' once ultra modern interior. Bourdelle's fresco *Leda*, his *L'Ame Passionée* (*Impassioned Soul*), are suggestive in their mood quality, of the "inspiratrice."

Most commemorative and admired is Bourdelle's famous marble haut-relief, "La Danse," on the theater's exterior, above the entrance doors. A single figure in the preliminary design phase, "La Danse" then became two graceful, rhythmic forms, one facing the other, and both Isadora. Several revisions and versions later, the figures in their final state were male and female, face to face and in a "trance" of dance. Described by Bourdelle to his students during a sculpture class, they were Isadora and Nijinsky. "Two figures facing one another . . . she, her fine head tossed back, closes her eyes to dance within in her pure emotion . . . and he . . . who carries within him the winged genius of birds."

A complex of three theaters in one, the Théâtre des Champs-Elysées proved to be a monument to the decorative arts. Assembled along with Bourdelle for this extraordinary collaborative project were some of France's eminent artists, each contributing in his métier to the decorative scheme inspired by Greek mythology. Of special note for their creative interest in Isadora Duncan were Ker Xavier Roussel, whose drop curtain for the Salle de Comédie (adjoining the main concert hall) was entitled *Fête Dionysiaque* and portrayed nymphs, fauns, Venus, and a Bacchus cortège, and Maurice Denis (theorist of the group of painters known as the NABIS), who dedicated his painting of the cupola of the main auditorium to the glorification of music and dance. The eye travelling around the colorful dome can encounter Orpheus, Bacchus, and a landscape peopled with figures tunicked à la Duncan, with a central figure said to represent Isadora.

On the mezzanine floor of the large theater is the gilden bas-relief, "The Dance," by Maurice Denis. Six child dancers stand in a row, hands linked, their plump bodies in short, sheer chemises, each with a foot slightly raised in a forward movement . . . a scene of innocence and serenity. The Théâtre des Champs-Elysées, while a testimonial to the performing and decorative arts, renders homage as well to Isadora Duncan.

Bourdelle first saw Isadora perform in Paris in 1909 when her career was in full bloom and her appearances frequent. His notes of 1913 relate how, upon seeing her dance, "all the great masterpieces became suddenly animated." It was extraordinary to him that this young woman with so resplendent and supple a beauty of movement could convey the deepest of man's emotions. His amazement never abated. Dufet's *Bourdelle et la Danse* described the artist's astonishment at Isadora's "spirited, trembling flights . . . her frenetic despairs that evoked, at times, as much a powerful violence as a touching tenderness and love." He remained haunted by her sculptural style. Isadora, predisposed to the art of sculpture with its three-dimensional forms, wrote in her essay, "What Dancing Should Be," that "dance and sculpture are the two arts most closely united."[10]

In his pen-and-ink drawings, a technique most direct for capturing Isadora's fleeting gestures, Bourdelle's line images bring us closest to the very moment of the dancer's movement impulse. He rarely, if ever, sketched from the live model, although now and then during a performance (he claimed to have attended them all in Paris) he would make a brief marking to fix a particular detail in his mind, and then, fresh from the concert, would render his study from memory, in pen and ink, occasionally with wash.

In the quiet corner of a room near window light, Rhodia Dufet assembled for me a large number of drawings consisting of papers, roughly 6" x 9", on which the sculptor had produced his facile sketches. As though seized in mid-flight, Isadora is presented in a wide range of studies that bear dates from 1909–1912 and even later. Many of the works have movement titles, while others indicate their choreography source. Most, however, are unidentified.

A series of impressions marked *mouvement calme* reveals Isadora in a standing position and in varying states of relative stillness—a barely stirring hand or foot, a subtle nod of the head, a slight shift of body weight toward one side. For an instant, the observing eye takes in the minimal, outer gestures, but soon senses beneath the visible surface, an inner experience moving up from some deeper center. Bourdelle, in surprising economy of line, suggested the sensitivity, grace of form, and charm of manner rendered by the dancer. This group presents an Isadora of ease, clarity, and intelligence expressed with a dignity both simple and moving.

Bourdelle's individual movement titles allow us to consider Isadora's interpretive scope: Colère (Passion), Invocation, Désespoir (Despair), Espoir (Hope), Fuite (Flight), Le Salut (Greeting). Mood studies depict Furor, Rage, Joy, Turbulence, Triumph, Revolt, and Tempest. In *Les Roses Dispersées* (*Scattered Rose Petals*), and the highly provocative group, *L'Avertissement du Destin* (*Fateful Omen*), we face an Isadora quite different from what some written accounts have led us to believe. We see an intrinsic relationship between the shape of her movement forms and the substance of the drama being interpreted. The gestural expression seems to be evolving out of a reaction to the impact of fear. In an almost spontaneous collision of mind and body, the force of terror causes a sharp contraction of her torso; the hip, distorted, swings out, the head pitches forward, somewhat shielded from the impending blow by her extended arm. The other related pieces of this disturbing set show a grim apprehensiveness as she is impelled to glance behind her, the feet awkwardly arrested at the moment of terror, the body twisting to confront the unknown. Another study presents a startling and prominently drawn eye through which is mirrored her interior chaos. The body line is ungainly, hands and fingers are gripped in frenzy.[11]

Next was a series of unrelated images: A carefree Isadora, youthful and swift and nimble in her scarf play, gentle and bouyant in a light, skipping action with her knee high and her head inclining towards it, a floral garland in her hair; a rapturous Isadora playing the flute while in a delirium of Dionysiac dance. In contrast are the scenes of her in vigorous strides, elastic runs, thrusts, and lunges—the kinetic energy leaping off the small sketch papers.

Certain dances were given numerous treatments, such as the one in which Isadora scored her greatest theatrical appeal—the *Marseillaise*. Bourdelle's pen lines seem to vibrate as they outline the heroic stance and militant expression of its interpreter. Even the fabrics suspended from her outflung arms appear electrically charged. Other illustrations belonged to her repertory staples: compositions from the popular Gluck operas *Orfeo* and

Iphigénie. By far, the most interesting impression from the latter work is the series entitled *Danse des Scythes*. These are robust and compelling delineations from a high point in Isadora's *Iphigénie en Tauride*. They have particular significance when analyzed from a group perspective in that there is obvious sequence of movement transitions, logical conception and structure. They also leave little doubt that this dance revolutionary was aware of movement as spatial design. So related do these individual pieces appear, and so fractional does the interval of time duration between each of them seem, that I was frantic to come up with some imaginary gesture that would act as a passageway from one to the other, thereby setting the Scythian dance in motion.

The strong sculptural quality of Isadora's poses and transitions and the emotional and musical nature of her creative material captured Bourdelle's admiration. His impressions of her over the years affirm certain paramount features of her artistry: the individuality of her performing manner, the graceful curve and elegant line of her body motions, the strength of gestures that gave weight and certainty to her actions, and her riveting expressiveness.

One might well consider the Musée Bourdelle and, by extension, the Théâtre des Champs-Elysées the most unique of repositories reflecting the work of two creative people, one, an artist of the dance whose vitality of movement generated the inspiration of the other, a twentieth-century master of the art of sculpture.

Michel Georges-Michel

This would be my first and only meeting with Michel Georges-Michel, a man who for decades traversed the wide spectrum of French art and theater in the first half of our century. An amateur talent at painting and drawing, he sustained a life-long fascination for the arts and artists. As writer and journalist he recorded the pulse-beat of intellectual and fashionable society of his era. The towering personalities he counted among his friends—Apollinaire, Diaghilev, Duncan, Cocteau, Vlaminck, Picasso, Renoir—were then re-shaping the culture of our age.

In his role as Parisian chronicler, Georges-Michel profiled the "who's who" in pre- and post-World War I France. His news columns were written in an urbane, conversational style marked by satirical humor, sprinkled with wittily sharp observations and no small flair for the melodramatic. He enjoyed a lengthy career as an author and a journalist during which time he reported frequently on Isadora's activities in the concert hall, in her studios, and in her life. Neither his *entre-nous* style nor his seizing of every opportunity to make journalistic capital of what was amusing or eccentric in Isadora Duncan, could disguise his deep admiration for her as woman and as artist.

Illustrative of his more typical literary form is his review of one of Isadora's evenings at the Trocadero, in March 1920. She chose to include on her program Tchaikovsky's *Marche Slav*; the audience's contentious reaction to her interpretation became the subject of Michel Georges-Michel's commentary, "Danse Bolcheviste"?

> They argued fiercely . . . while Isadora Duncan interpreted the *Marche Slav*, an almost unknown work by Tchaikovsky. Here's what happened. During the entire symphonic execution the artist, in the center of the stage, remained in a fiercely crushed position, hands bound behind her back, the face severely contorted, both legs ready to give way—and before this trembling symbol of slavery, the audience gasped. . . . With the opening bars of the old tsarist hymn theme . . . and with each beat, Isadora yields still more . . . sinking to the floor first with one knee, with the other, with a hand, the head, and then, collapses, just as the imperial anthem rises in an exalting and radiant crescendo.
>
> Then, we look at one another. The March continues; Isadora is still down. She stays there until the cannon sounds. At first, she doesn't seem to comprehend, but then she becomes aware that her hands are unbound. She hardly dares to bring them forward in front of her. When she does do so, it is only slowly, ever so slowly. . . . Something happened then that one rarely experiences in the theater—a gesture of interpretive genius such as inspires but one or two in a century: those hands, those pitiful hands, deformed by chains, she brings before her eyes and regards them with so joyous and incredulous a bewilderment that spectators were weeping—not from the horror, but from profound emotion.
>
> It was in the moment when quiet returned that a voice from a loge was heard. 'She is free of Bolshevism!' Then came the storm. 'No, of Tsarism!' . . . other voices shouting out. 'No, from Bolshevism, since you do hear the Russian anthem.' 'Why, no, it's precisely at the moment when the anthem is played that Isadora is weighed down.'

Georges-Michel went on with his story, picked up again several hours after the performance. Several people had gathered in the wee hours of the morning for a supper with Isadora. Present were some titled Englishmen, the "stunning Miss Violet Buckingham Selfridge (all Anglo-Saxon rose splendor under a cowboy hat), the Polish composer Eugene de Morowski (a sad Beethoven with binoculars), the pianist Rummel (the profile of Liszt and the hair of the conqueror, Pezon), M.de Sercy (the face of Laurent-Tailhade and the profile of Nebuchadnezer), Mme. Dalliès (Salome of the Independents), and Rabani (who conducted this *Marche Slav* as fiercely as Isadora danced it)."

The writer's roving eye next caught sight of Isadora as she moved to a Greek chaise where, alone, she sat re-attaching an emerald clasp to the shoulder of her gown. An Englishman approached her and Georges-Michel presented the following dialogue between them.

"Now, tell me, are you liberated from Bolshevism or Tsarism?"

"I don't know."

"How's that—you say you don't know?"

"No. I am free. Isn't that enough? Isn't being free enough?"

"But free of what?"

"I no longer want to know. I want to forget my tyrants . . . "

"I beg of you. It's important for my notes."

"Good heavens, my dear, isn't it sufficient that we are here among friends—free?"

"But free of what?"

"You are really persistent. Here it is three o'clock in the morning, we are having supper, we are free. But you want me to tell you at this very moment, from what I am free?"

"Please!"

Touching her temple with her index finger, Isadora began: "At this hour, I am free of maids, chauffeurs, train travels, restrictions, unlit streets, greeting people I don't know. It's time for me to dance a little, don't you think?"

Isadora arose to dance. "We are not assuming that she danced for or against Bolshevism at the Trocadero and if, as Paul Reboux assured me in the lobby, she risked winding up in the ditches of Vincennes. But we got Isadora to dance for us . . . and that satisfies even the English," wrote Georges-Michel.

My appointment with Monsieur Georges-Michel was arranged for six o'clock at his apartment in a quite modern-looking apartment house on rue Clement-Marot, just off the fashionable Avenue Montaigne, famous for its Théâtre des Champs-Elysées and *haute couture* salons of Christian Dior (to this present day), and in previous years, of Guy Laroche and Madelaine Vionnet, among others. Large-framed and looking his eighty-some-odd years, Georges-Michel admitted me into his narrow hallway cramped by the profusion and protrusion of paintings. Ceiling to floor canvasses, framed and unframed, in oils, watercolors, and pastels necessitated navigational commands from him.

Among the recognizable Dufys and Renoirs, one canvas drew my attention. I paused to view it more closely. The writer held it up for my inspection. "It's Diagilev, Picasso, Massine, Cocteau and myself," he explained. "I painted this many years ago for *Parade*."[12]

The hallway obstacle course had temporarily ended. We entered a large, comfortable living room. There was no dearth of paintings, sculpture, and objets d'art in this area, either, but it all was arranged to effect an attractive room decor. We sat facing the massive desk that dominated the front of the room. Behind it, the long French windows were hung with heavy, burgundy-colored floor-length drapes. "And there," he nodded towards his desk and its scattered papers, "is my present project—my memoirs. Isadora will be among them." He shrugged his shoulders and seemed especially weary. "I am in my eighties already. It is difficult to work at too much at a time." His English was limited and halting and interspersed with French. He asked permission to resume in his own language.

From his desk Georges-Michel produced an informal photo of Isadora by Steichen. "You know, I knew Isadora before she joined Loie Fuller's troupe [1901–1902]. Years later I acted as her impresario for a large French War Relief benefit. Isadora was always generous in such matters—always ready to help important causes."

It was a day before that event, Georges-Michel recalled, that she announced to him her intention not to perform. He remembered how enraged he was by her irresponsibility and demanded to know how she could dare to destroy all the efforts that had already gone into the preparations, and practically at zero hour. Isadora was unmoved by his outburst. She related a story about a strange woman who had come to her that day with a warning: should she dance the next evening, women and children would be killed in Russia. For Georges-Michel, this was an absurdity to madden him. Enough with premonitions! However, for Isadora, susceptible to presentiments, no coercing or making light of the incident would alter her decision. At frantic pitch, Georges-Michel, in the company of a police deputy, subsequently tracked down the lady of the dire prophecy. He threatened her with imprisonment unless she retracted her statement. The woman retracted; Isadora danced.

"Yes, she was an incredible person—frequently difficult, her temperament most trying at times." Georges-Michel began to chuckle. "She could easily heave a plate of soup across the table at you if you really displeased her in some way; and don't think I didn't come prepared. I knew to protect my vest and jacket beforehand," he assured me. Then there were those other times when she was "si gentille comme une femme, comme une maitresse" (so gentle like a wife, or a mistress).

He was interested in knowing if I, in the course of my research, had come across any recording of her voice. "Such an unusual voice." He expressed disappointment that hearing Isadora speak would never be possible for others. He had hoped that I would bring him news of discoveries of films of her dancing.

What about Isadora's dancing? I asked him. What was she like as a dancer? He sat there for a moment and then responded. "Isadora's dancing—une expérience suprême." Michel Georges-Michel shook his head slowly from side to side, as though in disbelief. "She could stand on stage, a tremendous stage, all alone—barely moving; just a hand would move up like *this* [he sat up straight and raised his right hand slowly and deliberately to above head height, palm open] or her head, like *that* [from his chest where he lowered his gray head, he began to lift it up, keeping eyes fixed straight ahead on some object] and no more; and the audience thundered applause. You must realize, she was only one person on stage. You have never seen such wonder. I tell you, there has been no one like her since." The little demonstration offered by this large, tired-looking man had curiously affected me. I chilled at the thought of what once was the magnetism of Isadora Duncan.

The conversation turned back to the present. Georges-Michel wished me well with my explorations into Duncania and I expressed keen interest in awaiting the publication of his memoirs. We moved on into the hallway. Almost at the door, he stopped to ask if I had been to see the actress, and staunch friend of Isadora, Cecile Sorel. "Very aged but very intelligent woman."[13] He then mentioned one incident to be included in his memoirs that took place on the Riviera some time after Isadora's return from Russia in 1924. Russia had been a disillusionment for her toward the end. One could say she was down and out, living a hand-to-mouth existence. In Nice along the Boulevard, Michel Georges-Michel ran into her. A Rolls Royce had pulled up alongside him. He glanced in and saw behind the chauffeur, in a white fur-lined luxurious interior—Isadora. Quite stupified, he called out: "Isadora! How is this possible? Why, you have barely been able to feed yourself, and now—in a Rolls?" Her reply to his question was purely Isadorian in its logic. "I couldn't afford to travel any other way."

NOTES

1. Abraham Walkowitz obituary, *New York Herald Tribune*, January 28, 1965.
2. Olga Schatz, *Juval Sings into the Spirit of Art*, p. 77.
3. Alfred Werner, "Abraham Walkowitz," *Jewish Heritage Magazine*, p. 50.
4. Carl van Vechten, "An Appreciation," in Abraham Walkowitz, *Isadora Duncan in Her Dances*, p. 8.

5. Arnold Genthe, *As I Remember*, p. 196.

6. Shaemas O'Sheel, "The Quality of Isadora's Art," in Abraham Walkowitz, *Isadora Duncan in Her Dances*, p. 12.

7. Raphael Soyer, *Self-Revealment: A Memoir*, p. 51.

8. Abraham Walkowitz interview by the author, January 1965.

9. Letter from Auguste Rodin to Antoine Bourdelle in Elizabeth C. Geissbuhler, *Rodin's Later Drawings*, p. 53.

10. Isadora Duncan, *The Art of the Dance*, p. 42.

11. The story associated with these drawings was told to me by Rhodia Bourdelle, which reveals her father's strong sense of premonition. (Isadora was highly subject to prophecies and forebodings as well.) It was during Isadora's season at the Châtelet Theater, on Friday, April 18, 1913, that Isadora's appearance onstage gave rise to Bourdelle's concern, who was in the audience. A strange foreboding took hold of him as he observed her fearful movements. Upon leaving the theater he saw the black car that arrived to chauffeur Isadora back home after the concert. Bourdelle remarked to his wife how hearselike it seemed. The next day the children of the dancer met death in that car when it accidentally plunged into the river.

12. *Parade* was a satirical, innovative work choreographed by Leonide Massine for Diaghilev and his Ballets-Russes. It was, for its day, a controversial ballet of cunning, sophisticated burlesque and avant-garde music and decor. Premiering in Paris in 1917 at the Châtelet Theater, it was regarded by critics as a cubist ballet that would usher in the new spirit in art.

13. It was during one afternoon's wanderings in search of material on Isadora that I came across a dealer in rare theatrical memorabilia on rue St. Sulpice who was the first to tell me of Cecile Sorel. He had no mementos of Duncan and frankly admitted he had never liked her art, however important it was to the dance. His passion was the theater and its flamboyant celebrities. Among the prize possessions shown to me were his collections of letters, plaster casts of heads, hands and feet, dresses, gloves, plumes, fans, haircombs, and jewels belonging to such greats as Rachel, Sarah Bernhardt, *La Belle Otero* ("Now there was a face, a figure—the supreme of the Epoque!") and Cecile Sorel.
The long-standing friendship between Sorel and Isadora was known to him.

> Cecile Sorel, you know, is still alive. She is ninety-six years old and is a ridiculous-looking figure. The ruination of age is a fright to behold. Her dress is that of the religious—the religion of the theater. Her hair is flaming red, her make-up heavily and gruesomely applied in her desperate attempt to retain an illusion of youth. The effect is a horror. But how glorious she once was! Now she lives in a chateau, the interior resembling Versailles, and she sleeps in Madame du Barry's bed. Always she has very young boys around her.

I was unable to arrange an interview with Cecile Sorel during that stay in Paris. She died before my next visit to France.

CHAPTER EIGHT

Little Brother

"A man of strong convictions unfettered by conventions. He is self-sufficient in a wobbly world."

CATHERINE CASEY
Daily Mail [Paris]

RUE DES BEAUX ARTS extends but one short block. Strategically it connects rue Bonaparte (at the approach to the courtyard of the historic Ecole des Beaux Arts) with rue de Seine and its curious mixture of bustling food markets, art and antique galleries, neighborhood cafes, bookstores, and the Akademia Raymond Duncan, installed in 1929.

Eccentric, shrewd, talented, and resourceful, "little brother Raymond" was the sibling closest to Isadora as children. They shared a vision then of a life dedicated to purposeful existence through creative endeavors. Both brought from their native California to Europe an adoration for Greece, so that the spirit that marked the high intellectual attainments of the ancient world became the substance of their youthful fantasies. Isadora records in her autobiography how Raymond, who was "very clever with his pencil . . . had copied all the Greek vases in the Louvre," and, in his exuberance for things Greek painted Athenian columns around the walls of their first studio in Paris.[1]

Predictably, these ardent Hellenists did reach the country of their inspiration. Self-disciplined and energetic, Raymond remained in Greece for years after Isadora resumed her evolving career in Europe, living in peasant villages, learning farming, weaving, batiking, and pottery making—the basic crafts and skills for a survival virtually unchanged from the days of Pericles. During those years he studied the science of movement and Greek music which, with his own theory of movement, became the foundation for all his later teaching.

Shortly before that first trip to Greece in 1903, Isadora's brother had already begun to espouse an unconventional mode of dress—the Grecian toga and barefoot sandal. The *beau monde* posture of the past—wine, cigars, and dapper clothes had been permanently superseded by the new attire and a diet of yogurt, goat cheese, fruit, and milk. In time "he wove tunic and chlamys by hand and made sandals of leather for himself and his sister."[2]

The sandal design, one of utmost simplicity and freedom for the foot, consisted of an arched sole and a thong. Its elementary beauty and function, when introduced by the Duncans to Europe and the United States, revolutionized concepts of modern footwear. Quite plausibly, the effective transmigration of this Grecian sandal from its earliest habitat in mythology to the concrete pavements of our day should be credited to Isadora's younger brother. With his long, silky gray hair and headband, the neat, conspicuous Raymond walked among us, to the end of his long life, toga-clad and sandal-shod. And when seated in a chair, he did so with the "dignity of a Roman emperor."[3] Isadora, on the other hand, was later drawn to the *haute couture* creations of Poiret, Fortuny, Callot-Soeurs, and Babani.

Simply put, Raymond viewed a modern society that judged a man "by the cut of his pants," as stupid. And so, what might have originated as a refutation of the motto "clothes make the man," resulted in this man making the clothes and forever freeing himself from the commercialism and tyranny of fashion whims. Still, the value and reliability of the toga had to be frequently defended by Raymond. He saw it as the ultimate practical garment, simple to work and move about in and functional for all weather. (Although one writer of the period, mentions seeing Raymond in Paris, in the height of winter, shivering in his tunic and sandalled bare feet. "It was on Boulevard St. Michel—even the dogs were shocked."[4])

Pressure from friends and family couldn't dislodge Raymond's defiance of convention. "My friends have always frowned on my way of life, but no man who wants to do anything in the world should listen to his friends. Like the treasure seeker in the fairytale, he must pursue his lonely way."[5] Raymond's contemporaries went on to view him as a curiosity, but the public's growing familiarity with his benign diversity tempered its attitudes. The media, for whom his eccentricities were always good copy, had begun to respect his audacity and his tenacity of ideals and on occasion even registered a measure of affection for him.

As our modern age accelerated its headlong rush into industrial technologies, Raymond proclaimed his self-sufficiency as a response to the omnipotent machine. The value of living that he put forth as his personal doctrine lay in work activity, not in an end product, not in monetary gain. Promoting his hand-over-machine convictions, he established teaching centers and workshops in several cities, the most permanent of these Akademias in Paris. Equipped with hand looms, spinning wheels and shuttles, he taught and produced the ancient crafts, turning out woven garments of utility, as well as decorative textiles and hand-dyed silks of original design or motifs borrowed from antiquity.[6]

The Duncan Akademias proved to be lucrative despite Raymond's lack of interest in financial reward. He went on to produce woven rugs, tapestries, and batiks, as well as sculpture, pottery, and his immensely successful sandal. In light of his entrepreneurial flair I am reminded of a comment made to me by Abraham Walkowitz: "Raymond Duncan is a complete contrast to his sister. He is a businessman, not an artist."

One vital function of Raymond's Paris shop centered around its printing press on which he, having designed and set his own type by hand, issued limited editions of articles written by his sister on the dance, publications about her, writings by contemporary poets, his own literary pieces, and general correspondence. Characteristic of his communication from his press to acquaintances and family is a New Year Greeting: "Lucky for us / To have caught the same train / To have met / And to be in the same hour."

Raymond's epic poems and lyric dramas are evocations of a staunch pride in his American ancestry; his free verse told of his love for his country and family. There remained a chronic nostalgia for his native San Francisco. "My building on rue de Seine is as much a part of San Francisco as though it stood on the corner of Pine and Montgomery Streets."[7] From his poem "You 48 States": "The Heart is elastic stretching / And like a Pendulum beauty / Swinging from side to side / Paris to San Francisco / rue de Seine to Telegraph Hill."[8] He returned with frequency to the United States where in New York he maintained an Akademia, offering in addition to exhibits and sale of his craft products, lectures and body-movement instruction.

Towards the end of the 1920s, in his gallery on 57th Street in New York City, a young dance enthusiast enrolled in Raymond's dance class. She recalls

Raymond Duncan as being "very philosophical and imbued with the Greek ethic."[9] The teenager thought him a kind man with shoulder-length hair, dressed in a toga, who maintained an impersonal manner throughout the months she studied with him. Around the gallery were paintings and woven items, and during their body-movement session Aia, his companion, sat in one corner of the studio at a loom, weaving.

The pupil recollected the nature of Raymond's dance instruction as being less than dance and more of an animated but literal representation of figures as pictorially depicted on surfaces of Greek vases. According to Aia's article in *Exangelos* (a periodic newsletter issued by the Paris Akademia), Raymond practiced a gymnastic system that was based on a thorough synthesis of movements related to man's work activities. In his further consideration of Raymond's anachronistic movement style, "measured, angular, clearly ritualistic gestures of Greek dancing,"[10] O'Sheel speaks of his productions of *Alcestis* and *Electra,* noting that "he dances as the chorus did in the ancient theater and does it worthily." While not being able to accomplish "the miracle which is his sister's, of showing us . . . the very essential flow of moods through the spirit in all its subtle variations, Raymond Duncan does effectively present the visible beauty of Hellenic posturing."[11] Whereas his sister depended on music's rhythms to rouse her body's rhythmic response, Raymond believed that a dancer need not be limited to the rhythm of formal music; he danced without music. His dancing was executed almost entirely in profile in order that clearly outlined movements would make more comprehensible the dancer's portrayal.

During 1909, Raymond and his first wife, Penelope, toured the major United States cities with a supporting troupe of Greek artists, presenting Sophocles' *Electra* in its original text. Raymond maintained that his productions brought to the stage, for the first time since antiquity, authentic woven and spun garments of ancient Greece.

For the inveterate talker who loved conversing with people on a wide range of topics, lecturing came naturally to Raymond. At a party of the rich and famous in London, in 1900, Isadora danced, her mother played the piano, her sister, Elizabeth, read verses from the early Greek poets, and Raymond gave a short talk on "dancing and its possible effect on the psychology of future humanity."[12] A series of lectures given in New York more than sixty years ago was characteristic of the man who flouted the commonplace and asserted the provocative: "The War of Art Against Nature," "The Value of Failure," "Love in Spite of Tradition," and "Freud, Smoke and Sex." But when expounding his philosophy of action or actionalism, Raymond was at his vigorous best. "To forge the hinges of your life and not hang on the hinges forged by others . . . Back to the rootal beginnings—back to the Action and build afresh . . . What must be done, t'is you to do it. That living Action / Leaving in its wake / A vast and deep churning / Of the world's movement."[13]

Theaters in the United States and Paris presented Raymond's solo renditions of his dramatic verse. I saw him for the first time in 1947 at Town Hall in New York City. An odd sight was this one-man cast, with barely a theatrical prop on stage, performing his poet-missionary act in a recitation-with-gestural illustration delivery. To laugh or not to laugh posed a momentary dilemma for many members of the small but intrigued audience. The man with the long gray hair who looked like an unbearded Ulysses dispelled the uncertainty in fairly short order. He was compelling in his imaginative pantomime, witty, endearing, and surprisingly touching and profound.

That same year Raymond also brought his one-man show to the Shubert Theater. "You With Me" was reviewed for *Dance Magazine* in May 1947. Raymond Duncan "brightened this metropolitan corner recently when he appeared . . . at the Shubert Theater. Duncan called upon the spirit of Isadora and other dear ones from the past to come down and join him on the stage, and they *did*."

In 1961 Carnegie Hall presented the world première of Raymond's solo drama, "One Man Against the World." On the occasion of his ninetieth birthday in 1964, he performed for the last time in that great hall, in a premiere of yet another dramatic poem, "Ship Ahoy." The program for that event contains this message from the author-artist: "What a joyous hour you will give me when you come. I want all New York to celebrate my Birth Day."

In Paris the following year, I was hopeful for an interview with Isadora Duncan's little brother. An introductory letter sent him had not been acknowledged but I went to the rue de Seine building anyway. The windows of the Akademia fronted on the busy, colorful street. Displayed were well-designed, hand-dyed scarves of silk and posters (printed in the workshop) announcing art exhibits, music, and poetry events. At the far end were two small photographic portraits of his famous sister.

Inside the Akademia a pleasant staff member indicated that neither Raymond nor Aia were in Paris but that the center could be freely explored. The intimate, dark auditorium theater with its small stage was the hub of its intellectual life. Here were presented the new voices among poets and musicians. The eminent Chopinist, Victor Gille, had long performed his piano recitals there. Artists and their latest paintings and sculptures were accorded opportunities for exhibitions. Raymond's own paintings were on display.

Every May 27, Isadora's birthday, Raymond would arrange a celebration. He would hang his stage with blue curtains; on exhibit were yellowing

photos of his sister, a "violet cloak, orange tunic and wreath of her red roses."
Those who came were faithful friends and pupils. There were men, those who
had adored the vibrant Isadora; and there were aging women, chattering and
delighted by the occasion, " . . . still coiffed in the 1925 dernier cri hair
style."[14]

These celebrations were simple affairs. Raymond would make no
speeches. A pianist and flutist on stage contributed to the nostalgia and someone from among the intimates would talk about the honored one. When it
was all over, everyone would be visibly content, and expressing pleasure, it
was understood—next year, same time, same place.

Among my papers on the Duncans is the message from Raymond's Aia
to friends and relatives. "Raymond Duncan left this life August 14, 1966. But
since then there has not been one day not dedicated to him—His house
[Akademia] is open to all. His activities—Exhibits—Classes in Music
Mouvement—Weaving—Spinning and Printing are continuing. His museum,
which he installed himself, contains thousands of documents, pictures and
newspaper clippings covering his long active life and that of his ancestors.
Raymond Duncan is here with us. He is living through image and his
indomitable spirit and the loving remembrance of his friends."

On a return trip to Paris in 1970, I met with Aia Bertrand. In her long
homespun robes, revealing only her face, hands, and feet, she moved about
the rooms and corridors of his temple as resolutely and piously as a Mother
Superior in the execution of her religious duties. She spoke of the youth of
today and their surprising interest and response to the old crafts. More classes
had been opened at the Akademia. More and more visitors were seeking
information and avidly perusing materials related to Isadora and her work in
the dance. With its documents and memorabilia of Raymond, Isadora,
Augustin, and Elizabeth, the center had become a Duncan family museum
where the public continue to pay them homage.

Maxwell Bodenheim's My Life in Greenwich Village relates an amusing
anecdote of Raymond. When Jews were fleeing Gestapo terror during World
War II, Raymond offered them refuge in his Paris studio and kept them hidden
until their safe removal could be secured. Re-telling his story to Bodenheim,
Raymond remarked: "Hitler's maniacs thought I was cracked. They didn't
think a citizen of the first century would have any interest in the affairs of the
twentieth. My toga not only saved my life but the lives of others."[15]

The day the American army entered Paris, Raymond made the most
spectacular of all his gestures. In Paris, as the Yankee tanks and jeeps were
making their victorious entry, he ran to the American Embassy to welcome

his compatriots and unfurled an American flag, all the while hoarsely and hysterically singing, "Yankee Doodle."

In the last decade of his life, Raymond maintained his remarkable vigor and could still talk up a storm (sometimes to the distress of others). He proclaimed himself the last of the rugged, independent American spirits, and even had a thought or two on the Beat Generation. "They're fault-finding, not artists; their natural expression is criticism. When I was young and angry with the world . . . I went out to Greece and discovered a new world."[16] By anyone's standard Raymond Duncan could be considered a unique man. By his own standard and admission . . . "the most remarkable man in the world."

Addendum

In May of 1984 I revisited the rue de Seine and its venerable landmark, only to find it in the process of being demolished. Scaffolding, drop-cloths, workmen in white coveralls, plaster and concrete debris signalled the *dénouement* of an epoch made memorable by the Duncans. As I drew closer to the site, the individual letters that spelled Akademia and Raymond over the front facade became visible where they lay in a heap on the sidewalk; up above, the name Duncan waited to join them.

NOTES

1. Isadora Duncan, *My Life*, p. 68.
2. Ardee Duncan, *The Sole and Thong*, p. 19.
3. Kay Boyle and R. McAlmon, *Being Geniuses Together*, p. 296.
4. Pierre Mille, "Miss Isadora Duncan," *Le Théâtre*, February 1909.
5. "Ambassador Without Portfolio—or Pants," *The American Weekly*, December 3, 1944, p. 17.
6. A square block-print of yellow silk with a tree motif, signed by Raymond Duncan, is in the Isabella Stewart Gardner Museum, Boston, Massachusetts.
7. Raymond Duncan, *Pages from My Press*, p. 72.
8. *Ibid.*, p. 144.
9. Louise Craig Gerber interview by author, 1985.
10. Shaemas O'Sheel in Isadora Duncan, *The Art of the Dance*, p. 35.
11. Shaemas O'Sheel, *Forum*, February 1911.
12. Isadora Duncan, *My Life*, p. 53.
13. Raymond Duncan, *Pages from My Press*, p. 102.
14. Nicole Rigal, "En Souvenir," *France Libre*, May 29, 1947.
15. Maxwell Bodenheim, *My Life in Greenwich Village*, pp. 90–91.
16. "Talk of the Town," *The New Yorker*, June 13, 1959.

CHAPTER NINE

Among the Immortals

"I seldom go out, but when I feel myself flagging, I go and cheer myself up in Père Lachaise. . . . While seeking out the dead I see nothing but the living."

HONORÉ DE BALZAC,
Permanent Parisians

THE SUDDEN AND VIOLENT death of Isadora Duncan in Nice on September 14, 1927, stunned not only France but the whole of the world where she had made known her dance and her vibrant personality. What did strike many of those reflecting on the highly publicized and bizarre event was how glaringly the symbols of both the life and the dance were coupled in their macabre finality: the shawl she wore on that fateful day—an endearing image of her colorful scarves, so lively and harmonious an accompaniment to the consummate beauty and order of her dance—and a sports car of *grande vitesse*—the great speed she so loved, driving her faster out of paradise lost.

The Parisians were, perhaps, the most bereaved. From those who had disclaimed her art came acknowledgements, posthumously, of her preeminent role in illuminating a new esthetic in the dance. André Levinson wrote

Nothing that we today call rhythm or plastic dance, would have
been possible without her. All that one generation had wanted
or dreamed of doing in dance had been accomplished, thanks to
her—or in opposition to her; never without her. He, who writes
these lines devoted himself to the restoration of the French
classic dance. How did he begin? By attacking Isadora
Duncan. . . . Whether the future historian of dance appreciates
this era as a period of renewal or decadence, he will have to
inscribe in it at the chapter head devoted to our times, the name
of Isadora Duncan.[1]

Those who, from the beginning, were drawn into the luminosity of her
interpreted visions and unfalteringly stood by all the ensuing personal griefs
and artistic triumphs, became mute from shock. Finally, Fernand Divoire in
the *Revue de France*, December 1, 1927, found his voice. "For many weeks I
have written nothing on the dance. Isadora Duncan is dead. Like so many
others, I admired her with such fervor, that today, still, I remain dumb before
my paper, not knowing where to begin, how to say a little of what has to be
said."[2]

Michel-Maurice Levy called for committee to move quickly on the subject of a monument to the woman who had inspired so many artists and intellectuals. The monument should be created by Bourdelle, said Levy. To raise
funds, *Comoedia*, the theater publication, would act as a host for gala festivals
to be held at the Opéra, the Opéra Comique, and the Théâtre des Champs-
Elysées. France must rise to this endeavor. "The memory of Isadora should be
as enduring as the Parthenon, as Music."

A monument to honor Isadora Duncan was proposed in the first decade
or two after her death. For many including this writer, such a tribute has long
been overdue. But time is on Isadora's side. She has eternal patience.

The telegram Paris Singer dispatched from Nice to Isadora's friend,
Mary Fanton Roberts, in New York, bore a brief and poignant message: "She
died painlessly. Mary [Desti] and Raymond [Duncan] watching her." (Singer,
ill and grieving, was not able to attend the final rites in Paris.) In her studio
on the Promenade des Anglais, surrounded by her blue curtains, she lay on a
divan covered with a long white cloth. Encircling the funeral bed were urns
overflowing with chrysanthemums and carnations, scented memories of the
fresh flowers that wreathed Isadora in her dances. Photographs of those dear
to her were arranged on the wall behind the divan. Friends kept the vigil.

At the Gare de Lyon in Paris a group awaited the train from Nice bearing Isadora. Fernand Divoire, Lisa Duncan, Fred Sides, Victor Seroff, Michel
Georges-Michel, André Arnyvelde, George Denis, Cecile Sartoris, Lotte

Yorska stood with others. At Raymond Duncan's Paris studio, friends reverently attended to the funereal chamber. The casket of oak embellished with silver disappeared under the masses of floral tributes crowned with gladioli and red roses.

Monday, September 19, 1927, at 11:00 a.m. under a gray Paris sky, the funeral convoy began making its way to the cemetery of Père Lachaise. Faithful in carrying out Isadora's wishes, those closest to her were resigned to the ordeal of the cremation rite that lay ahead.

At the cemetery and along the road to the crematory, more than four thousand people crowded the area when the cortège arrived two hours later. The nearby chapel, limited in capacity, had to close its doors against the surging crowds. During the cremation, which lasted more than an hour, pianists Victor Gille and Ralph Lawton performed Bach and Chopin in keeping with the dancer's requests. The Calvet quartet presented a symphonic medley from composers associated with the Duncan repertory, transporting many listeners to visions of her movements, of her ineffable grace. Fernand Divoire delivered a moving eulogy, less a speech than a poem immortalizing Isadora's genius, her love of life and her passion for the dance which alone had brought her joy, exaltation, and solace.

Outside, the crowds pushed against the barriers. Raymond Duncan came out to address them evoking his immense love for the world and requesting a tender respect for his sister's memory. It was to him that the small urn of ashes was given; it was concealed under Isadora's violet cape and an American flag. Observed leaving the crematorium were Raymond's companion, Aia, sculptor José Clará, Elizabeth Duncan, conductor Albert Wolff, and author/actress of the Comédie-Française, Mme. Georgette Leblanc, former wife of Maurice Maeterlinck.

Among my papers is an unpublished manuscript handwritten in pencil by Georgette Leblanc that I purchased at Claude Labarre's exceptional shop of theater memorabilia on rue Dauphine. Dated Tuesday, September 20, 1927, the day following the services, the manuscript appears to be unedited notes and comments, presumably intended for publication.

INTERMENT OF ISADORA
NO—A ROASTING!

Odius [sic] spectacle . . . What you see is ugly and stupid; what you feel is degrading. And you can never avoid it . . . I could very well have done without this. Arriving at 4 o'clock today would have been just perfect . . . We did see Yorska in the first row, all in black with a grotesque clown head [?], everyone laughing at her;

[Yorska] rehearsing the scene for the arrival of the body, Yorska throwing herself on the coffin just as others began to come forward, crying "Excuse me, excuse me," as though *she* was *born knowing* Isadora. With her arms and her cries, it was all too much and embarrassing, two furious journalists, near me, told me.

Picture a cold room of stone . . . a sort of platform cut off by curtains . . . not large . . . five hundred persons crowding, suffocating and stifling, without air, unable to budge. Four or five men attendants of the ovens push through the crowds. "Let us pass, let us pass." The casket carriage arrives, the black curtains part just enough to glimpse the tip end of a large box. The coffin disappears from view . . . How like at a fair when one always wonders where did the little bird disappear to . . . strong clicking sounds are heard . . .

At that moment, music starts in the wings behind the curtains where we know there is a second large stone room at the bottom of which is a furnace!! . . . nothing more . . . but for the directors who grow restless and run from one room to the other, lifting the curtain and asking "Is it done?" . . . Naturally from the curtain emanated an appalling odor of burning flesh!

At the moment of the coffin's disappearance, a noise as of an igniting furnace is heard . . . the body then passes from the coffin into a container made of wicker, like a chicken cage, (because oak is expensive!) . . . Lawton through an opening could see how an immense gust of flame engulfed the body which seemed to writhe and swell up as if coming to life again!!

Music once more was heard. First Lawton then Gille *who was a thousand times better*, then a singer. The unfortunate brother [Raymond], garbed in his robes as were his disciples, and having acted out a tragedy throughout this affair, went outside and on the steps harangued the people, Paris, and the heavens, in Comédie Française style. The whole event was provincial theater.

Forty five years later on October 28, 1972, I came to Père Lachaise to locate the columbarium and the vaults containing the ashes of Isadora and her children. I was unprepared for the extent and nature of the cemetery's geography. Through this vast and populous city of the dead, there was no simple terrain to traverse, but multi-level territories with slopes and rises ascended by steps which then fanned out into districts bounded by boulevards with avenues, streets, and lanes. Whatever it meant to be alive in Paris that caused people to migrate there from the four corners of the world also seemed to have induced many to die there.

Every conceivable architectural form designed to reflect man's social, intellectual and religious existence through the ages was represented in miniature replicas in death: from unassuming to elaborate sepulchers, to temples, pyramids, mosques, cathedrals, chapels, basilicas, obelisks, and memorial sculptures. Abélard and Héloise lie side-by-side in a structure resembling a canopied four-poster bed. Chopin's gravesite was infinitely moving with its ceramic female figure holding a lyre and the heartfelt inscription of homage from his intimate circle.

At the crematory it was necessary to inquire within for the exact location of Isadora's niche in the columbarium wall. Once informed, I quickly located the columbarium wall. My search had ended. As I regarded the facade with its undistinctive plainness, I was shaken by disbelief. How could it be? It seemed inconceivable that this woman who had emancipated the dance from its constrictions, whose largeness and vitality of spirit that reverberates to this day, could be contained in a cubicle of such pitiful smallness, nothing more for the future onlooker to know than the inscription: ISADORA DUNCAN, September 14, 1927.

NOTES

1. André Levinson, "Isadora Duncan," *La danse d'aujourd'hui*, p. 147.
2. Fernand Divoire, *Revue de France*, December 1, 1927.

Epilogue—
The Heritage

OUR HERITAGE FROM ISADORA Duncan ranges beyond that of fascination, inspiration, or idolization. Part of her legacy can be found in her collected writings: *The Art of the Dance*, *Ecrits sur la Danse*, and *Tanz der Zukunft*
(Dance of the Future); her autobiography *My Life* through which are abun-
dantly scattered her visionary beliefs and explicit ideas; and miscellaneous
essays, interviews, and comments in news journals around the world. The
written observations are perhaps the principal contribution to our understanding of the root and meaning of the form and spirit of her dance in its
esthetic, social, and creative character. Her affirmation of fundamental truths
concerning what is timeless and universal in nature and in man, her discoveries of movement as self-revelation and liberating power, assume greater relevance and clarity when absorbed and transmuted in their passage through the
dance expressions that have succeeded hers.

More immediately relevant to the active world of dancers, choreographers, and archivists, is another part of this legacy, the body of work—her *oeuvre*—the choreographies. Not unlike great figures in dance today who have

achieved a lifetime of uncommon creative accomplishment, Isadora also questioned the ultimate fate of her work and its continuity. The dispersal of her disciples and the downward spiral of her last years made more acute her concerns. But unlike those of her modern colleagues who have availed themselves of state-of-the-art techniques (systems of notation, films, video, and computer), Isadora neither believed in nor would accept the less than precise documentary devices available to her then. Moreover, it is altogether unlikely that she ever intended for her dance compositions in and of themselves, to be her legacy. They were the inevitable outpourings of an urgent longing to live her life through expressive movements and set forth her esthetic philosophy in visible form. They became her insignia. That they today are treasures of archives would have becalmed those devoted to her person and artistry who deplored the disappearance from their world of her "immense radiance" and despaired of not seeing her dances again.

Throughout the review of printed materials on Isadora, there is every indication that she considered her true legacy to be the formation of schools of dance for the young—not at all a career-shaping institution, but one where the child's still developing mind and natural exuberance for life would be nurtured in a harmonious artistic environment that would enrich both intellect and soul. "It was an attitude toward life through the dance that she wanted to create," explained Duncan authority Julia Levien.

But the choreographies that survived were a reality to be dealt with. A considerable number of Isadora's concert and studio repetory existed in the minds, bodies, and hearts of those who, resembling an act of consecration, committed themselves to the beliefs, practice, and furtherance of Isadora's life's work. Those dances that have come down through the years have rested on an oral tradition made visible and tangible through teaching and an all-too-rare performance. They have descended lineally from Isadora to her Isadorables and from their studios to those most talented and receptive to this art form.

No smooth paths facilitated the transmission of this heritage. There was no leadership, no central organization forthcoming from Isadora's three disciples in the United States. Not within the scope of this work is the dramatic story of the survival of the Duncan dance movement between the 1940s and the 1970s when an interest and a curiosity in the progenitor of modern dance showed signs of resurfacing. Singly ("each man for himself"), and geographically apart, the younger dancers, groomed for the tradition, were determined to hang on and defy the threat to its transiency. That story, the identity of particular individuals, both central and peripheral, who sustained, sheltered, and led this legacy into its future, and those of the present generation who have embraced the dances of Isadora and who will, hopefully, "carry the banner forward," is an integral part of the history of modern dance in America and deserves its own full study and independent acknowledgments.

No longer was there any doubt when the 1970s approached that American dance, in its phenomenal rise and development, would seek its roots and claim them in Isadora Duncan, her influence having been absorbed into almost every facet of contemporary theater expression. Isadora may have gained her fame in Europe, but first and foremost she identified herself with her native country. To America she did indeed bequeath the greatest of her legacies—a major dance art. In this dancer's exultant spirit and in her unfettered gestures, she captured the image of an America in the passion of its pioneering ideal and in the majesty of its scenic vastness. If her revered poet, Walt Whitman, captured the fervor of America singing, Isadora, as the self-proclaimed spiritual daughter of the poet, envisioned young dancers gesturing freely over America's mountains and plains.

As a new generation of students, dancers, and historians took to the library in search of documents on Isadora's life and its impact on our times, the media turned a commercial eye on the century's most famous "adventuress." Public awareness added to the momentum pushing for the rediscovery of Isadora. One could only regard with astonishment and question the *why* of this wave of attention, unabating these past two decades. Nor has this been solely an American manifestation. Across both our oceans could be noted the rising tide of attraction to this harbinger of a new art expression.

Russians today admit to a compelling appeal for the colorful Isadora and her inspiring performances. Though long gone is the last physical remnant of the school in Moscow that she and Irma had directed, memories survive among the older population, while for the young, curiosity and a broadened dance awareness have kindled strong sparks of inquiry into the history of this dance and its charismatic dancer. On June 22, 1988, the Russian newspaper *Izvestia* announced an exhibition entitled "We Remember the Famous Isadora," held in Konstantinova, Ryazan, the native region of Isadora's poet husband, Serge Essenin.

More recent surveys published on the history of dance in Russia made note of Isadora's artistic innovations in terms of costume, decor, and choreographic content. Of particular importance to the Russians was the introduction of an ethical consciousness into her expressive works.

Isadora's legacy can be seen throughout the world. Her principles of natural movement are the basis of dance instruction for young children in a school of dance in Czechoslovakia today. In Japan, a week-long festival, "Isadora Duncan's Birth Memorial" was held in May 1991. Guest American dancer Hortense Kooluris, one of those closest to the "pure" Duncan "doctrine," beguiled the Japanese audience of students and professional dancers with several of Isadora's charming and lyrical pieces. It was dancing, wrote a viewer, like "a fountain of love."

When, in 1983, the Sorbonne in Paris hosted an international seminar on dance, among its participants was a group of young Americans, dancers from the lineage of the Isadorables, Anna, Theresa, and Irma. Quite possibly they met their French counterparts from the school of Lisa Duncan for the first time. The contemporary Duncans on both sides of the Atlantic recognized in each other's performances a shared dowry. Observable variations and differences notwithstanding, the basic structure and gestural style had weathered surprisingly well the seventy years since first introduced by its creator.

Neither the nod to a celebrated name in the historic register of dancers, nor our American penchant for reviving and making trendy the styles and auras of yesterday's personalities, can alone account for the absorbing inquisitiveness into all details of the life, the death, the concepts of her dance, the content and manner of her motions, and more scholarly pursuits related to her influence on her era. Some answers may be suggested by the increasing discourses on the future direction of the dance as an artistic medium. Concerns are raised from within the community of art that the over-technicalization of post-modern dance has left audiences with an emotional void. A distinctly human trait among lovers of the theater arts is the desire for closer emotional ties with the material expressed (a trait that Isadora intuitively understood and consciously utilized). Periodically, contemporary dance sounds a mournful note: Something has been lost; where have the intimate, the beautiful and loving, the ecstatic, gone?

Coming full circle, we again find ourselves at the point in our evolutionary voyage when the body once again revels in its virtuosic glories and self-consciously strives for a theatrical effectiveness, to the eclipsing of the communicating, feeling element. As I write this I recall a comment written by journalist Mike Gold more than fifty years ago when he took issue with the then new modern character in dance. It "substituted geometry and technique for emotion and spirit . . . it was deliberately unintelligible and over-technicalized . . . it had no beauty . . . no simple, humanist approach of Isadora." Sixty-five years ago, Fernand Divoire also touched on this salient feature of Isadora's appeal—its universal communicability. "From the workers of Baku to the students of Paris, from audiences of fashionable society or differing professional criticisms, there are no estrangements from the human spirit."

Isadora Duncan's birth centennial celebrated in 1977–1978 proved to be the event that galvanized energies for a full blown Duncan commemoration, the dominant focus of which centered around performances of her choreographies. For the first time in more than a generation, many of the choreographies were seen in recreations and reinterpretations in several major cities of the United States. A body of work that could have become a lost treasure but for the determination to preserve, the commitment to train and reveal this art to others, and the sheer resolve of its veteran caretakers, is today a living heritage. There were no "estrangements from the human spirit" for the contemporary audiences who witnessed dances—some dating from our century's beginnings—and who responded warmly to the freshness of spirit and beauty of the Duncan forms. Retaining their capacity to stir viewers, the dances of Isadora were a tribute to both her artistry and the soundness of her creative imagination.

This largely unfamiliar choreography brought questions from dance critics and from the more discerning public. How faithful were these replications to their origin, to Isadora Duncan's own performances? Eminently valid questions that echo artist Segonzac's lament that all would become extinct without her, her powerful creativity, her feeling for life. He and others knew only too well that Isadora's uniqueness ceased with her.

The illusion of recreating an Isadora through her dance is just that—an illusion. The artistic dimensions of any artist cannot be cloned (at least, not yet). During her lifetime she addressed those wishing to emulate her: "I wanted to make you free—not to make you Isadora." To be free in dance, she believed, was to search and create anew for oneself. Her legendary ability to touch hearts in performances that made her dance an incantation should not be expected from current reinteptetations, nor will the revival of her choreography produce, as did she, "something new in the world, new and heart shaking." But the collection of her dances, each structured independently, with its own esthetic properties, has retained the potential for survivability apart from the specific qualities she personally invested in them. Chopin was said to be the greatest interpreter of Chopin and undoubtedly Isadora will be her own greatest interpreter, but his music and her dances are living organisms of art; the music thrives anew in the technical skill and poetic readings of his scores by others, and the dances re-animate through bodies physically disciplined, technically mature, and emotionally perceptive. Only then can an artistic recreation be realized. As Isadora discovered for herself when studying Grecian statuary, the interpreter can "breathe its life, recreate it in one's self with personal inspiration."

For the continued well-being of our heritage from Isadora, it would be crucial for those entering such a disciplinary study to understand that the ideas of this dance and the dances themselves were created by an artist of rare magnitude who conceived them with a love and reverence for life and for the dance that celebrates that life. They are her gifts to a world she deeply honored, notwithstanding her outspoken criticism of that world. These individual works must be respected, studied, practiced, and prepared as art. To do otherwise incurs falsification and misrepresentation, and diminishes not only the creation, but also the creator.

The legacies of Isadora Duncan have taken on an extended life in our time. Scholars and dance students search her writings for the source of her inspiration and her creative ingenuity. Colloquia, teaching residencies in universities, dance festivals, and lecture-recitals probe into aspects of her art as an outgrowth and a reflection of our century's transformation. Dance enthusiasts, sensing a corollary between the depressing invasiveness of our urbanized and troubled society, yearn for the releasing effect of their bodies in movement unencumbered, unaffected, and spiritually uplifting. Eager to experience the pulsing rhythms and spirit of her gesture, they continue to flock to centers of Duncan dance in the Untied States and abroad. For the essence of vital living that permeated her life and art, Walt Whitman might well have declared himself her "spiritual father" and in unison go forth, "Afoot and lighthearted . . . healthy, free, the world before me."

CHRONOLOGY

1877   (May 26, revised from long-established date of May 27, 1878)
       Born Angela Isadora, daughter of Mary Isadora (Dora) Gray
       and Joseph Charles Duncan, in San Francisco. Youngest of
       four; siblings: Elizabeth, Augustin, and Raymond.
1892   Teaches social dancing with sister Elizabeth in the Oakland
       area.
1895   (June) Leaves for Chicago with her mother to seek work
       opportunities as a dancer. Appears for three weeks on Masonic
       Roof Garden.
       (October) Joins Augustin Daly's theater company and leaves
       for New York.
1896   Gets a small part in Daly's production of *Miss Pygmalion*, with
       Parisian comedienne Jane May. Tours for several months with
       the company, dancing the fairy in *A Midsummer Night's Dream*
       and appearing in *The Geisha* and *Much Ado About Nothing*.
1897   (August) After a minor role in *Meg Merrilies*, leaves with
       Daly's troupe for England. While in London, studies briefly
       with the Empire Theatre's ballet mistress Katti Lanner. At
       Stratford-on-Avon, dances with others in a Shakespeare play.
1898–1899   Back in New York, quits the Daly company to give salon
       recitals.

(March) Recital at the Carnegie Lyceum with composer Ethelbert Nevin. Dances to Khayyam's *The Rubaiyat*, with recitation by Justin McCarthy.

(April) Gives farewell concert at the Lyceum.

Leaves for London, this time with Elizabeth, Raymond, and Dora [mother] Duncan. Dances in private homes of society matrons. Scrutinizes Greek and Roman antiquities in the British Museum. Meets George Watts, Holman Hunt, Burne-Jones.

1900   (February) Joins the Benson Shakespearean Company season in London, appearing briefly in *Henry V* and *A Midsummer Night's Dream*.

(March 16, July 4, and July 6) Three recitals at the invitation of Charles Hallé, director of the New Gallery. Programs include dances based on texts of Greek odes with recitation ("Happier Age of Gold" Suite), dances inspired by paintings and set to seventeenth-century music, and new dances to music of Chopin.

Prominent figures in the literary, music, and art circles lend her their patronage and assistance, among them Andrew Lang, Holman Hunt, Henry James, Sir Hubert Parry, Walter Crane, Arnold Dolmetsch, Sir Lawrence Alma-Tadema, and Jane Harrison.

(Late Summer) Leaves London to join Raymond in Paris. Visits the Louvre (Greek and Roman art). Admires Carpeaux's sculpture *La Danse*, of the Paris Opéra and the Arc de Triomphe's sculpture of the *Marseillaise* by Rude. Attends the Universal Exposition, highlighted by the Pavillion with Rodin sculptures and the theater of Loie Fuller, with the Japanese dance-acting performances there of Fuller's protégée, Sada Yacco.

Attends Sophocles' *Oedipus Rex* at the Trocadéro and is deeply moved by the performance of Jean Mounet-Sully. Sees Gluck's *Orphée* at the Opéra-Comique and his *Iphigénie en Tauride* at the Comédie-Française.

1901   Establishes a studio-apartment at 45 avenue Villiers.

Teaches and gives informal recitals.

Forms a close friendship with painter Eugène Carrière and his family.

Meets Rodin and forms a long-lasting friendship.

Appears in the homes of Parisian socialites: Mme Saint-Marceaux, Countess Greffuhle, Prince and Princess de Polignac, and the Duchess of Uzès, where she meets André Messager, Jean Lorrain, and Maurice Ravel.

Invited by Loie Fuller to join her troupe of female dancers. Goes with them to Leipzig and Munich.

1902   (February) Fuller arranges for her debut in Vienna before
        an artistic gathering. Impresario Alexander Grosz proposes
        a contract of appearances in Hungary. Leaves the Fuller
        company.
        (April) Successful debut at the Urania Theatre in Budapest.
        Choreographs the *Blue Danube* waltz and a stirring dance to
        Liszt's *Rakoczy March*. Dances for several weeks in Hungary,
        traveling with Oscar Beregi, popular Hungarian actor and her
        first lover.
        Makes debut in Munich at the Künstler Haus and is admired
        by Wagner's son, Siegfried.
        Feted by well-known German artists, among them Fritz von
        Kaulbach. His painting of her appears on the cover of the
        Munich journal *Jugend* in 1904.
        Enlarges Chopin repertory.
1903   (January) Dances at Kroll Opera House in Berlin and capti-
        vates artists, who call her "heilige Isadora." Responds to the
        intellectual life in Berlin and becomes acquainted with the
        influential young Nietzschean, Karl Federn.
        (March) Lectures to a press club on her "Dance of the
        Future," which becomes the substance and title of her first
        publication, *Der Tanz der Zukunft* (Leipzig: E. Diederichs,
        1903).
        Two bronze statuettes of her in motion are done by the
        German sculptor Walter Schott.
        Returns to Paris, where statesman Georges Clemenceau gives
        a short lecture for her studio preview recital.
        (May 30–June 13) Official Paris debut at the Théâtre Sarah
        Bernhardt. Programs include *Dance Idylls* suite, Chopin
        pieces, accompanied by Arnold Dolmetsch and a quartet of
        baroque instruments, and piano.
        (June 30) Guest in Vélizy at a special outdoor celebration of
        Rodin's promotion to Commander of the Legion of Honor,
        where she dances on the "greensward." Other guests are vio-
        linist Fritz Thaulow, painter Paul Albert Besnard, writer
        Octave Mirbeau, sculptor Kathleen Bruce (later Scott, later
        still Lady Kennet), sculptors Antoine Bourdelle and Charles
        Despiau.
        Receives an invitation from Cosima Wagner to dance in
        Bayreuth the following year.
        (Summer and Fall) Tours Germany.
        The Duncan family makes its first trip to Greece, where fur-
        ther exposure to Greek culture shapes her dance philosophy
        and style.
1904   Presents a singing and dancing version of Aeschylus' *The
        Suppliants* in Athens, using ten Greek boys.

Tours with the boys' chorus, but is not well received in Vienna, Munich, or Berlin. Boys return to Greece.

(February) Premieres in Germany of her new Beethoven program, consisting of two piano sonatas and the Seventh Symphony.

(May) Beethoven Soirée at the Trocadéro in Paris is received with great enthusiasm.

(Summer) During the Bayreuth Festival in Germany, appears in *Tannhäuser* as the principal Grace in the Bacchanale. Causes controversy by appearing in her own dance- and dress-style amid a traditional theatrical decor.

Invites noted biologist and Darwinian, Professor Ernst H. Haeckel, to visit her in Bayreuth.

Creates new dance to music of Gluck's *Iphigénie*.

Buys a villa in the Grunewald suburb of Berlin and, with Elizabeth, opens her first school of dance.

(Mid-December) While dancing at the Kroll Opera House, she is seen by stage designer Edward Gordon Craig, son of the English actress Ellen Terry. They become lovers.

(December 26) Debut in St. Petersburg in the Hall of the Nobles, performing a Chopin program. Influences Fokine and impresses Bakst, Benois, Diaghilev, Pavlova, and Kschessinska.

1905   (February) Returns to Russia, with Craig.

(February 3) Beethoven recital in St. Petersburg. Dances in Moscow, where actor-director of the Moscow Art Theatre Konstantin Stanislavski sees her for the first time.

Dances in Kiev.

(Late February–March) Dances in Germany.

(March 25–30) Dances at the Alhambra in Brussels.

(April 12–13) First appearances in the Netherlands. Amsterdam program is *Dans-Idyllen* and *Iphigénie*, accompanied by the Haarlem Municipal Orchestra.

(October) Second Netherlands tour of major cities, with a program of new works: Brahms waltzes and German dances of Schubert.

Appears in Stockholm. Expresses disapproval of Swedish gymnastic dance.

Settles in summer cottage in Nordwijck, Holland, to await the birth of her child.

(September 26) Deirdre, daughter of Gordon Craig, is born. Instrumental in effecting rapport between actress Eleanora Duse and Gordon Craig over his original decor for Ibsen's *Rosmersholm*.

1906–1907   Craig publishes his six lithographic movement studies of Isadora, *Sechs Bewegungsstudien*.

(Late December–January) Performs in Warsaw.

(February) In Holland. Fatigue and illness causes cancellation of schedule. Recuperates in Nice.

(April) Resumes engagements in Holland, Belgium, and Scandinavia.

(December) Arrives in Russia with several Grunewald pupils.

1908 (January) Dances *Iphigénie* with children at the Maryinsky Theatre in St. Petersburg.

Meets with Stanislavski.

(July) Appears with children at Duke of York Theatre in London. Author John Galsworthy and Ruth St. Denis attend performance.

(August) Children return to France. School at Grunewald permanently dissolved.

Makes first return to the United States since 1899. Dances *Iphigénie* and *Dance Idylls* at the Criterion Theatre in New York. Seen by Walter Damrosch.

(November) Dances at the Metropolitan Opera House, with Damrosch as conductor of his New York Symphony Orchestra. Program includes the Beethoven Seventh Symphony.

Tours with Damrosch to Boston and to Washington, D.C., where President Theodore Roosevelt comments favorably on her dancing.

Meets personalities of the New York cultural scene: sculptor George G. Barnard, painters Robert Henri and George Bellows, writer Max Eastman, and theater impresario David Belasco.

Purchases large house and studio in Neuilly, near Paris.

1909 (January 27–February) Gives several matinees at the Théâtre Lyrique de la Gaîté in Paris, presenting her *Iphigénie* there for the first time. Assisted by Camille Chevillard and the Concerts Lamoureux Orchestra, the programs are highly successful. Paris debut for several of the pupils.

Meets Paris Eugene Singer (the "Lohengrin" of her memoirs).

(May–June) Second engagement at the Gâité Lyrique, with pupils and accompanied by Edouard Colonne and his Orchestra Colonne. Continues to receive acclaim. Artists, sculptors, and photographers study and sketch her.

(October–December) Appears in the United States with Damrosch and the New York Symphony Orchestra. After farewell recital at Carnegie Hall returns to France.

1910 Travels on a holiday cruise with her wealthy lover, Paris Singer.

(May 1) Patrick, son of Paris Singer, is born in Beaulieu, France.

Singer and Duncan host a gala at the Trianon Palace Hotel in Versailles. Among the guests are Diaghilev, theater director Lugné-Poë, Vaslav Nijinsky, conductor-composer Gabriel Pierné and his orchestra.

Attempts a brief domestic interlude with Singer at his Paignton, Devon, estate in England.

Returns to Paris to work on a fuller adaptation of Gluck's *Orphée*, including the dramatic segment, Danse des Furies.

Folio of pen-and-ink sketches by Jean-Paul Lafitte, *Les Danses d'Isadora Duncan*, published by Mercure de France, with a preface by art historian Elie Faure.

La Danseuse de Diane, line drawings by André Dunoyer de Segonzac with a preface by Fernand Divoire, published in a limited edition.

1911   (January 18–February) Premiere of new version of *Orphée* at the Châtelet Théâtre in Paris. Programs also include *Iphigénie*, *Schubert Waltzes*, two dance movements from Bach's *Suite in D major*, and the Bacchanale from *Tannhäuser*.

(February 15) Dances excerpts from Wagner's *Parsifal*, *Tannhäuser*, *Die Meistersinger*, and *Tristan* at Carnegie Hall. Tours with Damrosch before returning to Paris.

Elizabeth Duncan inaugurates her School of Dance in Darmstadt, Germany, under the patronage of the Duke and Duchess of Hesse. Artist Jules Grandjouan commemorates occasion with a rare album of pastel sketches.

1912   Grandjouan produces twenty-five pastel drawings of Isadora in movements from her well-known dances, published in a limited edition by Rieder.

(April) Performs in Rome at Teatro Costanzi.

1913   (January) Accompanied by pianist Hener Skene, tours Russia. Experiences premonitory visions of tragedy.

(March) Appears at the Trocadéro with the original Grunewald pupils, the Isadorables, who arrive from Elizabeth's school. A major presentation, *Orphée*, is given, with chorus and orchestra of the Concerts Colonne conducted by Pierné, Mounet-Sully of the Comédie-Française, and singer Rodolphe Plamondon of the Opéra. The children and Isadora dance together in Beethoven's *King Stephen*, *Brahms* and *Schubert Waltzes*, and *Marche Militaire*.

(April 9) Begins a series of concerts at the Châtelet Théâtre, with *Iphigénie* the major offering.

Controversial art-deco Théâtre des Champs-Elysées opens. Interior and exterior of the new building shows direct and indirect influence of Duncan on the art work and decorations by Antoine Bourdelle, Ker-Xavier Roussel, Maurice Denis, and others.

Dunoyer de Segonzac's XXX *Dessins*, which incudes line drawings of Duncan and her pupils, is published by Les Editions du Temps Présent.

(April 19) The children Deirdre and Patrick die accidentally by drowning in the Seine.

Leaves France for the south of Europe.

1914 (January) Occupies a former mansion, the Paillard Hotel and Restaurant, in Bellevue on the outskirts of Paris; a gift of Paris Singer for a residence and new school of the dance. The six core pupils join her; others are sought in Russia. Celebrities— Rodin, Eleanora Duse, Gabriel D'Annunzio, Bourdelle, Cécile Sorel—come to Bellevue (Duncan's "Dionysion") to observe lessons and informal recitals.

(June 28) Dionysion officially opens with a performance of all the children at the Trocadéro; Duncan does not dance, near-ing confinement with her third child.

(August) A son is born and dies within hours. World War I complicates progress of school. Gives building to authorities for use as a military rehabilitation center.

(November) Returns to New York; joins pupils who are already there.

(December) Isadorables debut in the United States at Carnegie Hall, with Isadora. A new dance set to Schubert's *Ave Maria* is presented.

1915 Additional new choreographies are performed in New York: Schubert's *Unfinished Symphony* and his *Funeral March*. Improvises the *Marseillaise* at the Metropolitan Opera House.

(March–April) Financier-art patron Otto Kahn offers use of the Century Theater in New York to stage a festival of music and dance.

Returns to France.

1916 (April 9) Appears in a benefit matinee for the Armoire Lorraine at the Trocadéro. Presents new, more dramatic com-positions: Tchaikovsky's *Symphony No. 6* ("Pathétique"), Franck's Symphonic Interlude from *Rédemption*, and the *Marseillaise*.

Gives a second matinee performance, a benefit for Cooperation des Artistes.

(May) Leaves Paris with new musical director and pianist, Maurice Dumesnil, for South America via New York.

(May 25) Makes an unannounced appearance at the Stadium of the College of the City of New York, and participates in celebrating the Shakespeare tercentenary.

(July–September) Dances in Argentina, Montevideo, and Brazil.

(September) Returns to New York.

Performs at the Metropolitan in a benefit to aid families of French theatrical and musical artists.

1917   Isadorables and Isadora perform at the Metropolitan.

Visits her native city, San Francisco, after an absence of twenty years. Performs with the orchestra. Meets renowned pianist Harold Bauer.

1918   Performs an all-Chopin recital with Bauer at the Columbia Theater in San Francisco.

Returns to Paris via London. Meets Debussy's distinguished pupil, pianist Walter Morse Rummel (the "Archangel" of her memoirs). Together they work on choreography to Liszt's *Les Funerailles* and *Bénédiction de Dieu dans la Solitude*.

Develops material from Chopin music into a program entitled *Chopin Festival*.

1919   To benefit restoration of the Bellevue mansion, gives an intimate recital in the dance salon. Financially unsuccessful; Bellevue is sold.

Finds a house in Passy with a studio, Salle Beethoven.

Isadora Duncan, Fille du Prométhée, with drawings by Bourdelle and text by Divoire, is published.

1920   (March–April) Commences music and dance festivals with symphonic orchestra in major theaters of Paris; at the Trocadero, the program consists of Beethoven, Wagner, Schubert, Chopin, Tchaikovsky, and Franck.

(May–June) At the Théâtre des Champs-Elysées, the program includes *Chopin Festival* and works to Liszt, Brahms, Wagner, and Berlioz.

Revisits Greece with the Isadorables upon their return from the United States. Tries to revive Greek government interest in a school of dance in Athens, but is unsuccessful. Edward Steichen accompanies and photographs them, producing pictures of great distinction.

(November–December) Appears again at the Trocadéro with four Isadorables in an all-Wagner program.

Collection of line drawings by Lucien Jacques is issued in Paris.

1920–1921   Van Saanen Algi's folio of line drawings of Duncan, Karsavina, and Nijinsky is published in Paris.

1921   (January 25–31) Completes year-long festival of dance at the Champs-Elysées, with Rummel and the four Isadorables participating.

Takes a brief tournée with Rummel, revisiting Belgium and Holland. Terminates relationship with Rummel.

Dances in London at the Prince of Wales Theatre, with the London Symphony Orchestra.

(July) Departs for Russia with disciple Irma to meet offer for a school of dance in Moscow.

Moscow School opens with a gala performance at the Bolshoi
Theater.

Begins work on new choreography to music by Scriabin.

Russian sculptor Alexander Konionkov does several wood
sculptures of her.

1922 (May) Marries esteemed Russian poet Sergei Essenin and
embarks on travels outside Russia with him.

Returns through France on her way to the United States.

(October) Arrives in New York; detained at Ellis Island as a
Soviet citizen and interrogated.

Performs in Carnegie Hall and addresses cheering audiences.

Angry, inflammatory speeches in Boston cause bad press and
cancellation of concerts.

Deteriorating health and disturbing episodes of Essenin's alco-
holic, violent behavior aggravate ill-fated American tour.

Tours the Midwest, where poet Hart Crane reacts enthusiastically to her art.

(December 25) Winds up tour dancing at the Brooklyn
Academy of Music, assisted by her tour pianist Max
Rabinowitch.

1923 (January) Gives farewell concert at Carnegie Hall. Sails with
Essenin back to France, after making speech to reporters vow-
ing never to return to the United States.

(May) Rehearses in rue de la Pompe studio for two performances at the Trocadéro.

(August) Returns to Moscow with Essenin. Visits the
Caucasus—Kislovodsk, Batum, Baku, Tiflis—with Irma for
rest and performances. Estranged from Essenin.

(November) Appears with Moscow pupils at the Bolshoi.

1924 (January) On death of Lenin, composes two funeral marches.
Dances in Kharkov, to overwhelming success, and in Kiev.

(June) Tours the Volga region with pianist Mark Metchick, a
pupil of Scriabin, to aid Moscow School's financial crisis.

(September) Dances to Scriabin, Liszt, and Chopin at the
Kamerny Theater in Moscow, with Russian pupils. Premiere
of latest compositions set to Russian songs and dances.

(September 29) Gives final concert at the Bolshoi before
leaving Russia permanently. Receives most tumultuous reception of her career.

Travels to Germany by airplane. Gives two Berlin concerts to
unfavorable reviews.

Reaches Paris, finances depleted.

1925 (January–February) Margot, an Isadorable, dies.

Stays temporarily with Raymond Duncan on the Riviera.

Rents a small studio in Nice and hopes, fruitlessly, to have
Irma and the Russian pupils join her.

(December) Essenin commits suicide in Leningrad.

1926   Becomes acquainted with the Russian pianist Victor Seroff.
(September 10) Before a select audience and accompanied by
pianist Orakli Orbeliani dances a new work to music of Liszt,
sonata *After Reading Dante*, along with his *Funerailles*, and
Legend of St. Francis Preaching to the Birds.
(September 14) Dances as Jean Cocteau reads his "Orphée"
and other poems.
(November) House in Neuilly is sold at auction for default of
mortgage payment. Committee of friends and distinguished
individuals forms to buy back the property for her.
Begins to write the story of her life for publication to ease
financial stress.

1927   (February) Returns to Paris.
(April) Prints newspaper appeals for financial support of
Neuilly campaign. Sale of art objects to benefit the fund takes
place at Comoedia's hall in Paris.
(July 8) At the Mogador Theater in Paris, with the Pasdeloup
Orchestra under the baton of Albert Wolff, gives last concert.
Program consists of Franck's *Rédemption*, Schubert's *Ave
Maria* and his *Unfinished Symphony*, and Wagner's Bacchanale
from *Tannhäuser* and Isolde's Love-Death from *Tristan*.
Returns to Nice.
(September 14) Dies accidentally of strangulation.
(September 19) Cremation and funeral service are held at
Père Lachaise cemetery in Paris.

BIBLIOGRAPHY

Books

Aguilera. *José Clará*. Barcelona, 1967.

Amory, Cleveland. *The Last Resorts*. New York: Harper Brothers, 1952.

Anderson, Jack. *Dance*. New York: Newsweek Books, 1974.

Armitage, Merle. *Dance Memoranda*. New York: Duell, Sloan & Pearce, 1946.

Arvey, Verna. *Choreographic Music—Music for the Dance*. New York: Dutton, 1941.

Aschengreen, Erik. *Jean Cocteau and the Dance*. Copenhagen: Gyldendal, 1986.

Aveline, Claude, and Michel Dufet. *Bourdelle et la Danse*. Paris: Arted, 1969.

Bablet, Denis. *Edward Gordon Craig*. New York: Theatre Arts Books, 1966.

Beerbohm, Sir Max. *Last Theatres, 1904–1910*. Introduction by Rupert Hart-Davis. New York: Taplinger, 1970.

Benois, Alexandre. *Reminiscences of the Russian Ballet*. London: Putnam, 1947.

Bie, Oskar. *Der Tanz*. Berlin: Julius Bard, 1923.

Blair, Frederika. *Isadora: Portrait of the Artist as a Woman*. New York: McGraw-Hill, 1986.

Bodenheim, Maxwell. *My Life and Loves in Greenwich Village*. New York: Bridgehead Books, 1954.

Boehn, Max von. *Der Tanz*. Berlin: Volksverband der Bücherfreunde, Wegweiser-Verlag, 1925.

Bolitho, William. *Twelve Against the Gods*. New York: Simon & Schuster, 1929.

Bordeaux, Jeanne. *Eleanora Duse*. New York: George H. Doran, 1924.

Boyle, Kay, and Robert McAlmon. *Being Geniuses Together*. Garden City, NY: Doubleday, 1968.

Brandenburg, Hans. *Der Moderne Tanz*. Munich: G. Müller, 1921.

Brooks, Van Wyck. *John Sloan: A Painter's Life*. New York: Dutton, 1955.

Brownell, Baker. *Art is Action*. New York: Harper Brothers, 1939.

Buckle, Richard. *Nijinsky*. New York: Simon & Schuster, 1971.

Caen, E., et al. *Georges Pomiès*. Paris: Editions Pierre Tisné, 1939.

Caffin, Carolyn and Charles. *Dancing and Dancers Today*. New York: Dodd, Mead, 1912.

Caldwell, Helen. *Michio Ito: The Dancer and His Dances*. Berkeley, CA: University of California Press, 1977.

Campbell, Margaret. *Dolmetsch: The Man and His Work*. Seattle, WA: University of Washington Press, 1975.

Cannon-Brookes, Peter. *Emile-Antoine Bourdelle*. Cardiff: National Museum of Wales, 1983.

Charles-Roux, Edmonde. *Chanel*. New York: Alfred A. Knopf, 1975.

Cladel, Judith, ed. *Rodin: The Man and His Art*. New York: Century, 1918.

Clará, José. *Isadora Duncan: Soixante-douze Planches*. Paris: Editions Rieder, 1928.

Cocteau, Jean. *La Difficulté d'Etre*. Monaco: Editions du Rocher, 1953.

———. *My Contemporaries*. Edited and Introduction by Margaret Crosland. Philadelphia: Chilton, 1968.

Cohen, Selma Jeanne, ed. *The Modern Dance: Seven Statements of Belief*. Middletown, CT: Wesleyan University Press, 1966.

Cowles, Virginia. *1913—An End and a Beginning*. New York: Harper & Row, 1967.

Craig, Edward A. *Gordon Craig*. New York: Alfred A. Knopf, 1968.

Craig, Edward Gordon. *Index to the Story of My Days*. New York: Viking, 1957.

———. *The Theatre—Advancing*. Boston: Little, Brown, 1919.

D'Acosta, Mercedes. *Here Lies the Heart*. New York: Reynal, 1960.

Daly, Joseph F. *The Life of Augustin Daly*. New York: Macmillan, 1917.

Denby, Edwin. *Looking at the Dance*. New York: Pellegrini & Cudahy, 1948.

Denis, Maurice. *Journal*. Vol. 2. Paris: La Colombe, 1957.

De Osmo, Guillermo. *Mariano Fortuny: His Life and Work*. London: Aurum Press Ltd., 1980.

Der Ling, Princess. *Lotus Petals*. New York: Dodd, Mead, 1930.

Descharnes, Robert, comp. *Auguste Rodin*. Texte de Jean-François Chabrun. Lausanne: Edita, 1967.

Desti, Mary. *The Untold Story*. New York: Liveright, 1929.

Dewey, John. *Art as Experience*. New York: Capricorn Books, 1958.

Dickson, Edward R. *Poems of the Dance*. New York: Alfred A. Knopf, 1921.

Dictionnaire du Ballet Moderne. Paris: F. Hazan, 1957.

Dictionnaires des Peintres, Sculpteurs, Dessinateurs et Graveurs. Paris: Librairie Grund, 1949.

Dillon, Millicent. *After Egypt: Isadora Duncan and Mary Cassatt*. New York: Dutton, 1990.

D'Indy, Vincent. *Cesar Franck*. London: John Lane the Bodley Head Ltd., 1922.

Divoire, Fernand. *Découvertes sur la Danse*. Paris: Editions G. Grès, 1942.

———. *Isadora Duncan, Fille de Prométhée*. Illustrations by Antoine Bourdelle. Paris: Editions Muses Françaises, 1919.

———. *Pour la Danse*. Paris: Editions de la danse, Saxe, 1935.

———. *Les Spectacles à Travers les Ages*. Paris: Editions du Cygne, 1934.

Dolmetsch, Mabel. *Dolmetsch: A Personal Recollection*. New York: Macmillan, 1958.

Donoghue, Denis, ed. *William Butler Yeats*. London: Macmillan, 1972.

Dos Passos, John. *U.S.A.* New York: Modern Library, Random House, 1937.

Drummond, John. *Colour, Rhythm and Dance: Paintings and Drawings of J. D. Ferguson and his Circle*. Scottish Arts Council. Edinburgh: John Swain and Son Ltd., 1985.

Dufet, Michel, and I. Jianou. *Bourdelle*. Paris: Arted, 1965.

———. *Emile-Antoine Bourdelle*. Paris: Arted, 1970.

Dumesnil, Maurice. *An Amazing Journey*. New York: Washburn, 1932.

Duncan, Ardee. *The Sole and the Thong*. Provincetown, MA: Sandal Shop, 1948.

Duncan, Irma. *Duncan Dancer: An Autobiography*. Middletown, CT: Wesleyan University Press, 1966.

———. *Isadora Duncan: Pioneer in the Art of Dance*. New York: The New York Public Library, 1959. (Reprinted from The New York Public Library *Bulletin*, May 1958.)

———. *The Technique of Isadora Duncan*. New York: Kamin, 1937.

———, with Allan Ross Macdougall. *Isadora Duncan's Russian Days*. New York: Covici-Friede, 1929.

Duncan, Isadora. *The Art of the Dance*. New York: Mitchell Kennerly, 1928.

———. *The Dance*. New York: The Forest Press, 1909.

———. *La Danse*. Paris: Akadémia Raymond Duncan, 1927.

———. *Ecrits sur la Danse*. Paris: Editions du Grenier, 1927.

———. *Memoiren*. Zurich: Amalthea Verlag, 1928.

———. *My Life*. New York: Boni & Liveright, 1927.

————. *Der Tanz der Zukunft*. Leipzig: Diederichs, 1903.

Duncan, Raymond. *Pages from My Press*. Paris: Akadémia Raymond Duncan, 1947.

Eastman, Max. *Artists in Uniform*. New York: A. A. Knopf, 1934.

————. *Enjoyment of Living*. New York: Harper Brothers, 1948.

————. *Heroes I Have Known*. New York: Simon & Schuster, 1942.

————. *Love and Revolution*. New York: Random House, 1964.

Edwards, George W. *Paris*. Philadelphia: Penn Publishing Co., 1924.

Emmanuel, Maurice. *The Antique Greek Dance*. New York: John Lane, 1916.

[Essenin] *Serge Essenine*. Translated and commentary by Sophie Laffitte. Paris: Editions P. Seghers, 1959.

Flaccus, Louis. *Spirit and Substance of Art*. New York: F. S. Crofts, 1941.

Flanner, Janet [Genêt, pseud.]. *An American in Paris*. New York: Simon & Schuster, 1940.

————. *Paris Was Yesterday, 1925–1939*. New York: Viking Press, 1972.

Fletcher, I. K. and A. Rood. *Edward Gordon Craig; A Bibliography*. London: The Society for Theatre Research, 1967.

Flint, R. W., ed. *Marinetti: Selected Writings*. New York: Farrar, Straus & Giroux, 1971.

Flitch, J. E. Crawford. *Modern Dancing and Dancers*. London: Grant Richards, 1912.

Flockhart, Lolita W. *A Full Life: The Story of Van Deering Perrine*. Boston: Christopher, 1972.

Fokine, Michel. *Memoirs of a Ballet Master*. Boston: Little, Brown, 1961.

Ford, Hugh, ed. *The Left Bank Revisited: Selections from the Paris Tribune 1917–1934*. University Park, PA: Pennsylvania State University Press, 1972.

Freeman, Joseph. *An American Testament*. New York: Farrar & Rinehart, 1936.

Frisch, G., and J. Shipley. *Auguste Rodin*, New York: Frederick A. Stokes Co., 1939.

Fuller, Loie. *Fifteen Years of a Dancer's Life*. Boston: Small, Maynard, 1913.

Galsworthy, John. *A Motley*. London: Ballantyne, 1910.

Geissbuhler, Elizabeth. *Rodin; Later Drawings*. Interpreted by Bourdelle. Boston: Beacon Press, 1963.

Genthe, Arnold. *As I Remember*. New York: Reynal, 1945.

————. *The Book of the Dance*. New York: Mitchell Kennerley, 1916.

————. *Isadora Duncan: Twenty-Four Studies*. New York: Mitchell Kennerley, 1929.

Georges-Michel, Michel. *From Renoir to Picasso*. Boston: Houghton Mifflin Co., 1957.

Gibbons, Herbert A. *Paris Reborn*. New York: Century, 1915.

Gide, André. *Journals*. New York: Alfred A. Knopf, 1947.

————. *Notes on Chopin*. New York: Philosophical Library, Inc., 1949.

Ginner, Ruby. *The Revived Greek Dance*. London: Methuen, 1933.

Goldscheider, Cecile. *La Musique et la Danse*. Paris: Rodin Museum, 1973.

————. *Rodin et la Danse*. Paris: Arts de France, 1962.

Gomez, Joseph. *Ken Russell*. London: Frederick Muller, Ltd. 1976.

Gosling, Nigel. *Paris 1900–1914*. New York: William Morrow, 1978.

Green, Martin. *The Von Richthofen Sisters*. New York: Basic Books, 1974.

Guilbert, Yvette. *Song of My Life*. London: G. G. Harrap, 1929.

Hahn, Reynaldo. *Notes: Journal d'un Musicien*. Paris: Plon, 1933.

Hale, William H. *The World of Rodin 1840–1917*. New York: Time-Life, 1969.

Haskell, Arnold. *Balletomania*. London: Victor Gollancz, 1934.

————. *Dancing Around the World*. London: Victor Gollancz Ltd., 1937.

————, and Walter Nouvel. *Diaghilev—His Artistic and Private Life*. New York: Simon & Schuster, 1935.

Hawkins, Eric, and Robert Sturdevant. *Hawkins of the Paris Herald*. New York: Simon & Schuster, 1963.

Henri, Robert. *The Art Spirit*. Philadelphia: Lippincott, 1939.

Homer, William I. *Robert Henri and His Circle*. Ithaca, NY: Cornell University Press, 1969.

Huddleston, Sisley. *Bohemian Literary and Social Life in Paris Salons, Cafés, Studios*. London: G. G. Harrap, 1928.

Humphrey, Doris. *The Art of Making Dances*. New York: Grove Press, 1959; reprint edition, Pennington, NJ: Dance Horizons, 1989.

Huneker, James. *Chopin: The Man and His Music*. New York: Charles Scribner's Sons, 1900.

Hurok, Sol. *S. Hurok Presents*. New York: Hermitage House, 1953.

————, and Ruth Goode. *Impresario*. New York: Random House, 1946.

Joyeux, Odette. *Le Monde Merveilleux de la Danse*. Paris: Librairie Hachette, 1967.

Karsavina, Tamara. *Theatre Street*. London: Constable, 1947.

Kemeri, Sandor. *Visage de Bourdelle*. Paris: Librairie Armand Colin, 1931.

Kendall, Elizabeth. *Where She Danced*. New York: Knopf, 1979.

Kennet, Lady [Kathleen Bruce Scott]. *Self-Portrait of an Artist*. London: John Murray, 1949.

Kessler, Harry. *Diaries of Harry Kessler—In the Twenties*. New York: Holt, Rinehart & Winston, 1971.

Kinel, Lola. *This Is My Affair*. Boston: Little, Brown, 1937.

Kirstein, Lincoln. *Movement and Metaphor*. New York: Praeger, 1970.

Krasovskaya, Vera. *Nijinsky*. New York: Schirmer Books/Macmillan, 1979.

Kravchenko, Konstantin, ed. *Sergei Konionkov*. Leningrad: Aurora Art, 1977.

Kschessinska, Mathilda. *Dancing in St. Petersburg*. Garden City, NY: Doubleday, 1961.

Lampkin, Lucy. *The Dance in Art*. New York: J. Fischer & Bros., 1935.

Lawler, Lillian. *The Dance in Ancient Greece*. London: A. & C. Black, 1964.

Lecomte, Valentine. *The Dance of Isadora Duncan*. Paris: Studio of Raymond Duncan Akadémia, 1952.

Leslie, Anne [pseud. of Anita Leslie]. *Rodin: Immortal Peasant*. New York: Prentice-Hall, 1937.

Lever, Maurice. *Isadora-Roman d'une Vie*. Paris: Presses de la Renaissance, 1987.

Levinson, André. *La Danse d'aujourd'hui*. Paris: Editions Duchartre & Van Buggenhoudt, 1929.

————. *La Danse au Théâtre*. Paris, 1924.

Lifar, Serge. *History of Russian Ballet*. New York: Roy, 1954.

Liszt, Franz. *Chopin*. Oliver Ditson Co., n.d.

Lloyd, Margaret. *The Borzoi Book of Modern Dance*. New York: Alfred A. Knopf, 1949.

Lucas, Edward V. *A Wanderer in Paris*. New York: The Macmillan Co., 1911.

Lugné-Poë, Aurélien-Marie. *La Parade III—Souvenirs de Théâtre*. Paris: Gallimard, 1933.

Luhan, Mabel Dodge. *Movers and Shakers*, Vol. 3. New York: Harcourt Brace, 1936.

Macdougall, Alan Ross. *Isadora: A Revolutionary in Art and Love*. New York: Thomas Nelson & Sons, 1960.

Magnus, Maurice. *Memoirs of the Foreign Legion*. Introduction by D. H. Lawrence. New York: Knopf, 1925.

Magriel, Paul. *Isadora Duncan*. New York: Henry Holt, 1947.

Martin, George. *The Damrosch Dynasty—America's First Family of Music*. Boston: Houghton Mifflin, 1983.

Martin, John. *America Dancing*. New York: Dodge, 1936.

Maynard, Olga. *American Modern Dancers*. Boston: Little, Brown, 1965.

McBride, Henry, et al. *One Hundred Drawings and Paintings*. New York: B. W. Huebsch, 1925.

McVay, Gordon. *Esenin—A Life*. Ann Arbor, MI: Ardis, 1976.

————. *Isadora and Esenin*. Ann Arbor, MI: Ardis, 1980.

Miomandre, Francis de. *Danse*. Paris: Flammarion, 1935.

Moore, Lillian. *Artists of the Dance*. New York: Thomas Y. Crowell Co., 1938.

————. *Images of the Dance*. New York: The New York Public Library, 1965.

Morgan, Charles H. *George Bellows—Painter of America*. New York: Reynal, 1965.

Morris, Lloyd. *Postscript to Yesterday*. New York: Random House, 1947.

Morse, Peter. *John Sloan's Prints*. Catalogue raisonné of the etchings, lithographs, and posters. New Haven, CT: Yale University Press, 1969.

Nietzsche, Friedrich. *The Birth of Tragedy*. New York: Doubleday Anchor Books, 1956.

O'Sheel, Shaemas. *Jealous of Dead Leaves*. New York: Boni & Liveright, 1928.

Ostrom, Nicki N. *The Gordon Craig—Isadora Duncan Collection: A Register*, Bulletin of the New York Public Library, Vol. 76.

Palmer, Winthrop. *Theatrical Dancing in America*. Philadelphia: Ruttle, Shaw & Wetherill, 1945.

Pandelli, Jacques. *Ballerinas et Danseurs*. Paris, 1969.

Parker, H. T. *Eighth Notes*. New York: Dodd, Mead, 1922.

Parry, Albert. *Garrets and Pretenders*. New York: Covici-Friede, 1933.

Perugini, Mark E. *A Pageant of the Dance and Ballet*. London: Jarrolds, 1946.

Poiret, Paul. *King of Fashion*. Philadelphia: Lippincott, 1931.

Pound, Reginald. *Scott of the Antarctic*. New York: Coward-McCann, 1966.

———. *Selfridge*. London: Heinemann, 1960.

Radir, Ruth. *Modern Dance*. New York: A. S. Barnes, 1944.

Rambert, Marie. *Quicksilver*. London: Macmillan, 1972.

Rather, Lois. *Lovely Isadora*. Oakland, CA: Rather Press, 1976.

Reid, Benjamin L. *Man From New York—John Quinn and His Friends*. New York: Oxford University Press, 1968.

Reiss, Françoise. *Nijinsky, ou la Grace*. Paris: Editions d'Histoire et d'Art/Plon, 1957.

Richardson, Lady Constance Stuart. *Dancing, Beauty and Games*. London: A. L. Humphreys, 1913.

Rodgers, Audrey T. *The Universal Drum: Dance Imagery in the Poetry of Eliot, Crane, Roethke, and Williams*. University Park, PA: Pennsylvania State University Press, 1980.

Roger-Marx, Claude. *Segonzac*. Geneva: Pierre Cailler, 1951.

Rolland, Romain. *Essays on Music*. New York: Dover, 1959.

Rose, Sir Francis. *Saying Life*. London: Cassell, 1961.

Rosemont, Franklin, ed. *Isadora Speaks*. San Francisco: City Lights, 1981.

Rosenfeld, Paul. *By Way of Art*. New York: Coward-McCann, 1928.

Roslavleva, Natalia. *Era of the Russian Ballet, 1770–1965*. New York: Dutton, 1966.

St. Denis, Ruth. *An Unfinished Life*. New York: Harper Brothers, 1939.

St. John, Bruce, ed. *John Sloan's New York Scene*. New York: Harper & Row, 1965.

Savinio, Alberto. *Isadora Duncan*. Milan: Franco Mario Ricci, 1979.

Saylor, Oliver M. *Revolt in the Arts*. New York: Brentano, 1930.

Schatz, Olga. *Juval Sings into the Spirit of Art*. Berkeley, CA: Circle, 1949.

Schneider, Ilya. *Isadora Duncan: The Russian Years*. London: MacDonald, 1968.

Séchan, Louis. *La Danse Grecque Antique*. Paris: Boccard, 1930.

Seroff, Victor. *The Real Isadora*. New York: Dial, 1971.

Shaw, Martin. *Up to Now*. London: Oxford University Press, 1929.

Shawn, Ted. *The American Ballet*. New York: Henry Holt, 1926.

———. *Every Little Movement*. Pittsfield, MA: Eagle, 1954.

Shirer, William. *Twentieth Century Journey: A Memoir of a Life and the Times*. New York: Simon & Schuster, 1976.

Siblik, Emanuel. *Isadora*. Prague: Aventinum, 1929.

Sloan, John. *The Gist of Art*. New York: American Artists Group, 1939.

[Sloan, John.] National Gallery of Art. *John Sloan: 1871–1951*. Washington, DC, 1971.

Solane, Janine. *Pour une Danse Plus Humaine*. Paris: Editions Jacques Vautrain, 1950.

Sorel, Cecile. *Autobiography*. New York: Ray Publishers, 1953.

Sorell, Walter. *The Dance Has Many Faces*. New York: World, 1951.

———. *The Dance Through the Ages*. New York: Grosset & Dunlap, 1967.

Soupault, Philippe. *Terpsichore*. Paris: E. Hazan, 1928.

Soyer, Raphael. *Self-Revealment: A Memoir*. New York: Random House, 1967.

Splatt, Cynthia. *Isadora Duncan and Gordon Craig: The Prose and Poetry of Action*. The Book Club of California, 1988.

Sprigge, Elizabeth, and Jean-Jacques Kihm. *Jean Cocteau: The Man and the Mirror*. New York: Coward-McCann, 1968.

Stanislavski, Constantin. *My Life in Art*. New York: Theatre Arts Books, 1924.

Starr, Kevin. *Americans and the California Dream 1850–1915*. New York: Oxford University Press, 1973.

Steegmuller, Francis. *Your Isadora*. New York: Random House and The New York Public Library, 1974.

Steichen, Edward. *A Life in Photography*. Garden City, NY: Doubleday, 1963.

Sterne, Maurice. *Shadow and Light*. New York: Harcourt, Brace and World, 1965.

Stokes, Sewell. *Isadora Duncan: An Intimate Portrait*. New York: Brentano, 1928.

Terry, Ellen. *The Russian Ballet*. New York: Bobbs, Merrill, 1913.

Terry, Walter. *The Dance in America*. New York: Harper & Row, 1971.

———. *Isadora Duncan: Her Life, Her Art, Her Legacy*. New York: Dodd, Mead and Co., 1963.

Theocritus. *The Greek Idylls—Theocritus, Bion, Moschus*. Translated by Marion Miller. Lexington, KY: The Maxwelton Co., 1926.

Ullmann, Lisa. *The Mastery of Movement: Rudolf Laban*. London: Macdonald and Evans, 1960.

Untermeyer, Louis. *Makers of the Modern World*. New York: Simon & Schuster, 1955.

Vaillat, Louis. *Historie de la Danse*. Paris: Librairie Plon, 1942.

Varenne, Gaston. *Bourdelle par Lui-Meme*. Paris: Fasquelle, 1937.

Varèse, Louise. *Varèse: A Looking-Glass Diary, Vol. I: 1883–1928*. New York: W. W. Norton, 1972.

Vorobëv, Marevna. *Life in Two Worlds*. London: Abelard-Schumann, 1962.

Wagonknecht, Edward. *Seven Daughters of the Theatre*. Norman, OK: University of Oklahoma Press, 1964.

Walkowitz, Abraham. *Isadora Duncan in Her Dances*. Girard, KA: Haldeman-Julius, 1950.

Weaver, Mike. *William Carlos Williams*. The American Background. London/New York: Cambridge University Press, 1971.

Weber, Brom, ed. *The Letters of Hart Crane*. New York: Hermitage House, 1952.

Weinstock, Herbert. *Chopin: The Man and His Music*. New York: Knopf, 1949.

Werner, Morris R. *To Whom It May Concern*. New York: Cape & Smith, 1931.

Wharton, Edith. *A Backward Glance*. New York: D. Appleton & Century, 1934.

White, Eric W. *Stravinsky: The Composer and His Works*. London: Faber, 1966.

White, Palmer. *Poiret*. New York: Clarkson N. Potter, 1973.

Whiting, Lilian. *Paris the Beautiful*. Boston: Little, Brown, 1911.

Wigman, Mary. *The Language of Dance*. Middletown, CT: Wesleyan University Press, 1966.

Wiser, William. *The Crazy Years: Paris in the Twenties*. New York: Atheneum, 1983.

Articles and Reviews

Alexandre, Arsène. "L'art qui danse," unidentified source, July 1, 1928.

———. "L'art, les luttes et les projets d'Isadora Duncan," unidentified source, April 4, 1920.

———. "La nouvelle école des femmes et des formes," *Comoedia*, April 12, 1914.

"L'ascension d'Isadora Duncan," *Bulletin de l'Oeuvre*, November 1911.

Amaya, Mario. "Isadora and the sculptor," *Dance and Dancers*, August 1962.

———. "Rodin's dancers," *Dance and Dancers*, March 1963.

Arnyvelde, André. "Isadora Duncan va rouvrir son école sous le patronage de l'état," *Comoedia*, May 12, 1920.

———. "Reapparition d'Isadora Duncan," *La Vie Parisienne*, July 28, 1919.

———. "L'école de danse gratuite d'Isadora Duncan," *Le Temps*, April 12, 1914.

Ashton, Sir Frederick. "Unforgettable Isadora Duncan," *Readers Digest*, September 1968.

Ballet News, Vol. 3, no 8, February 1982.

Bardsley, Kay. "A Dancing Isadorable: Maria-Theresa," *Dance Scope*, Vol. 11, no. 2, 1977.

———. "Isadora Duncan's first school," *Dance Research Collage* (CORD Annual no. X), 1979.

Bauer, Harold. "Portrait of the artist as a young man," *Musical Quarterly*, April 1943.

Bazalgette, M. "Isadora Duncan," *Renaissance Romantique*, July 1909.

Bernouard, F. "La plus belle danseuse du monde," *Bulletin de l'Oeuvre*, November 1911.

Besdini, M. "Mrs. Oedipus Has Daughter, Too." *Psychology Today*, March 1971.

Bienstok, J. W. "Le mariage russe d'Isadora Duncan," *Mercure de France*, October 1, 1927.

Bluemner, Oscar. "Kandinsky and Walkowitz," *Camera Work*, 1913.

Boissie. "Mme Isadora Duncan revient à la danse," *Excelsior*, February 9, 1914.

Boncour, Paul. "L'art de la danseuse sublime," *Le Figaro*, May 22, 1909.

————. "Une oeuvre." June 23, 1914.

Bourdelle, Antoine. "Pensées-sculpture et danse cahiers," *Comoedia-Charpentier*, April 1942.

————. *National Sculpture Review*, Winter/Spring 1963–1964.

Byronianas, A. "Como conoci Isadora Duncan," *Revista de Revistas*, April 20, 1930.

Caffin, Charles. "Henri Matisse and Isadora Duncan," *Camera Work*, Vol. 25, 1909.

Cannell, Kathleen. "She moved through the air as though she belonged in it," *Christian Science Monitor*, December 4, 1970.

Charpentier, R. "Festival de musique et de danse d'Isadora Duncan," unidentified source, March 23, 1920.

Clará, José. "Isadora Duncan," *L'Art Décoratif*, August & September 1913.

Cohen, Dorothy H. "The Heritage of Isadora Duncan for Today's Child," unpublished paper, 1978.

Collier, John. "The stage, a new world," *Survey*, June 3, 1916.

"Consacré à Isadora Duncan," *Bulletin de l'Oeuvre*, November 1911.

Cortissoz, Royal. "Isadora Duncan, reflections apropos of her work," *New Music Review*, March 1909.

Craig, E. Gordon. "Gordon Craig and the Dance," *Dance Index*, Vol. 11, No. 8, August 1943.

————. "The Artists of the Theater of the Future," *The Mask*, Vol. 1, No. 3 & 4, May–June, 1908.

————. "Memories of Isadora Duncan," *The Listener*, June 5, 1952.

Dallal, Alberto. "La gran precursora," *La Danza Moderna*, December 1975.

Dalliès, Christine. "Isadora," *Entr'acte*, October 1927.

De Laban, Juana. "The triumph of the ego—the legacy of Isadora Duncan," *Dance Magazine*, July–August 1950.

Delaquys, Georges. "Isadora Duncan," *Revue Hebdomadaire*, May 29, 1909.

————. "Isadora Duncan," *Mercure de France*, December 15, 1906.

————. "Isadora Duncan, reformera-t-elle nos corps de ballet?", *Excelsior*, November 30, 1910.

————. "Prière pour Isadora Duncan," *Comoedia*, November 27, 1936.

De Meeus, M. "A Star Danced," *Cornhill Magazine*, London, May 1932.

De Mille, Agnes. "The revolution of Isadora Duncan," *New York Times Magazine*, September 14, 1952.

Der Ling, Princess. "Recollections of Isadora Duncan," *The Mentor—World Traveler*, September 1930.

D'Houville, Gerard. "Lisa Duncan," *Revue deux Mondes*, June 15, 1935.

Divoire, Fernand. "La danse," *Revue de France*, December 1, 1927.

———. "Non, Isadora n'était pas grecque," *Panorama*, March 16, 1944.

———. "Sur l'urne d'Isadora Duncan," *L'Illustration*, September 24, 1927.

Doob, B. R. "Conversation with Sir Frederick Ashton," *York Dance Review*, No. 7, Spring 1978.

Dowd, Harrison. "The art of Isadora Duncan," *Theatre Guild Magazine*, February 1929.

Draegin, Lois. "After Isadora: Her Art as Inspiration," *Dance Magazine*, July 1977.

Duncan, Isadora. "L'Art de la danse," *Exelsior*, January 18, 1911.

———. "Ce que je pense de la danse," *Femina*, April 1, 1914.

———. "The Dance in Relation to Tragedy," *Theatre Arts*, October 1927.

———. "Fragments from a dancer's philosophy," *Dance Magazine*, June 1927.

———. "Les Idées d'Isadora Duncan sur la danse," *Société Internationale de Musique*, January 18, 1912.

——— and Elizabeth Duncan. "The dance and philosophy," *New York Times*, February 16, 1898.

[Duncan,] Maria-Theresa. "As I Saw Isadora," *Dance Magazine*, November 1928.

———. "Does Classical Dancing Pay?" *Dance Magazine*, June 1929.

D'Udine, Jacques. "Isadora," *Courrier Musical*, February 1, 1911.

Dunning, Jennifer. "The Spirit of Isadora Dances On," *The New York Times*, January 6, 1978.

Eastman, Max. "Isadora is Dead!" *Nation*, September 28, 1927.

Erdman, Jean. "Contemporary dancer looks at her heritage," *Dance Magazine*, December 1960.

Eschelier, R. (Lisa Duncan review) *Revue Deux Mondes*, January 15, 1931.

Etscher, Gaspard. "The renaissance of the dance," *Forum*, September 1911.

Evan, Blanche. "The child and dance," *Dance Magazine*, January 1949.

Faure, Elie. "Isadora Duncan," *La Revue de la Femme*, November 1927.

Flament, Albert. "Isadora," *Revue de Paris*, October 1926.

———. "Une automobile tombe dans la Seine," *Excelsior*, April 21, 1913.

Frejaville. "Isadora Duncan," *Journaux des Débats*, September 23, 1927.

"G. B." "Le beau rêve d'Isadora Duncan," *L'Ilustration*, May 22, 1909.

Gamson, Annabelle. "On dancing Isadora's dances," *Ballet Review*, Vol. 6, no. 4, 1977–78.

Ganne, Gilbert. "Le retour d'Isadora Duncan (La danseuse aux pieds nus)," *L'Aurore*, April 15, 1969.

Gazeau, Jeanne. "Isadora Duncan," *Les Entretiens Idealistes*, December 25, 1909.

Geddes, Minna B. "Isadora: the last year," *Dance Magazine*, January 1978.

Genthe, Arnold. "Revival of classic Greek dance in America," *Dance Magazine*, February 1929.

Georges-Michel, Michel. "Dans la chapelle d'Isadora Duncan," *Paris-Midi*, November 26, 1920.

————. "La Danseuse Nue," *Gil Blas*, December 7, 1911.

————. "Les Ennuis et les rêves d'Isadora Duncan," December 3, 1911.

————. "Les Funerailles Paienne des deux enfants d'Isadora Duncan," *Comoedia*, April 23, 1913.

————. "Isadora—Isadora," *Gil Blas*, September 6, 1912.

————. "Isadora—Isadora, au soleil de la Riviera," Paris-Midi, November 1924.

Getty, Charles N. "The Incomparable Isadora," *About the House*, Vol. 6, #2, Spring 1981.

Gilland, H. "Die Adoptivtöchter der Isadora Duncan," *Kölnische Illustrierte Zeitung*, 1930.

Gille, Victor. "Nous parlous de la Grande Artiste," *L'Illustration*, September 24, 1927.

Gold, Michael. "The Loves of Isadora," *New Masses*, March 1927.

Gregory, John. "Isadora—a transient muse," *Dancing Times*, October 1969.

Hall, Fernau. "Isadora Duncan—Julia Levien in lecture and demonstration," *Ballet Today*, November–December 1969.

Handler, Louis. "Isadora Duncan au Théâtre des Champs-Elysées," *La Danse*, January 26, 1921.

Hardy, Jérôme. "Le Correspondence de Mme Isadora Duncan," *La Danse*, December 1921.

Harris, Marguerite T. "Erika Lohmann. A Life of Dancing, Painting, and Joyful Religion," (Obituary), *Darien News-Review*, May 24, 1984.

Herdies, E. "La reforme orchestique d'Isadora Duncan," *La Revue d'art Dramatique et Musical*, Paris: No. 20, 1906.

Hering, Doris. "To Dionysius with Love," *Dance Magazine*, December 1957.

Hubert, Diane. "The Prophet of Paris," (Raymond Duncan), *The Dance*, August 1927.

Joel, Lydia. (Conversation with Sophia Golovkina), *Dance Magazine*, January 1961.

Johannet, René. "Une Vie," *Le Gaulois*, July 13, 1928.

Johnson, H. "Isadora Duncan and Walt Whitman—their infatuation with America," *Dance Observer*, February 1949.

————. "Isadora Duncan as a source woman of the dance," *Dance Observer*, March 1948.

Jones, Robert E. "The Gloves of Isadora," *Theatre Arts*, October 1947.

Jowitt, Deborah. "Images of Isadora: The Search for Motion," *Dance Research Journal*, 17/2 and 18/1, 1985–1986.

Kaye, Joseph. "The Last Chapters of Isadora's Life," *Dance Magazine*, April–July, 1929.

Kisselgoff, Anna. "What Happened to Isadora in Russia?," *New York Times*, August 31, 1969.

La Fouchardière, G.de. "Un Assassinat," *Oeuvre*, January 22, 1927.

Lalo, Pierre. (Critique of Isadora Duncan), *Le Temps*, January 24, 1911.

Laloy, Louis. "Le ballet moderne," *Revue de Paris*, 1920.

———. "Isadora Duncan et la danse nouvelle," *La Revue Musicale*, May 15, 1904.

Laurent, Jean. "L'Isadorisme," *Les Nouveaux Temps*, June 27, 1941.

Lavedan, Henri. "Miss Isadora Duncan," *L'Illustration*, January 30, February 6, 1909.

Layson, June. "Isadora Duncan—A Preliminary Analysis of Her Work," *Journal of the Society for Dance Research*, London, Vol. 1, No. 1, Spring 1983.

Legrand-Chabrier. "Isadora Duncan à Bellevue," *Paris Magazine*, September 10, 1919.

Levien, Julia. "Sources of style in the dances of Isadora Duncan," *Ballet Review*, Vol. 6, no. 4, 1977–78.

Levinson, André. "L'Apogée D'Isadora Duncan," *Comoedia*, September 14, 1928.

———. "Art and Meaning of Isadora Duncan," *Ballet Review*, Vol. 6 #4, 1977–1978.

———. "La danseuse aux pieds nus—sa destinée—sa vie," *Comoedia Illustré*, September 16, 1927.

———. "Une revolution dans la danse: Isadora Duncan," *Oeuvre Hebdomadaire*, September 24, 1927.

Levy, Junia. "Une livre tchèque sur Isadora Duncan," (review of Emanuel Siblik book), *Comoedia*, December 21, 1930.

Liebman, Marjorie. "Isadora Duncan—a vignette," *Christian Science Monitor*, April 12, 1968.

Loewenthal, Lillian. "Isadora Duncan in The Netherlands," *Dance Chronicle*, Vol. 3, no. 3, 1979–80.

———. "Isadora Duncan and her Relationship to the Music of Chopin," *Journal of Society of Dance History Scholars*, February 1987.

Louppe, Lawrence. "Elizabeth Schwartz et Rodin," *Pour la Danse*, February 1988.

Lugné-Poe. "Isadora! et nos oeuvres," *Revue Politiques et Litteraires*, January 7 and 21, 1933.

Lydon, Susan G. "The Other Isadora," *Ramparts*, May 1969.

Macdonald, Nesta. "Isadora, Chopin and Fokine," *Dance and Dancers*, December 1983.

———. "Isadora Reexamined: Lesser Known Aspects of the Great Dancer's Life," *Dance Magazine*, July–December 1977.

Macdougall, Allan Ross. "Isadora and the Artists," *Dance Index*, March 1946.

———. "Dancer Speaks," *Touchstone*, February 1921.

MacMillan, Kenneth; Clement Crisp. "About the ballet 'Isadora'," *About the House*, Vol. 6 #2, Spring 1981.

Martin, John. "Dance Since Isadora," *Theatre Arts Monthly*, September 1940.

Marty, André E. "Miss Isadora Duncan et son école d'enfants," *Comoedia Illustré*, February 1909.

———. "Isadora Duncan au Châtelet," *Comoedia Illustré*, February 1911.

Marsh, Lucile. "The shadow of Wigman in the light of Duncan," *Dance Magazine*, May 1931.

Mason, Arthur, "Mistress of the Dance," *Green Book Album*, January 1909.

Mason, Redfern, (Isadora Duncan-Harold Bauer recital review), *San Francisco Examiner*, January 4, 1918.

Mauclair, Camille. "Danseuse," *Le Progres*, Lyon, December 24, 1911.

Meunier, Mario. "Isadora Duncan," *Musica Noel*, December 12, 1912.

Mille, Pierre. "Isadora Duncan," *Le Théâtre*, February 1909.

"Music impersonated—the art of Isadora Duncan." *Review of Reviews*, May 1921.

Newman, E. "Dances of Isadora Duncan," *Living Age*, June 4, 1921.

Noble, Hollister. "Isadora Duncan, liberator of the dance," *Musical America*, September 24, 1927.

Norman, G. "Appreciation of Isadora Duncan," *The Theatre*, February 1905.

O'Sheel, Shaemas. "Isadora," *The New Republic*, October 26, 1927.

———. "Isadora Duncan, Priestess," *Poet Lore*, November 1910.

———. "Isadora Duncan—Artist" in *The Art of the Dance*, p. 33.

———. "On with the Dance," *Forum*, February 11, 1911.

Ovion. "Les danses d'Isadora Duncan," *Mercure de France*, March 1, 1910.

Pastor, Grace. "A Remarkable Family," *Physical Culture Magazine*, April 1910.

Pavlova, N. "Essenine et Isadora Duncan," *Revue Mondiale*, January 1, 1930.

Polignac, Princess Ed. de "Memoirs," *Horizon*, August 1945.

Pyros, Odile. "Lisa Duncan," *Journal of the Sorbonne*, July 1983.

Regnier, Henri de. "Danse et Isadora Duncan," *Débats*, January 23, 1911.

Reuillard, G. "Isadora Duncan-Fresque où Statue parfaite à jamais renouvellé," *Les Hommes du Jour*, May 3, 1913.

Reynard, P. "Gallant Old Trouper [Augustin Duncan]," *Parade* May 12, 1946.

Rigal, Nicole. "En souvenir d'Isadora Duncan," *France Libre*, May 29, 1947.

Roberts, Mary F. "Dance of the future as created and illustrated by Isadora Duncan," *Craftsman*, October 1908.

———. "France honors Isadora Duncan and helps her establish a free school of dancing," *Touchstone*, July 1920.

———. "Isadora Duncan—The Dancer," *Denishawn Magazine*, July 1925.

———. "Isadora Duncan's Schools," in *Dionysion*, Vol. 1 #1, c. 1915.

Rodin, Auguste, "La renovation de la danse: Loie Fuller, Isadora Duncan, Nijinski," *Le Matin*, May 30, 1912.

Roger-Marx, Claude. "Les danses de Loie Fuller et d'Isadora Duncan," *Comoedia Illustré*, February 1, 1912.

———. "Sous le Signe D'Isadora—l'âme de la danse," *Le Figaro Litteraire*, June 3, 1966.

Rose, Sir Thomas. "Isadora Duncan," *Vogue*, July 1969.

Roslavleva, Natalia. "Prechistenka 20: the Isadora Duncan school in Moscow," *Dance Perspectives* 64, Winter 1976.

———. "Stanislavski and the ballet," *Dance Perspectives* 23, 1965.

Sauret, Henriette. "Chez Isadora Duncan," *Chanticler*, July 23, 1927.

———. "Isadora Duncan Imperatrice Errante," *Revue Mondiale*, March 15, 1928.

Saylor, Oliver. (On Isadora Duncan), *Footlight and Lamplight*, September 15, 1927.

Schwartz, Elizabeth. "Isadora Duncan: la transmission invisible," *Pour la Danse*, May 1984.

Seldes, George. "What Love Meant to Isadora Duncan," *The Mentor*, February 1930.

Sergines. "Les échoes—Isadora Duncan," *Annales Politiques et Littéraires*, October 1927.

Sorell, Walter. "Isadora Duncan—An American Memento," *University of Kansas Review*, Winter 1954.

Spaeth, Sigmund. "Isadorables," *New York Mail*, June 27, 1918.

Spiesman, M. "The Isadora Duncan schools," *Dance Magazine*, December 1950, February 1951.

Stieglitz, Alfred. "Exhibition of drawings and paintings by Walkowitz," *Camera Work*, January 1913.

Suares, André. "Danse et Musique," *Revue Mondiale*, Paris, December 1921.

Svetlov, Valerian. "Isadora Duncan," *Dancing Times*, December 1927.

Tarn. "Miss Isadora Duncan's matinees at the Prince of Wales Theatre," *The Spectator*, April 23, 1921.

Taylor, Deems. "Isadora Duncan," *New York World*, October 12, 1922.

Terry, Walter. "The legacy of Isadora Duncan and Ruth St. Denis," *Dance Perspectives* 5, Winter 1960.

Tobias, Tobi. "Remembering the Matriarch of Modern Dance," *New York Times*, May 22, 1977.

———. "She [Annabelle Gamson] Brings Duncan's Artistry Back to Life," *New York Times*, November 14, 1976.

Torquet, Charles. "La Rentrée D'Isadora Duncan," *La Vie Parisienne*, August 15, 1919.

Tugal, Pierre. "Isadora Duncan, la géniale novatrice," *Rolet*, September 2, 1954.

Tyler, Parker, and Anna Duncan. "A conversation," *Ballet Review*, Vol. 3, no. 1, October 1969.

Untermeyer, Louis. "The dance," *Seven Arts Magazine*, November 1946.

Valogne, Catherine. "Il y a vingt aux mourant Isadora Duncan," *Arts*, September 12, 1947.

Van Vechten, Carl. "Dance criticisms," *Dance Index*, Vol. 1, nos. 9–11, September–November 1942.

Vautel, C. "Pour Isadora Duncan," *Polemiques*, Paris, June 1920.

Watkins, Mary F. "An Heiress of Isadora Duncan," (Anna Duncan) *Dance Magazine*, May 1928.

———. "Dance Festival in Memory of Isadora Duncan" (Maria-Theresa), *Dance Magazine*, May 1929.

———. "With the Dancers" (Isadorables), *N.Y. Herald Tribune*, January 13, 1929.

Weiss, David. "Isadora Duncan—Actress," *Dance Magazine*, February 1960.

Werner, Alfred. "Abraham Walkowitz," *Jewish Heritage Magazine*, Winter, 1966/1967.

Yorska, Lotte. (On Isadora Duncan and Neuilly), *Comoedia*, February 28, 1927.

———. "Isadora Duncan," *Arts and Decoration*, August 1927.

Clippings, Papers, Miscellany

Alexandre, Arsène. "L'art qui danse," unidentified source, July 1, 1928.

———. "L'art, les luttes et les projets d'Isadora Duncan," unidentified source, April 4, 1920.

"L'Ascension d'Isadora Duncan," *Annales Politiques et Littéraires*, December 15, 1930.

Ballet News, Vol. 3, no. 8, February 1982.

Boncour, Paul J. "Une oeuvre," June 23, 1914.

Bourdelle, Antoine. *National Sculpture Review*, Winter/Spring 1963–1964.

Charpentier, R. "Festival de Musique et de Danse d'Isadora Duncan," unidentified source, March 23, 1920.

Chefs d'oeuvre de l'Art. *Grand Sculpteurs—Bourdelle*, Paris: Hachette, 1969.

Cohen, Dorothy H. "The heritage of Isadora Duncan for today's child," unpublished paper, 1978.

"Consacré à Isadora Duncan," *Bulletin de l'Oeuvre*, November 1911.

Coulard, Marcel. "Isadora Duncan," unidentified source, March 2, 1920.

"Dance," *Salmagundi*, Nos. 33–34, Spring–Summer 1976.

Die Elizabeth Duncan Schule. Marienhöhe, Darmstadt, Jena: Eugen Diedericks, 1912.

"Dance at the Temple of the Wings—the Boynton-Quitzow family in Berkeley," Vol. 1: Interviews with Charles and Sülgwyn Quitzow, conducted by S. Riess and M. Mitchell, Bancroft Library, University of California at Berkeley, 1973.

Duncan Dance Guild. *Newsletter*, April 1956.

"Duncan dancers," (Isadorables), *New York Mail*, April 7, 1920.

"Duncan dancers from Moscow," *Literary Digest*, January 19, 1929.

"L'école d'Isadora Duncan à Moscow," *Théâtre et Comoedia Illustré*, November 1, 1924.

"Emotional Expression" (on Isadora Duncan) *The Director*, Portland, ME: Melvin Ballou Gilbert, March 1898, Vol. 1 #4.

"F. L." "La Prière sur l'acropole d'Isadora Duncan," *L'Illustration*, Paris, March 12, 1904.

"G. B." "Le Beau Rêve d'Isadora Duncan," *L'Illustration*, May 22, 1909.

George, Valdemar. "La danse et l'esprit moderne," unidentified clipping, July 26, 1920.

Gignoux, Regis. "La Rentrée d'Isadora Duncan," (Benefit performances of April 9 and 30 at the Trocadéro), April 3, 1916.

"Isadora Duncan Anniversary Memorial," *Exangelos* (Periodic Newsletter of Raymond Duncan Akademia) Paris, May 27, 1970, #256.

"Isadora Duncan on training the child," *Physical Culture Magazine*, March 1915.

"Isadora Duncan refuse l'heritage du poète Essenine," *Paris-Midi*, November 25, 1926.

"Isadora Duncan's art," *Literary Digest*, May 1, 1915.

"Isadora Duncan's artistic credo," *Literary Digest*, October 8, 1927.

"Isadora Duncan's triumphs and tragedies," *Literary Digest*, October 8, 1927.

Julien, Jean. "La danse," Program, Teatro Costanzi, Rome, April 22, 1912.

Leblanc, Georgette. "Cremation and funeral services of Isadora Duncan," unpublished document, September 20, 1927 (author's collection).

"Miss Isadora Duncan," various illustrated items, *Jugend*, Nos. 5, 11, 13, 28, 1904.

"Miss Isadora Duncan en haar school te Grunewald biz Berlijn," *Elseviers Geillustrierte Maandschrift*, 1906.

Montabré, M. "Les nymphs ont dansé," review of the Isadorables, unidentified clipping, June 29, 1914.

"New dance of Kinzel, Duncan," *Illustrated London News*, September 25, 1920.

Noel, Guy. "Isadora Duncan," unidentified clipping, July 22, 1919.

Saint-Marceaux, R. "L'Art d'Isadora Duncan," *Annales*, 1909.

Scize, Pierre. "Isadora Duncan," (unid.) April 14, 1920.

The Sketch Supplement. London. May 29, 1912.

Sue, Louis. "Isadora Duncan, météore génie," in *Sous le Signe d'Isadora*, catalogue of the exhibition, Musée Bourdelle, Paris, 1966.

"Trois élèves d'Isadora Duncan," *La Danse*, April 1922.

"Two Dancers," *Harper's Weekly*, November 29, 1913.

Exhibitions, Exhibition Catalogues, and Specialized Materials

Arnold Genthe. Staten Island Museum, September–November 1975.

Art and Dance: Images of the Modern Dialogue 1890–1980. Institute of Contemporary Art, Inc. Boston, 1982.

Cassou, Jean and Philip Rhys Adams. *Antoine Bourdelle*, Slatkin Galleries, New York, 1965.

Clará, José. *Isadora Duncan, Portfolio of Seventy-Two Plates* Pen and Ink and Watercolor. Paris: Rieder, 1928.

Craig, Gordon. *Sechs Bewegungstudien Isadora Duncan* [Portfolio of six lithographic studies]. Leipzig: Insel Verlag, 1906.

Drawings by Jules Grandjouan. Palace of the Legion of Honor, San Francisco, California, 1956.

Edward Gordon Craig and the Theatre of the Imagination. Stanford Universities Libraries, California, 1985.

Gordon Craig et le Renouvellement du Théâtre. Paris, Bibliothèque Nationale, 1962.

Grandjouan, Jules. Folio of engraved pastel/crayon drawings on the occasion of the inauguration of the Elizabeth Duncan School at Darmstadt, Germany. 1911.

――――. *Isadora Duncan* [Twenty-five studies]. Paris: Editions Rieder, c. 1912.

Lafitte, Jean-Paul. *Les danses d'Isadora Duncan* [Drawings]. Preface by Elie Faure. *Mercure de France,* 1910.

Lecomte, Valentine. *Album of Line Drawings of Isadora Duncan.* Paris: Raymond Duncan Akademia Press, 1952.

One Hundred Artists and Walkowitz. Brooklyn Museum, 1944.

Ornement de la Durée [Rodin and Fuller, Duncan, St. Denis, Vellany]. Musée Rodin, Paris, September–November 1987.

Pourchet, M. *Charpentier-Mio et la danse* [Text]. Gallery Gilberte Cournand, Paris, n.d.

Rood, Arnold. *Edward Gordon Craig: Artist of the Theatre 1872–1966.* New York Public Library, September–November 1967.

Sous le Signe d'Isadora [Catalogue of the exhibition]. Musée Bourdelle, Paris, 1966.

Théâtre des Champs-Elysées: Cinquante Années de Créations Artistiques 1913–1963 [Catalogue of the exhibition]. Paris, 1963.

Van Saanen Algi. *Croquis* [Drawings of Karsavina, Nijinsky, Isadora Duncan] Text by Jean-Louis Vaudoyer, Paris, c. 1920.

INDEX